FARM
GATE
DEFENSE

Available in the United States from:

North American Farm Alliance Publications
Box 8445, Minneapolis, Minnesota, 55409
(612-827-6056)

The Story of the Canadian Farmers Survival Association

Allen Wilford

FARM GATE DEFENSE

Introduction by Wayne Crytz

NC Press Limited
Toronto, 1984

Canadian Cataloguing in Publication Data
Wilford, Allen, 1948 -
   Farm gate defense

ISBN 0-920053-40-8 (bound). - ISBN 0-919601-85-5 (pbk.)

1. Canadian Farmers Survival Association. 2. Farmers - Canada
- Political activity. 3. Agriculture - Canada - Economic aspects.
4. Wilford, Allen, 1948 -

HD1486.C2W54 1984   338.1'06'071   C83-098789-4

We would like to thank the Ontario Arts Council and the Canada
Council for their assistance in the production of this book.

New Canada Publications, a division of NC Press Limited, Box
4010, Station A, Toronto, Ontario, M5W 1H8

Printed in Canada.

Contents

Acknowledgements

I would like to dedicate this book to the men, women and children around the world who work the soil. Those who have given so much to so many for so little. But more particularly I would like to dedicate it to those involved in the struggle for justice and the survival of the family farm.

I would like to first thank Wendy, my wife, and my children — Tracy, 15, Terry, 11, Timmy, 6, and Tony, 3, for the sacrifice of their time to the Survival Association and to the writing of this book. Also I would like to thank the many people who wrote or phoned in their support, and of course the many people who have influenced my life.

A special thanks to the people of NC Press who supplied so much help, namely, Caroline Walker, Mary Lea, Karen Alliston and Joe Solway, and who made the writing of this book a pleasure.

I also wish to thank the Royal Bank of Canada, whose indefatigable efforts have encouraged me to pursue my present activities.

Foreword

I think that if there was ever a time when North American farmers
needed to get off their backsides and down on their knees and then
stand up on their feet that time is now. The North American
farmers have got a solution to the economic problems of our
countries.

I believe that there is more justice in our two countries than
anywhere else in the world, but that justice is not always brought
and set in your lap. Sometimes you have to stand up and reach for
it, and for every person who is treated unjustly and doesn't stand
up, then the next person who does must stand a little taller. If people treated unjustly don't stand up then justice may be got out of
reach of us all.

Allen Wilford impressed me. When he came to Missouri, he told
us that there were no instant solutions to our problems. He said
that what we were fighting for was worth the lengthy struggle it was
going to take; that it would not take violence or bloodshed. All we
need is the involvement of good people to turn the present economic
conditions around.

I am proud of Allen for being willing to reach out for the justice
he believes in. He's willing to go just a little further to make up for
the others who don't or can't.

Wayne Crytz
American Agriculture Movement

Introduction

Someone ripped me off for a quarter of a million dollars. This was the beginning of my awakening. My story is an integral part of the Canadian Farmers' Survival Association. How did a boy, who started out with a Bible and ten dollars, get a quarter of a million dollars in equity? Was it real? Was it just inflation? What is inflation?

Why did the federal government force double-digit interest rates to support the dollar, sacrificing the backbone of our industry and commerce? Was inflation a move to deliberately destroy, a move of desperation, or just plain ignorance? Why would farmers, one of the hardest working, most honest segments of society be reduced to tears, desperation and poverty? The cornerstone of our society was being eroded. Was it Progress or was it deliberate policy? Its causes, effects, cures, are perhaps the most crucial questions in the latter half of the twentieth century. Could world peace hinge on the farm crisis?

Why would farmers pick up guns, defy the law? What were the social implications? A Biblical prophecy fulfilled, the beginning of a class struggle, or a flash in the pan of history?

In the 1830s Canadian farmers picked up guns; in the 1880s the farmers led a tremendous political upheaval in the United States. In the 1930s farmers were shot and killed. Why did these farm revolts seem to happen every fifty years? Was there a pattern, could the causes be understood, could the cures be discovered? Is it possible to organize farmers? What about labour? Is the farmer a businessman? Or is this theory a deliberate ploy to separate him from his fellow workers?

The real-life drama of men and women, their families, politics, and economics, are all part and parcel of the struggle of the Canadian Farmers' Survival Association. Is it possible to take on the huge financial institutions whose smallest member is two-and-a-half times larger than all the oil companies in Canada? Are they really the enemy? Are they crooked men running an honest business, or honest men running a crooked business? Are we farmers victims of our greed, or masters of our destiny?

Perhaps the best way to get at the story is to start at the beginning. But where is that, at the Black Farm in June of 1981, or my personal upbringing and views on life? Small forces have won tremendous battles with their courage; tremendous forces have lost important battles due to cowardice. In the farm rebellion of 1837, William Lyon Mackenzie's first rank opened fire, then lay down to allow their comrades to fire over them. Their comrades, mistaking the prone positions for death, fled. Can we fight ignorance, can we overcome cowardice long enough to get the job done — or will we be just another farm organization?

This is the story of some very brave individuals who put their own positions in jeopardy to help others.

My Story   1

My cow milks me — Ralph Waldo Emerson 1803-1882

Back to the beginning. We moved to the farm from the city
when I was three years old because the doctor told my father
that he must move to the clean air and out of his job at the rubber factory. My first memories of the farm were tremendous
— fresh air, open spaces and freedom. My free spirit must have
been worrisome, especially for my mother, as I played almost
continually in a creek not far from the house.

My mother passed away when I was seven, but not before
instilling in me a reverence for the Lord, and a contagious charity which I took to be natural and which I have found, time and
time again, in mankind around the world. Twenty-five years
after her death a businessman donated a sign in her memory
because she had given much, much more than she had ever
received.

The years that followed were ones of learning and growing
self-sufficiency. There is always work to be done on a farm,
although, on looking back, Father probably spoiled me. My
early realization of our lack of money was not so much a problem as a simple reality. It was totally irrelevant in exchange
for the freedom, the rich home life and the community spirit,
etc. And I add the etcetera because words cannot describe the
pleasures I received from watching birth, watching the flowers
and birds develop; seeing new plants in spring. I must con-
fess total shock at the city people who have no desire to live in
the country but prefer to live in the smog, in a community-less
society where you don't even know your neighbour, much less
those for miles around.

At a very early age I realized that it was fact that the city people were well off by country standards. As children, we stood in awe of people who could actually buy a new car, take a holiday, eat in a restaurant, or wear new clothes. Times have changed but not that much. More farmers in the seventies were participating in the luxuries of life but very few were raised with running water, toilets, or central heating. So the memories of these stark realities weren't that far away. One farmer recently said to me that if he hadn't put the toilet inside, the banker never would have wanted the farm.

When I was 12, my father re-married. My new mother had her hands full. She was a generous and kind person, always helping others. But I was a headstrong boy who had known independence at a very early age. We moved to town when I was 15, where both my parents had jobs. We built a new house with the help of the farm sale. The move to a new large school from a small farm school was one of the major steps of my life: it was the first step away from the rural to the urban. A lot of the children were rural, as all the small country schools were being destroyed at this time and children were being bussed thousands of miles yearly. A fellow said, "We pick them up an hour earlier so they can ride in a bus to school and then they build a gymnasium to give them exercise." A person involved in physical fitness said that any of the old generation who walked to school, or in my case bicycled half the year, are no trouble to get back in shape years later. But in the next generation, no muscle base was being formed.

However the change was more devastating than mere physical fitness. The shifting of classes was such that any one teacher saw hundreds of students for only forty minutes each day. It was a step backwards from our high school where two teachers not only knew every student but they probably taught the parents. Its superiority was attested to in the fact that all the children who had been educated there did quite well when transferred to the large urban schools. Personal contact had allowed the teacher to spend more time with those who needed it. The destruction of personal contact and of individual concern can have nothing but bad effects on society.

I did very well in subjects with interesting teachers, or where the challenge interested me, but I was bored with French and Latin because I found memory work and the lack of logic in languages to be very boring. I skipped a lot of school because of my free spirit and my desire to hunt and fish. I worked after school — helped the caretaker, helped at a bake shop, shovelled snow — sometimes all the same day. I quickly found the monetary rewards of honest labour and business initiative, but as a teenager I spent all my money on wine, women and gasoline.

After high school I left home and started an apprenticeship as a tool and die maker — a very good trade to teach problem solving, hand skills, self-confidence, and responsibility. Because of the lack of monetary reward for the tremendous responsibility (and I can't emphasize that enough — you're constantly working with dies worth thousands of dollars, which can be destroyed in one wrong move) I find a great many tool and die makers who, like myself, have chosen other lines of work. Usually, large numbers of these people are self-employed.

Again, I had a tremendous impression of the houses, summer cottages, airplanes, and new cars that were owned by people who have no more invested than a lunch pail. I don't mean to imply that money was falling out of the sky because, as an apprentice with a young family, I found money extremely scarce, and I don't mean to say that these people did not deserve what they had. But I did see a vast difference in the hours, the type of work, and the monetary reward for the city people as opposed to their country cousins. In 1981 the average Canadian farmer's investment was $440,000, and average farm income was only $9,000.

One farmer said, "If they just paid me for the overtime I would be happy." The farmer's long hours bring very little monetary benefit, notwithstanding the quality of life, time with our families, benefit to our children, and the future hope that someday we'll have something to pass on. A farmer farms for his sons and the big benefit, which is so hard to describe, is possibly the creativity, the good feeling from seeing a good crop, knowing that you and Mother Nature did it. You should see the mess when she's left all to herself!

And now we are close to one of the major problems with farmers: total contempt for money. The reward is being present when a sow has her piglets. Or watching a small calf frisk in the sun. The money is just something that is used to pay bills, or exchange for something you need. The farmer, in his simplicity and his honesty, unconsciously realizes what money really is: simply a medium of exchange. Not a real substance; not anything to be cherished or worshipped. Money and how it is created comes up repeatedly in farm movements because the people who create these worthless bits of paper are constantly trying to take our land because it is real; it cannot be created.

I bought my first farm in 1971. It consisted of 100 acres, and I paid $19,000. I put $4,000 down, with a mortgage of $15,000. I worked off the farm, renting out the grass. About six months after purchasing it I broke my leg in an industrial accident. I was laid up for almost a year before I could walk properly, so the farm got off to a very slow start. In 1973 I bought my first cattle, just in time for the market to go from 74 to 40 cents a pound. I owned outright 22 head, borrowing the money for another 22, then selling them all the next year just to pay off what I had borrowed.

I started from scratch again in '74. It was the same old scenario — you couldn't make a living on 100 acres, or with 50 cattle, you had to have more than that. Like any young farmer starting out, I had to work out to get the money, pouring all my time, evenings and weekends, money and effort into the farm, trying to build it up to self-sufficiency. The problem is to get it large enough to be self-sufficient so that you don't have to work out. I was lucky that the job I had was on a piecework basis so I could work when I wanted. I would work for a week straight, then take a week off, spending the time on the farm.

Because I didn't have much capital to start with, the only farm I could afford was very rundown. An older bachelor in his early seventies, had been there for the last twenty years. The fences were held together with binder twine, the barn was a shambles. He had put in electricity the year before, but there was no running water and no central heating or bathroom in the house.

In the first year, all my time and effort went into trying to make the house liveable. At this point I had a wife and small child. The second year I spent on the barn, trying to make it useable. There was just a dug well, which had gone dry and wouldn't stand to do a washing (we had the washing machine draining on it), so I had to drill a well.

The other farms I bought were much the same, although the second house was in better condition. Because of all the stone, Grey-Bruce is not a good cash crop area. We're too far north for corn, which I tried growing for two years in a row and quickly found that the returns didn't equal the investment. Someone came out with the bright idea of feeding cornstraw or stover through beef cows, trying to make the cows work. Well, I wasn't making any money on the corn — the calves were selling for 32 cents a pound and costing me about 60 cents a pound to produce — and when I combined the two it just made me lose more money. So I quickly got out of corn.

I went into a hay-pasture rotation. Hay and pasture are soil-conserving and soil-building crops. My next door neighbour said don't ever worry about any feed you buy because it's a good investment. You put feed through the cattle and the manure out on the soil and it's the same thing as buying fertilizer. So I got into the habit of buying hay, and set myself up with a bale thrower — three wagons drawn by a truck. I continued to draw the hay onto the farms, into the barn, put it through the cattle, returning the manure to the soil.

Over the course of a few years I built up a very good soil base. My soil tests were in the high and the high plus range. I had dumped a lot of commercial fertilizer on at the beginning to try and get these farms growing, to get my soil tests up quickly, but as the manure became available I relied less and less on commercial fertilizer.

As I mentioned, the cow-calf business didn't work. I got into it quite innocently. I bought the heifers, the price went down, I bred the heifers and kept them for breeding cows. But they still didn't generate income; I was selling calves for 32 cents a pound and losing money. I realized that if I was losing money *selling* them for 32 cents I might as well be *buying* them for 32.

So I got rid of the cows and started what they call a background, or stocker, operation. This consists of buying western calves in the fall, wintering them on hay, pasturing them through the summer, taking them up to eight, nine hundred pounds and then selling them into a feedlot, where they are put on grain and "finished." I had good luck at this. Normally on a hay-pasture routine it was considered acceptable to double the weight — I got an average of 2.2 times in weight and sometimes 2.3; the calf would grow from 350 to 800 pounds.

There are a few problems with this, and they go to the heart of our industry: we are entirely dependent on the calf price. We literally have a choice of paying the going rate, over which we have no control, or going out of business. In my arguments with former Ontario Agriculture Minister Lorne Henderson, he said I paid too much for my calves. Having been a cowman, I didn't think the calves were overpriced given the cost of the inputs. However, we were competing against the provincial treasuries of Quebec and Saskatchewan, which have programmes to stabilize the selling price of beef. Their farmers could depend on a cost of production formula in bidding on these calves. Buying calves in Ontario it was just me against the Quebec treasurer.

Rene Levesque's government wanted Quebec to be self-sufficient and so strongly encouraged agriculture. It ultimately hurt the Quebec farmer by encouraging unrealistic expansion, and it knocked the hell out of us, because they were literally buying the beef industry out of Ontario for Quebec. Of course the Conservative government in Ontario didn't even know we had cattle so they weren't worried about it. They thought agriculture was a disease everybody else had.

I paid $1.10 a pound one year, $1.26 the next. As the price for replacements escalated each year, any profits I thought I was making were going back into paying more for inventory.

My bank loans kept climbing but my net worth, due mainly to inflation, also kept climbing to the point where my assets exceeeded my liabilities by $250,000. But there were danger signs. One could buy a tractor for $5,000, use it for five years, and sell it for $10,000, but it cost $40,000 for a new replacement. Did you make $5,000 on the old tractor or lose $30,000 in replacement cost? These were the facts which didn't show up in the books. One farmer's accountant kept telling him he was doing very well — right up to the time he went broke.

Then the collapse came. The $1.26 calves went out at 85 cents. We came back in, and because we were still competing with these other provinces the buying price held to $1.00, $1.10; and then those calves went out at 75 cents.

Then the double whammy of the interest rate and price hit us. Our financing was on floating rates which hit a high of 24.75%. Just as interest rates on my loans went wild, beef prices collapsed, since the consumer had to spend more on his mortgage and couldn't afford to eat steak.

Allen Wilford with Hereford steers.

I had, at this point, 440 acres and I rented a further 300 for hay or pasture. Some people criticize expansion, but all of my properties were still saleable for as much as I paid for them, despite dramatic drops in real estate prices. My downfall was the price of cattle. One could lose more on the cattle on the farm than the farm was worth, with bank estimates of $300 to $400 per head, or $120,000 on 300 head. If I had rented the land out and not farmed I wouldn't have had all these problems. The more one farmed the more one lost.

Another part of the problem was marketing. The Cattlemen's Association refused to have anything to do with marketing boards. Charlie Gracey, manager of the Canadian Cattlemen's Association, kept screaming free enterprise. I said it's hard to stick out my chest when my hip pocket is hurting. We have no control over our marketing. You can sell at the local market, and if the sun shines you get a couple of cents more than if it is raining, because people are optimistic. You didn't really know what you are going to get until the hammer comes down. If you don't like the price and are quick enough bidding them back, you have to load them on the truck and take them home. They are off their feed, and you pay the trucking both ways plus a modest commission. The other option is to try to sell the cattle to dealers, but you have to have your head up because some of these fellows aren't the most honest people in the world.

The large packers control the price several ways. The most obvious is direct sales. They buy cattle direct from the farmer at the price next Wednesday in Toronto. This saves the farmer a sales commission but the problem comes when the packers had purchased enough cattle direct. They don't have to bid on cattle in Toronto on Wednesday, so the price falls, or worse yet, they bring in extra cattle from the U.S. to dump on the Toronto market to depress the price. Packers lose as much as five cents a pound on importing these cattle, but win on the ones they bought direct. Iowa Beef Company controls 30% of the cattle in the U.S. and some people still believe every man for himself!

One of the answers that has come out of this chaos is video marketing. I was very enthusiastic, thinking it was a very good idea. You have your cattle shown on a video screen, and people bid on them without the cattle ever leaving the farm. If you sell them, fine and dandy, they arrange a pickup the next week. If you don't sell them, the cattle are still on feed, there are no trucking fees, and only a modest commission to cover the expenses of the video tape. It is a much superior method.

But the problem of price remained. Free enterprise: "Every man for himself," yelled the elephant as he danced among the chickens.

It became very obvious that the farming community was being forced to be cannibalistic. The only way I could make money in the stocker business was by stealing the calves from the cowman. The only way the fellow in the finish business could make money is if he stole them from me. He in turn would try and steal cheap grain. Everyone was fighting his fellow farmer, trying to keep ahead of the thing. It was a very dangerous way to go.

The Ontario Cattlemen's Association was now quite used to refusing to admit that cows are part of the beef cycle. (There are a lot of misconceptions floating around; for example, contrary to popular belief, the world's oldest profession is apple picking.) They were continually talking about bringing in cheaper calves from Western Canada or the U.S. to keep the price of calves down; this was a deliberate policy, as Charlie

Gracey, the manager, pointed; profit would come from cheaper calves, instead of controlling our price. It was very frustrating for the cowman. Lorne Henderson continued to blame the high price of calves and grain, which was in effect telling us we had to steal from the cowman and the grain man.

Duncan Allen, Ontario deputy minister of Agriculture, complained that we took "all" his help and used it to buy expensive calves from out of province. Well, the alternative to buying a 400-pound calf was not to buy and then someone else would have to buy a 1200-pound finished steer from out of province; it was the same choice as buying the steel or buying the finished car.

As the margins got smaller and smaller, we were forced to get big or get out — to increase our volume and try and make a profit that way. Looking through history we find that farm size and farm land prices increase as the price of farm product falls. This is contrary to popular conception.

With the expansion of herd and farm size came the updating of equipment — because economics dictated it. You couldn't afford to use an old tractor or old baler which might break down, because the hay you were putting in was literally worth $2,000 a day. At a dollar a bale, if you're putting in 2,000 bales of hay a day, and your baler breaks down when it starts to rain, the $2,000 will go a long way towards paying for the new baler. Another good example is the dehorning saw for cattle. It's a $300 expenditure, but if one steer bleeds to death, because you don't have it, you lose maybe $5-600. So you're forced to go for these capital expenditures to try to save money, because money is so vital.

Of course these added expenditures piled onto interest. The result in my case was that a debt of $150,000 at a compound interest of 18% skyrocketed; added to cattle losses this amounted to $400,000. Land, machinery and cattle valued at $500,000 dropped to $300,000 — my positive net worth vanished.

As my money vanished to high interest and low cattle prices, and the bank refused to renew my loans as I couldn't make the interest payments, I started to look for a solution. I did a lot of work to acquire a Small Business Development Bond which, through a tax reduction to the bank, could have halved the interest rate. I investigated a young farmers' assistance program which had been in effect for some years, and yet on examination it had only seven applicants in total, ever. The mountains of red tape for government programs which discourage many, only angered me and spurred me to dig deeper and deeper. The attitude of the bank and the fact that I was lied to, in order to acquire additional securities, got me into a fighting mood. The gauntlet was down and I accepted the challenge.

The stage had been set in England when Margaret Thatcher raised interest rates to support the pound on international markets, under the guise of stopping inflation. If interest rates are twelve percent in England, and ten percent in France, an investor with a huge sum of money will put it in England, selling his francs to buy pounds, and thus creating a demand for pounds and supporting the price. The problem of course is that this is not a permanent investment of bricks or stone to build factories or houses but rather a short term paper investment, thirty days or three months. When the principal is needed or if the interest rates are raised in France, the paper money comes back out, plus interest. Thus, the investor sells more pounds than he bought, decreasing the currency value and even worse, forcing the interest rate even higher.

So interest rates are really a tax to support the dollar because the federal government is broke and cannot afford to peg the dollar and support it out of the treasury. It is a tax without legislation. The tax collector — the banks — get fat, and the tax, as always, is on the poor, or those who have to borrow money. I knew that the charging of interest creates inflation and even when they started raising interest on the pretense of stopping inflation I naively thought they would see the error of their ways. I should have read history — they do the same thing every time.

This insane cycle spread to the U.S. and Canada. That the price of gold in the U.S. reached a thousand dollars in 1980 was an indication not of the value of gold but the lack of worth of the U.S. dollar. In Canada, the stage was set much earlier; in 1967 the federal government realized that it could not afford to support the dollar out of treasury because of insufficient income. Notice that I didn't say overspending. So it floated the dollar and, quite unnoticed, it floated the interest rate as well. At first, the increase was insignificant and few realized what was happening or why.

Mind you, since Confederation in 1867, it had been illegal to charge more than seven percent interest on a mortgage. In 1943 it was lowered to six percent. This restriction was removed in 1967 on the pretense of increasing the money available for mortgages and lowering the interest rate. Get that? I was getting out of high school in 1967, and by 1969, as I watched interest rates and inflation climb, I quickly realized that the charging of interest inevitably creates inflation.

If you're locked in a room and given ten marbles and then asked for eleven back, it's physically impossible. The eleventh marble does not exist. But if you melt the ten marbles down and make eleven smaller ones it might work; thus, inflation. More simply, as a manufacturer had to pay interest, it had to be added to the cost of production, increasing the product price.

Of course, the dummies teaching the economic courses said too much money chasing too few goods. Did you ever have too much money? Look at all the salespeople around selling things. Too few goods? Now, as our businesses are destroyed by high interest rates, there *is* a real chance of too few goods. The crunch started when prime rates of 12 % eventually rose to 24.75 % This move by the feds — for after all the Bank of Canada is supposed to be controlled and responsible to the federal government — had a three-fold effect on the cattle industry. First, it blew costs out of all proportion because farmers had borrowed on a floating interest rate, not a fixed one, as your mortgage might be for five years, but one that changed from week to week. A group of cattle purchased at 12% could quite easily be at 20% before they were sold. People who were forced to pay more and more for mortgage rates, car loans and so on, could not afford to eat steak and roast beef and started to cut back on the purchase of meat. High interest rates also had the effect of supporting the dollar, which decreased our depressing prices, as I mentioned before. If the dollar had been allowed to fall, the price we would have gotten for beef would have risen because it could have been sold on the international market — we could have shipped into the United States. But in 1981, 25 % of the finished cattle slaughtered in Ontario came from the U.S.A.

So the federal government, by keeping the dollar high, was decreasing the price the farmer was paid for meat. Increasing the cost of interest to the consumer further drove down the price of meat. The increasing interest rate moved the cost of production up. Increased costs were added onto every tire, every piece of machinery we bought; spare parts that sat on the shelves were financed at 20% interest so that when we eventually purchased them the price was inflated. This affected the farm scene not only in Canada but throughout North America and the world. The red meat industry was hit first, as we were still paying for what seemed like high-priced grain at that point.

Why did the fight start in Ontario, in Bruce County? The simple truth is that Bruce is the most highly concentrated beef county in Canada. The reasons are geography and history I suppose. We're nestled in between Lake Huron and Georgian Bay and the amount of limestone, especially in the upper layers, is such that cash cropping isn't really feasible. There's too much rough land. It's good pasture land, however, as the limestone keeps the soil acidity down and the rainfall from the lakes maintains the moisture level so that pasture grows. It is probably one of the best spots to grow alfalfa.

Throughout recent history, calves have been brought down from Western Canada where the rough, drier land could raise cows, but not fatten calves. Four-hundred-pound calves were shipped east and put out to our good pastures until they reached 900 lbs. and then put on grain. Thirty percent of calves shipped east of Manitoba went to Bruce County. The industry gradually evolved into feed lots as grain got cheaper and the demand for cash flow increased. There are now a number of feed lots, some very large, as the expertise and the knowledge of how to handle and look after cattle passed down from father to son.

It is a cattle area, so much so that when the cattle industry is hurting there aren't other profits to turn to. So much of our farm land is tied up in beef that when we started to get squeezed, our only recourse was to put our land on the market. This very rapidly decreased land values. There were 9,000 acres in Elderslie Township in the fall of 1981 for sale. That's a fifth of the township. It later got up to a third and nearly a half. At that point sales stopped and land values dropped by 50% almost overnight. The equity that we relied on, that we'd been financing against, was no longer there.

That's why now I can tell farmers exactly when they will go bankrupt. The moment the bank calls their notes — these are demand notes so the moment the banker demands payment they are due and payable and something must be sold — the greatest investment the farmer has is his land and he cannot sell the land. When you realize that your land has suddenly become worthless, you realize you're bankrupt and the fight begins.

It's interesting to note that because of the roughness of the terrain they say that Bruce County virtually breeds character. Our area produced Agnes McPhail, Canada's first female M.P., Nellie McClung, the suffragette leader, and Walter Miller, National Leader of the Farmer's union. I've read that when the Romans got to Scotland and its rough land, they built a wall between England and Scotland. There wasn't any sense in going up into those hills — you could kill ten people and the next day you'd have to kill ten more, and the next day you'd have to kill ten more — they didn't know enough to quit. Those mountain people were a hardy type and the land was definitely not worth the fight. Probably it is partly our Scottish ancestry, and partly the geography, the adverse farming conditions — the stones, and a climate that isn't very good for growing corn. Adversity and a streak of rebelliousness, I guess.

The Black incident was the first unified action to stop farm closures in the 1980s in North America. As I travel and organize around the continent, I constantly recount the story of these brave individuals because it was this spontaneous action that triggered so much.

All the things I've mentioned reached a pressure point at the farm of Marvin Black. Marvin was just another young fellow who went broke in the beef industry and he had a job to go to. But his 72-year-old father Clarence had guaranteed his loans for $15,000, six years previous. The Bank of Commerce, in anger at Marvin, said that they could *expand* those notes to include everything that Clarence had.

We realized, when we heard this, that these papers we had all signed at the bank weren't what we thought they were, in fact the banks could bring these guarantees ahead six years. In one later case I got into, the Bank of Montreal brought a guarantee ahead 20 years. A piece of paper signed 20 years ago under completely different circumstances was still valid! And it could be expanded; you could sign a guarantee for $15,000 and they could in fact expand it to as much as was owed. Of course, when you read the fine print on the thing, it was expandable.

The farmers in their honesty just signed everything that was put to them, with every intention of paying it back, and with complete trust in the banker. He was our friend, noted for his honesty. People who are not involved in financing — who get a mortgage and maybe take it to their lawyer — can't really understand what happens when you go into a bank once or twice a month, signing papers and more papers (every time you turn around, you sign papers,) to the point where you don't bother reading them. It doesn't do you much good, because you can't understand what they say, anyway, and you have to sign or you don't have the money to operate.

Farmers, of course, don't trust lawyers. This is deep-seated and probably well-founded, as the lawyer was someone who cost you a lot of money and didn't do much. And so, farmers would save the expense of the lawyer's fees, although looking back on it now, it should have been mandatory for all these things to be signed in front of a lawyer. As well, there should be government forms as the bank writes in everything it possibly can. It has the right to break and enter into your house and to use, to the exclusion of all others, anything and everything they want. You frequently waive your rights under bankruptcy: traditionally under farm bankruptcy practice you cannot be forced into bankruptcy and you're allowed to keep equipment and enough seed for a hundred acres, $2,000 worth of personal items, and so on. But when you sign some of these papers, such as the general security agreements, you waive all rights to those things — all your personal rights. It is much the same as demanding, when you get your driver's license, that you sign a piece of paper that says you promise to plead guilty to every and any charge, waiving your right to a court hearing.

So the Black affair had a real educational effect on Marv and his neighbours; we attracted some people from other areas who had gone through it before, and they explained some of the papers. That was a real benefit, a real awakening.

Marvin Black:
"Farmers Rebellion 1981" 2

*Justice and freedom do not depend so much on our willingness
to stand up and fight for ourselves as it does on our willingness to stand up and fight for the rights of others.*

The Black incident started for me two weeks earlier than the
rest, when I heard that Marv was being shut down. I'd been
hearing rumours for weeks. After consuming a considerable
amount of truth serum with a fellow farmer, discussing the whole
thing and deciding that something had to be done, I ventured
over to the Black's about 1:00 a.m., where I discovered Marv
and some other friends also discussing and cussing the problem,
the severity of the situation and its magnitude, the frustrations
and angers. We talked about a lot of things, and got pretty
hot about it. Not an awful lot came of it, but it did make us
aware that we had some mutual problems. I, at that time,
didn't really see that I had a problem, but I was very angry
about the money stolen from me — by the banks, by the failure
of the provincial and federal governments to address the problem, by the abdication of the Cattlemen's Association, and by
the "blame the victim" scenario so rampant in our society. When someone's in trouble you blame him, you don't
blame the fellow that did it to him.

About two weeks later the phone rang at eight o'clock on a
Saturday morning; George Bothwell was calling. I didn't
know George very well at the time and I suppose he got my
name from Marv. In the ensuing months I would be very impressed with his concern for his fellow human beings. His
message that morning got my heart to beating. "The bank is

closing in on Marvin Black and some of us are going to stop them. Do you want to help?''

Finally someone was doing something. Everything reflected back to one thing — if you want something done, do it yourself. And here was someone going to do something.

The game plan was to take guns and go groundhog-hunting on Marvin's front lawn. We figured we might be breaking the law but we would certainly wake somebody up. George would have liked to have seen everything disappear, with the bank left holding the bag for a million dollars. He thought it might get their attention.

The night before I got the call, George had called about fifteen farmers, starting about 1:00 a.m., saying something to the effect of get your ass out of bed and get over to Black's. Fifteen men responded in trucks and in the meeting that ensued they decided to stand and fight. The only real issue to fight on was Clarence Black, Marvin's father. Marv had a job to go to. But the bank had pulled out a guarantee, signed by Clarence six years previous, for $15,000 and said they could expand it and take everything the father had. (The only way to clear the banks of these guarantees is to change banks. They just hold everything forever.)

That was our issue. We said no, this just isn't fair. Another little kicker here was that there were two houses on the Black farm — one that Clarence lived in and one that had originally been an old log cabin that Marvin had fixed up with quite a bit of renovating. The bank understood that Clarence's house was supposed to have been severed from the property when Marv bought it from him and kept for himself. Of course the severance had never been done, and there was nothing on the mortgage to that effect. When the bank was foreclosing on the farm, they were kicking Clarence out of his house as well. Both you and your father will be at the road with your suitcases was the statement.

The other thing I should throw in here is that the problem, really, began with a 300 head of ''missing'' cattle, and perhaps with a lack of understanding on the bank's part of how farmers think. As everything had gone downhill, farmers used any means they could to stay in business. Now Marv had been running around 1,800 head, maybe 2,000. He'd had some significant death losses, due to disease, which is common enough with the type of animals Marv was purchasing, the bigger, rougher animals. Some viruses cannot be controlled. You can use vaccinations ahead of time, but once the actual disease is there, it's pretty well impossible to cure. Some viral diseases that get into cattle — IBR, VDB — don't kill the animal but weaken its digestive system to such an extent that it is malnourished; secondary infections come in, pneumonia and so on.

So Marv had about three runs of that, IBR and VDB, and another virus whose origin they never discovered. His losses, in my own rough calculations, amounted to about five percent. In that type of an operation, death losses should have been running around three to four. However the kicker here is that in order to maintain his equity position, Marvin never reported these death losses. The animals had died and he simply failed to tell the bank.

When it came down to collecting on the last 300 head, they weren't there, and the bank didn't really believe that they had died a year to two earlier. They thought that Marvin had taken them, sold them and pocketed the money. When they got to digging into it I think they eventually accepted the truth because there were no charges laid — on that. But it got the bank's dander up and, in all fairness to them, that's what started the confrontation.

Clarence was well-liked in the neighbourhood and we stood firm. Thirty or so neighbours took turns standing guard over the weekend and contacting quite a few people to support us.

On Monday, when the bank phoned to say they were coming, someone in the background shouted, "Tell them to come armed." They never showed. Thirty unarmed men had stopped the mighty Bank of Commerce. It took about a week to work out a deal. I wasn't involved at all in the negotiations. The bank had a second mortgage on the farm where Clarence lived. We got them to guarantee that if they foreclosed he would have a life lease on the house. As it turned out, the Farm Credit Corporation foreclosed on the first mortgage and then sold the farm back to Clarence. And we got his guarantee back; in other words his life savings were protected. We also got him half the proceeds of the corn crop because he'd been working away at the farm with Marv for no salary, just volunteer labour. As corn prices fell, it turned out to be a liability, but at the time we judged his half to be in the neighbourhood of $20,000.

Another very important item we got paid was a $20,000 fertilizer bill. A common bank tactic down through the years has been hooking in the small suppliers; the bank would get the fertilizer company to advance the fertilizer and spray; the feed company the feed. Then the bank would grab either the crop or the livestock and leave these unsecured creditors hang. One of the important aspects of the Farm Creditors Act we're fighting for is to prevent exactly that sort of thing.

To give you a bit of a background, the bank had indicated to Marv that *they* would pay for these inputs if he would just go ahead and put the crop in. But Marv kind of had his head up a bit and he knew what was likely going to happen. So he leased the land to his father and they put the crop in in Clarence's name, which would give him a bit of a bargaining point, although it didn't leave much when it was all finished at the negotiating table. But the key was that we fought to get the supplier paid and won!

Through the history of the Survival Association we have considered the small business person as an integral part of the farm community. We can't exist without him, he can't exist without us. In Rodney, Ontario, we occupied a farm supply store off and on for two weeks to stop the bank from selling off the stock and finally we negotiated a settlement. The Deputy Minister of Agriculture for Ontario said the reason he was in trouble was that the farmers were in trouble. If he could just have expanded that to the factories that supply the stores!

Newlife Mills was also a player in the Black case, although not when we were negotiating, since they had already looked after their position. They had $75,000 owing to them for feed that was in Marv's cattle when the bank was selling them and keeping all the money, refusing to pay for the feed. Newlife Mills said, "We've had enough trouble with the Canadian Imperial Bank of Commerce, they've done this to us once too often, give us a crack at them."

So they came in and loaded up two truckloads of cattle. It's very interesting because Marv informed the bank of this situation and they worked out a deal with Newlife Mills. If you've ever read *The Merchants of Grain* you'll understand that there are only seven families who run the world grain trade anyway. Newlife Mills' parent company is Perish and Heinbecker. Perish and Heinbecker is the Commerce's largest customer, so when Newlife Mills told them that they had the cattle, then they had to work out a deal. As it came out in the court proceedings, Newlife Mills gave the Commerce $30,000 from the proceeds of the cattle it sold.

Now here you have a situation where Newlife Mills took the cattle, the Commerce got half the proceeds, and the police in their ensuing investigation charged Marvin with stealing the cattle. The police investigated the Marvin Black case for about six months — where the cattle went, what happened, were there possible criminal charges, and so on.

There was a lot of night riding and it shook our fellows up quite a bit to have police crawling all over, asking questions. One of the funniest incidents — (the banks don't understand the farm mentality) — arose from a favour Marv did for a friend. That friend of Marv's had put some cattle out to feed. The guy who was feeding them did not do a good job; they came out in the spring in a very green, or thin, condition. The friend went to see Marv. Marv knew he was being shut down and said, "There's a grass farm that I've been renting over the years — It's a good price, good grass, and I'm not going to be able to take it this year so you might as well take it."

So they did just that, and they ran the herd over to Marv's (he had pretty good working facilities) because they needed to be wormed, de-horned, castrated, treated for lice and so on. So they conditioned them, put on Marv's brand to identify them, took them out and dropped them on this rented grassland. Naturally the police were convinced that these were part of the missing cattle.

In the ensuing investigation they were further confused in that it turned out that two partners in fact owned the cattle. They questioned the one partner who said, yes, he owned the cattle but had no receipts. The other fellow had the receipts at home for the cattle but didn't know where the cattle were. He went and got the receipts, saying that he'd been by the farm once when a local trucker had taken him, and he pointed out the trucker to the police. The police asked the trucker about it and, I guess in order to protect the innocent, he claimed he didn't know anything about it. This just made the police all the more suspicious. They dug through the books of the fellow who claimed to own them, who was in partnership with the guy who actually had the receipts, and they dug them out with the other receipts. The police said that they'd never believe that anyone could have $30,000 worth of cattle and not know where they were.

But what they didn't realize was the trust that farmers have for each other, that business deals worth thousands of dollars are done by word of mouth, not even a handshake really. One partner had complete trust in the other; he knew that his partner was looking after the cattle and that they were on good grass, that Marv or his dad would keep an eye on them for them, and so on.

Back when I started farming I rented my grass out. The farmer came in from quite a ways away, put the cattle in — we didn't really have anything in writing, just a verbal agreement — and he didn't come back until the fall to pick them up! I phoned him once about a steer which had quite a bit of pink eye, and I think he came out once to look at it, but other than that he had no worries.

For the bank and two policemen it was inconceivable. I think they are still convinced that the cattle actually belonged to Marv.

But with that kind of investigation going on — the police in unmarked cars travelling all over — the neighbourhood was in quite a bit of excitement. There was a lot of anger and frustration as well. The net result, (after six months of investigation the police had to do *something,* in my opinion, was that the Crown Attorney was overzealous. He charged Marv with two counts of theft: one for the cattle which Newlife Mills had taken (they never charged Newlife Mills or the Commerce, which received $30,000); and the other for sileage.

There had been a pile of sileage on the farm. Once sileage is exposed to the air, it has to be used for feed or it deteriorates very rapidly. It's not really a saleable item. Marvin managed to sell some of this sileage to pay some small bills — a mechanic who had done some work on an engine, and a mineral bill (the cattle had consumed the mineral). Again the bank had grabbed the cattle and to hell with the mineral bill. They charged him with stealing the sileage. Looking back on it, I am convinced they laid these charges just to associate farmers with thieves, and to discredit the organization. The two theft charges were just pure b.s.

The Commerce admitted at the hearing that they thought it was worthless, had tried to sell it and hadn't had any offers. There was a lot of sileage in the area because it's a traditional feed for cattle and so many cattle producers had been shut down.

A further charge, obtaining credit under false pretenses dealt with the juggling of the cattle count.

The police physically arrested Marv, which is a violation of his constitutional rights — under our new Constitution you're not subject to unwarranted arrest when a summons will do. Everyone knew where he was. The sheriff had been handing him summonses and court documents during all these proceedings. Marvin was a married man, working at a job. They wouldn't allow him to tell his wife that he'd been arrested, and wouldn't allow him to get his heart medication. Marv has an artificial valve in his heart and he's on blood thinners and has to stay on these pills three times a day. They wouldn't let him change his clothes, which had manure on them from working on the feedlot. His six-year-old son went to tell Mummy that Daddy had been arrested and of course the mother didn't really believe Andy and couldn't understand it, until one of the workers at the feedlot told her.

They detained him in jail in Saskatoon that night, flew him to Toronto and kept him a second night there, then they drove to Owen Sound and spent the next night there — all in order to go to a court where they were only setting a date for a hearing. The whole thing could have been done by summons. Actually Marv didn't even have to appear, as his lawyer could have made the arrangements. So this was simply intimidation.

The kicker, of course, is that Marv lost his job because he was arrested and taken away for three days. Fortunately Marv is a very good cattleman and subsequently got a better job at another feedlot — when he went back after they set the hearing date he had a job waiting for him. But that wasn't the whole of the story. The Royal Bank, which was financing the first feedlot, had earlier threatened to call its loan if Marv Black was manager. So the feedlot, in order to keep Marv on, put in a token manager who did very little work. Of course once they arrested him, the Bank wanted him out of there, and brought enough pressure that Marv was fired.

When Marv's trial came up July 20, 1983, the jury acquitted him on the two theft charges based on the evidence that came out at the trial. Members of the Association and local farmers made it the best attended trial anyone could remember. There were humorous moments as the "evidence" was trotted out. The bank officials who were sent out to count the cattle for the bank got so drunk that one had to be loaded into the car to go home. They weren't even sure just which farms they'd been to.

Marv was convicted of obtaining credit under false pretenses — not reporting the death of the cattle. In actual fact, by extending the time under the line of credit, he had stayed in business two more months and decreased the bank's losses as the price of cattle went up in the interim. Of the documents as to the number of cattle, which the bank claimed they relied so heavily on, two could not be found, one had no date and the other, the banker admitted filling in after Marv had signed it. The judge, however, ruled that the extension of time was an extension of credit. I think the jury was negatively influenced by the million dollar figures reported in the press which had nothing to do with the cattle count.

In speaking to sentence, Marv's lawyer presented about twenty letters from local farmers stating their support for Marv. Judge Elizabeth Robinson took them to mean that the farmers didn't feel that what Marv had done was wrong and decided to make an example of him. During sentencing she said that the ordeal of trying to keep his farm operating had been enough punishment for Marv, but that the publicity generated by the farm gate defense had made him "appear a victim of the CIBC rather than the offender." With no previous record he was sentenced August 8, 1983, to six months in reformatory. The next day Gerald Kaplan, the Federal Minister of Justice made a big speech about not imprisoning people convicted of non-violent crimes.

Why A Survival Association? 3

If doctors were as incompetent as lawyers we'd have no need for birth control.

After the incident at Black's we had quite a few meetings. Almost every night different farmers came in. We started off with an information meeting, which brought in one woman from Toronto who'd been through the mill. She gave us a good explanation of bank papers, what they had you sign, some of the illegal manoeuvers the banks make. Awareness I guess you'd call it; one fellow said it was the best day he'd ever spent insofar as being aware of what he'd been signing.

She informed us that in her case the bank had forged documents. One of our members had promissary notes that his wife had signed, "pre-dated," to cover debt two years previous. One ex-banker explained how you could hold the two copies against a window and trace the signature. We began to see that bank employees weren't necessarily honest. In digging through the Bank Act we found the banks were not always going by the law. As things progressed we found a real and increasing reluctance on the part of the banks to go to court.

A big part of the problem on the paper end of it was the volume of paper. Every time a farmer went into the bank there were always three or four documents to sign. Because the documents were written in legal jargon they were completely unintelligible to a layperson, even to some lawyers; moreover the farmer trusted the banker. He had fully every intention of paying the money back; there was never going to be any problem — he just signed his note. There were stacks of paper at a time, with a great deal signed blank, which the bank would fill in afterwards. It's a slightly different story now that a lot more people have been made aware of what these papers contain.

Another thing that began to surface were people with solutions. As soon as there is a thing in the paper about problems, there are always people with solutions. Some blamed it on Satan, for example. These were interesting people; I wouldn't criticize them too loudly, they all had their own beliefs. Some of their ideas resurface again and again as you go back in history, especially on the creation of money and debts, usury and interest, things like that. They keep kicking up again and again.

But the bad ones were the ambulance chasers — people who came for publicity or money, to ride the wave for their own benefit. Even today advisors are going around claiming to be with the Survival Association, bilking people of money. At Doug Dailey's sale in Ohio, the day before the sale, a lawyer came with a solution for $2,500. And when we would have no part of him, he went to the press and claimed we wanted the sale to go through.

As we talked among ourselves we began to realize the magnitude of the problem. The realization came to me that perhaps I was in trouble too, so many farmers in the beef business were in trouble. Land values were bound to fall. Whereas originally I felt that at anytime I could sell off some land and be fairly secure, I began to realize that if so many people were in trouble my land wasn't going to be worth anything. I still felt, though, that my bank was all right, and that I'd still make it through, since I would be able to refinance that fall. The long term looked rough but that fall I'd still be okay.

The desperation and the stress some people were feeling became quite evident. The human suffering was what got me involved more than anything else, I suppose. It was unbelievable. The interest rate kept climbing, completely beyond our control. The very government that was supposed to be protecting us was the one doing this to us, or allowing it to be done. We farmers were being raped by the banks and the government was holding us down.

First it was the beef business but, as we all knew, once the red meat sector (beef and pork) was hit, the grain farmers would follow. It was quite plain to a farmer. But the banks didn't seem to realize that by encouraging people to get out of red meat and into cash crops, they were adding to the inevitable disaster in these areas too. We have farmers, with good proof, actually suing the banks for forcing them to sell their livestock and go into corn production.

What also became very evident was the lack of competent legal advice. You go to one lawyer and are told one thing, another lawyer will tell you something different. Five lawyers will give you five different opinions. Lawyers in the rural communities tend to be general lawyers; to give them their due they know a little bit about everything. Or a lot of nothing; jack of all trades, master of none I suppose.

Some, including us at the beginning, didn't even realize that what we were talking about was litigation, and what we needed were litigation lawyers. About 80% of lawyers, in my opinion, shouldn't be practising law. They are nothing more than real estate lawyers — they know how to draw up a deed, maybe a mortgage, that sort of thing. As far as litigation goes, they're a complete waste. Ten percent then meant to help and tried very hard to help but weren't aware.

We had a lot of what might be construed as fraudulent conveyances, putting the farm in one's father's name in order to avoid creditors, that sort of thing. It was being done by farmers on their lawyer's advice and lawyers didn't even realize when they were doing it that they were setting their clients up for trouble.

These lawyers would transfer properties and then sit back and not contest the judgement. Once the bank got judgement they moved to roll back the conveyances. With good lawyers — and now we get to the ten percent who want and know how to help — we have not had one single case that I worked on where the banks were able to get judgement. These lawyers had to be filtered out, as one of our early goals was to get proper legal counselling. This would save money and the running around. We tried to create a structure whereby the lawyers and ourselves could be made aware of what was and wasn't working, keeping everyone well informed. This was something the banks had not counted on.

Good financial advice was pretty well nil. Chartered accountants couldn't work with red ink. Once the situation got to that point, you were bankrupt, and the normal course of action dictated that you declare bankruptcy or quietly go out of business and walk away. That sort of thing wasn't a viable alternative, not with the emotional commitment we had to the farms and with the severity of the situation. So we had to get some innovative financial consulting. We had to teach people to put proposals to the banks, proposals for write-offs, of what might be called irretrievable losses. This was something very foreign to the banks; they were doing it all the time for business but no they wouldn't do it for farmers.

We also had to make farmers aware of what little government help there was, get them to put pressure on their members of parliament, try and put a legislative package together and get some advice as to how it could get through.

A lot of what we did was literally survival: telling farmers how to deal in cash, and how to make sure they didn't leave money where the bank could grab it. This is another illegal move banks make constantly — seizing accounts in other banks without a court order. They comply with each other to steal, even stealing accounts of other family members. As for the police, the banks could do no wrong. We advised people how to hold the banks off by protecting themselves with a lawyer, making sure that they had grocery money — that their family was the first one looked after; that they could hang on, that help was on the way. How long it was going to take we didn't know, but we knew that sooner or later the government would have to address these problems.

For dealing in cash we had an underground set-up for buying and selling and cashing cheques. We discovered very quickly that banks could seize cheques at the source. Some of the worst incidents of this kind involved the milk and hog marketing boards, where all the farmer's money went through a centralized agency. Milk must be sold through the milk board, so if you're in the dairy business the bank knows that that is where the cheque is going to be, and so can grab it and keep 100%.

This is an interesting scenario because the most a court can garnishee from a working person in Ontario is 20%, and if he's making only a small amount they have to ensure that he has a decent standard of living before they can seize anything. If you're a farmer, however, they can take 100% of the milk cheque. That doesn't allow anything for feeding the cows, paying the hydro bills for the milkers — anything like that — let alone any consideration as to what is actually the farmer's share of the money for his work. Out of $100, the wage share might be $10 while the rest was for inputs but they were grabbing the entire $100.

In one case, the bank seized the full pig cheque and gave the farmer $173 to go on for three months. He then went back and asked for another $100 and they gave him $95. It is a good thing the man did not have my temper.

Although some of what we did could probably be construed as illegal, such as hiding of assets, I don't consider it illegal; it was a matter of survival.

How were we to stop the judgment process, challenge their documents? It became quite obvious, in the first few cases I got involved in, that banks worked through brute force. One outrageous case involved $20,000. The farmer and the banker had a fight in the morning. At noon the banker came out with a demand for the money. With two trucks, they loaded up cattle worth much more than the $20,000 the farmer owed. The cattle were taken off their feed and put them in a barn some miles away on straight hay, which set them back, weight-wise. Then the banker sat back and laughed while the farmer ran around trying to raise the $20,000 to get his $40,000 worth of cattle back. When he did get the $20,000 he found he had to pay another $2200 in bailiff's costs, trucking costs, plus the feed bill. The bills piled up and the bank had no concern about how high that cost went. In that case the bank didn't get to the receivership end of it. Receivership costs are all borne by the farmer. It was as if the banks were on a power trip, to punish the "bad farmer," to destroy him so that he wouldn't have enough money left to sue them.

One farmer cashed in an insurance policy for $1800 for family expenses. The Bank of Commerce grabbed the cheque in June, even though they knew the farmer had no other money.

"Your wife drives a school bus," was the banker's justification.

"But the buses don't run in the summer," was the farmer's meek reply.

"That's not my concern!"

The Vigilantes   4

The hottest places in Hell are reserved for those who in time of great moral crises maintain their neutrality. — Dante 1265-1321

The vigilantes were probably the most exciting and intriguing part of the farm movement at that time. It started with a remark Tom Clark, an Owen Sound area farmer, made at the provincial legislature. Tom had been instrumental in organizing farmers to fight interest rates about a year prior to our involvement as a group. In 1980, he led quite a few farmers (four hundred, I think) down to pack the Queen's Park visitors' gallery and brought a lot of pressure to bear. The Ontario government subsequently came out with a program that provided a maximum of $1300 to $1400 per farmer, just a drop in the bucket. Some of these farmers were paying more interest *per week* than the maximum they could get out of the program.

Then in November 1981, when Tom was back down in Queen's Park, he happened to mention that there were groups of people, whom he called "vigilantes," forming, who were prepared to fight to protect their land. Now that got a lot of media attention. They questioned Gary Gurbin, our federal Conservative MP, who confirmed that there were groups forming and that the mood in the neighbourhood was very militant. Emotions were running very high.

On December 2, pictures of three hooded men with guns, who vowed to fight to save their farms, appeared on the front page of the *Toronto Star*.   I was at home and a reporter had come over to do a television interview. At noon she got a call about the picture and the chase was on. For the next three days there were reporters crawling all over Grey-Bruce counties looking for the vigilantes, trying to line up meetings. Because of the press they were receiving, the vigilantes went underground.

Months and months later, I would be in farm homes with financial problems and they would bring that picture out and say it was the first sign of hope they'd had, that someone was finally doing something. The encouragement it gave to farmers in financial difficulty right across North America, I don't suppose, will ever be able to be measured.

The background to the vigilante picture, as it was told to me, is quite intriguing. Ours is a neighbourhood of old family farms, a lot of inter-marriages, people knowing people for miles around, local names for places. One of the most intriguing in our area is a little town called Desboro which consists of a feed mill, a hotel, a farm equipment dealer and a couple of houses. It has the nick-name Dodge City; even the ball team calls itself the Dodge City Flyers. So in some of the conversations, when the vigilante picture was being set up, there were references to Dodge City and other intriguing places. Everyone was convinced, because of the police nosing around Marv Black, that the phones were tapped. So a lot of the time, when referring to people, they'd call them by their wife's maiden name, that only an insider would know. It was quite a clandestine movement.

As it was reported to me, the actual picture was taken about five o'clock in the afternoon in December, when twilight comes around six o'clock, in a barn with no lights. The person who took the reporters there refused to go into the barn with them. There were more hooded men in other parts of the barn, all armed. One spoke out behind them and sent a chill down their backs.

It was quite an emotional thing. After the reporters left, one farmer was reported to have said that two years ago, who would have believed that farmers would take these steps? It was a real indication of how serious the situation had become.

Frank Reynold's article in the *Toronto Star* was nothing if not dramatic:

OWEN SOUND — They'll sacrifice their lives if need be to protect their farms, these members of a vigilante farm group in one of the province's hardest-hit areas.

They are furious at government inaction in providing financial aid to farmers. They're angry at the increasing number of farm foreclosures. They say they are prepared to fight with guns and pipes to keep bankers and sheriffs from closing them down.

"We've run out of alternatives," one vigilante said in an interview yesterday.

In a deserted barn on the outskirts of Owen Sound, five vigilante members, carrying rifles and wearing black masks to protect their identity, said they'd waited long enough for help, now it was time to take matters in their own hands.

Sitting on bales of hay, their rifles across their laps, with one pointed to catch any stranger walking in the door, the vigilantes said they were supported by many farmers, young and old, who feel fighting is the only way to make people listen.

"We all stand to lose our farms," one farmer said angrily. "Our roots start in these farms and the soil and if you pull them out we'll die. We'd rather die fighting than leave peacefully."

One farmer yelled, "Five years ago I had over $600,000 in my farm. Today, I can't even pay my heating bills. That's why I'm here."

One after another, the vigilantes said they were tired of paying gouging interest rates to the banks only to have them keep coming back and asking for more security on their loans.

The farmer at the door on the upper level with the gun pointed toward the ground yelled out, "We're tired of the banks charging us rates we can't begin to pay back, and telling us what to do."

The group members wouldn't elaborate on what they intend to do to protect their homes and

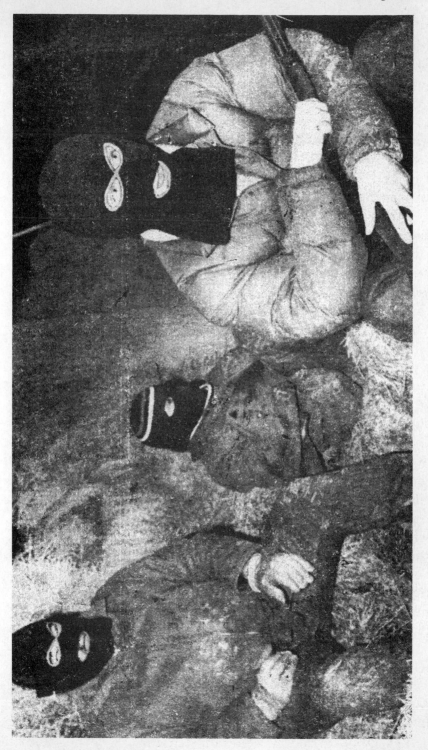

The sight of masked vigilantes on the front page of the Toronto Star (December 2, 1982) shocked its readers and forced them to regard farm problems as serious issues. This picture was the springboard for national focus on the farm community's activities.

farms other than to say they'll use whatever is necessary, whenever necessary.

"We kept being told to wait for the federal budget, that relief was on its way," yelled one angrily. "That budget did more harm to farmers than anything else has done in the last 30 years."

Of course a picture of that sort had to be coordinated. You don't just find people with hoods on walking through the fields at night. In one television report, some hooded farmers, who wished only to keep their identities concealed, let some of their anger and frustration out. A year later I was down in Minnesota, going through my scrapbook with reporters and, when they saw the vigilante picture they said, "Oh, we have a videotape of those people." They had a tape of these farmers with hoods, talking about their problems. So it did get quite a bit of international coverage, including the front page of the *National Enquirer*. The existence of the vigilantes is firm in my mind. I know from my own experience that the tensions running through the community were very real and that the availability of guns to the farmers was a matter of real concern to the OPP. They know that almost every farmer has a gun, and if things get pushed too far, well, the danger had already manifested itself in a number of suicides.

There is still a real possibility of bloodshed. I could never conceive of it as an organized thing, but I can conceive of individuals with their backs to the wall and their whole lives going down the drain, with no sense of hope, picking up a gun to defend their property. In North Dakota, a farmer shot three police officers. A baker in Ottawa fired twice at a bailiff, and a guy in Calgary holed up in his house to stop a foreclosure. In Minnesota in October 1983, as I write this chapter, a farmer and his son invited a banker and his loans officer out to the farm where they assassinated them. In Texas a P.C.A. loan officer was shot by a farmer. The potential for violence is very real. The Vigilantes did have a good effect — they got a lot of attention. And the vigilantes episode conveyed some sense of the desperation out here in the countryside to the city people, and to the government.

The Government Programs 5

I had lost $333 a head on stocker animals and the govern-ment paid me $20 per head to cover. They might as well stick it up their nose.

I had gone down to Toronto with the Cattlemen's Association that fall (1981) to put pressure on the then Minister of Agriculture for Ontario, Lorne Henderson, for a stabilization program to give some relief to the beef industry, because it was wholesale slaughter out there. The Ontario government had come up with a program that offered $40 a head to each pro-ducer of a fattened steer or slaughter animal. Absolutely nothing for farmers like myself.

I buy a 400-pound calf, I winter him and put him on grass in the summer and sell him off at about 800 pounds to a feedlot. I have that animal a whole year. Three to four months in the feedlot should have him finished and away he goes. The potential is there for a feedlot operator to collect that $40 three times a year. Not all of them get that; some take the 400-pound steer right through to the finish, and get the $40. But those of us in the background business, especially in Bruce County where cattle are fed a lot of grass, weren't going to get anything. Nor were the cow owners who produced the calf.

My first exposure to Lorne Henderson, as an individual, made me feel such disillusionment and anger that it's hard to express it. He had no comprehension. Bill Wolfe, a respected cattle-producer in the Grey-Bruce area, who at one time had over 10,000 head, had the documentation: receipts, bills and a very good set of books. He is a very knowledgeable and good producer — his rate of gain was up to four pounds per day, which is very good. I also had documentation that for my type of farmer, losses were far in excess of those who finish an animal. The interest rate was the problem at that point. We were up to about 18%, so I paid interest on an animal for a full year, while the short-keep fellow paid interest on it for three to four months.

Lorne Henderson insisted that the price of feed grain was too high, but to me that's just wrong, because you don't sacrifice one farmer to help the other. Things had to be stabilized. Cheap grain makes for cheap meat. To me there was no problem with the price of grain being high except that in the free-for-all market out there, it certainly hurt when the price of beef was down. When Bill Wolfe tried to explain this, Henderson stated that it was quite obvious that Bill didn't know anything about the cattle business. That angered me to no limit. Bill had forgotten much more than Lorne Henderson ever knew about cattle. We eventually got $20 a head which amounted to $3.40 for every person for whom I raised a year's supply of beef.

The other thing that came up at the meeting was that Marvin Black's assets were going to be taken over by a court receiver that day. Lorne Henderson happened to mention that, because of the pressure we had been putting on, they had set up a provincial review committee to look into these kinds of cases. So I asked him if he was familiar with the Black case, and what he was doing about it. He replied that Marvin was the fellow who had lost a million dollars of his father's money. It was no such thing. Marvin had bought the farm from his father. It was the bank that was out the money. I exploded. I don't even remember what I told him and I left right after. Later, I spoke to some of his aides, who were very sympathetic.

A few weeks later, we sat in the visitors' gallery in Queen's Park. The Opposition asked Henderson what he was going to do, and he got up and said it was a federal problem. I immediately came to a boil, remembering the frustrations I'd had talking to the man before. I jumped up and hollered, "Tell that to my wife and kids you stupid son-of-a-bitch," and gave him the arm gesture. Knowing I would have to leave, I turned and started to walk away. One of the Conservatives stood up and hollered something — questioning, I suppose, our abilities as farmers. George Bothwell then remarked, "Why doesn't this government get off its ass and do something? This Tory government stinks,'' and followed me out the door.

The television cameras showed security men leaping over chairs trying to get to us. We went out to the elevator, pushed the button and were surrounded by a huge mob of uniformed security guards. I guess they'd been watching and were waiting for us. They said they were going to take us outside. George said he'd been around the country long enough to know that when someone is going to take you outside it usually means something that isn't going to be in your best interests. So he turned to get the press, and the security guards tackled him, getting one handcuff on him. I went over to try to back them off a bit, and Eddy Sergeant (our local Liberal MPP), bless his heart, who by this time had gotten up out of the Legislature, bowled over some of the security guards, picked up George, got the handcuff off him and took us down to his office.

The press pestered us constantly, asking if we were vigilantes, and I certainly felt like one then. George later remarked that we had found the vigilantes — they wear blue uniforms and walk around Queen's Park. Eddy Sergeant later remarked, ''Those fellows down there (Queen's Park) will think I paid you to do that.'' Eddy is a very sympathetic person and did what he could but he was fighting a losing battle with the Tory government. A few weeks later, Lorne Henderson was to be replaced as Minister of Agriculture.

Three weeks after the incident in the legislature, we got together three busloads of Grey-Bruce farmers to meet with MPP's. When one of our members, who had driven down himself, went to park, a security guard warned him not to park there, as a group of angry farmers was coming to dump dead animals and manure! When we stepped off the bus in our three-piece suits, we found they'd rolled up the red carpet. Duncan Allan, then Deputy Minister of Agriculture, promised help before the house adjourned for Christmas.

The P.C.'s have always made the pretense of being a farm party, but nothing could be further from the truth. They act as if they have a complete lack of knowledge of the farming situation. They don't know where new wealth comes from. They think industry is the key to economic revival, a carryover from decades ago when they wanted to encourage industry. They don't tie unemployment to farm price.

Unemployment insurance is simply wealth redistribution, and at an average of $189 per week, it pays out more than the average farm family makes. It is denied to farmers. In 1981 the Ontario government gave more to subsidize urban transport than it spent on its total agricultural budget, which was mostly administration and research. It gave a subsidy of $84 million to the TTC — *in Toronto alone.*

The farmer is denied tax dollars for delivery or purification of his water and his waste. The federal housing program costs $400 million annually and farmers cannot participate. The farmer pays 30% more for hydro than the city dweller. Farm programs total less than one percent of federal and provincial budgets, and yet farming directly accounts for 20% of jobs, and is of course ultimately responsible for all employment.

The average farm debt to assets ratio is 5 to 10:1, whereas that of a normal business is 2 to 3:1. The impact is obvious: farmers are affected much more seriously by high interest rates.

Farm debts are collaterally secured by mortgages. Mortgages are simply deeds that transfer title to the lending institution until the debt is paid. The result is that the banks are daily securing ownership by default to more and more of rural Canada.

Questionnaires handed out at a meeting of farmers in Middlesex County in 1981 showed that average liabilities for each farmer amounted to $276,301, with interest payments averaging $41,133.

At the time when agriculture in Ontario was going down for the second time, the government spent $650 million to purchase a share in the Suncor oil company and ordered a $10 million jet with leather toilet seats for the Premier. That jet did have one good effect — it could only land at the seven longest Ontario airports and it employed a lot of farmers ''shortening'' runways!

What angers me more than anything is the difference between what governments promise when they do set up a program for farmers and what we actually get. The press hooplah after Tom Clark's delegation in the fall of 1980 promised $30 million. In actual fact, only $7 million was given out to farmers. The big press campaign was to cool out the farmers and get the sympathy of the city people, to make them think the government was really helping. In all these programs, help is limited to two cents a person and only then to people with one green eye and one blue eye. They build in limitations so the money isn't available, saying, well, we *had* $30 million out there but only $7 million was used! The newly-announced (January 1984) $62 million beef marketing program is the same. It's a five year program. It's not $62 million, but rather $12 million per year (if needed). Again, no money for the farmers, but a lot of talk of upgrading packing facilities. I call it the packers assistance program.

Perhaps as a result of our protest (and that of other groups), Lorne Henderson announced, at the beginning of the 1981 Christmas break (and the eve of his departure), a $60 million program: the Ontario Farm Adjustment Assistance. Only $16 million was ever actually used to help defray interest costs. The government got hooked into the guarantee program, I can only suppose, because of its ignorance. There were two factors: first, they didn't realize that the chartered banks were not the solution but rather the biggest part of our immediate problems; secondly, they didn't realize how serious the situation was. The government professed to believe it was going to get better: if they just left matters alone, the economy would right itself. So they came in with bank guarantees on operating loans, but only for those farmers whom they chose. You had to have ten percent equity, but a lot of us were already broke. By the time it was over, they had guaranteed about $42 million in loans with no intention of ever having to make good on the guarantees. This was a death knell for many farmers because, to collect on the guarantee, the bank had first to realize on all security, i.e., sell out the farmer.

The Ontario Department of Agriculture is free to do anything it wants, as long as it doesn't spend any money. They went into a state of shock a year later when those guarantees were called. In reality, of course, the banks had set them up. The banks had given them the problem cases, knowing full well things would get worse, and ensuring that the government would bail them out.

The program consisted of three parts:

> (1) A guarantee by the government to pay the interest when the farmer defaulted, if the bank would defer the interest for six months (no compounding), and calculate simple interest only;

(2) A maximum 5% subsidy on interest over 12% to those who qualified;

(3) A government guarantee on new operating loans.

The big problem was that you had to work through your banker and were subject to his whims. The second year, they allowed the farmer to bypass the banker if he was not cooperative.

One farmer, who had had his notes for $70,000 called, was not in the program. I asked the manager of the Owen Sound Bank of Nova Scotia why. "He didn't have a good enough set of books," was the answer! Five percent of $70,000 or $3,500 would have paid for one hell of a set of books!

After five months, only 732 farmers had received help. The government's own estimates were that 5,000 needed help. The program could have made a real difference if they had used the time it bought to address the commodity price problem.

There was another example of their lack of understanding. Part of the program was a five percent interest subsidy on money borrowed without benefit of this guarantee. (If the government guaranteed your loan, the interest rate went up to prime, and you were not eligible for the second part of the program.) Those farmers who were in enough difficulty to need the government to guarantee their loan, certainly needed the interest subsidy — all the help they could get — but it was specifically not available to them.

The first part involved a government guarantee so that the farmer would defer, or not pay, the interest for six months. The bank agreed not to compound the interest. This was an absolute nothing, because if a farmer couldn't make the interest payment, the bank already just added interest onto principal and increased his notes. The interesting thing about this, is that the government's calculations on this thing, when it first came out, was that on a $100,000 note, at 17% interest, the bank's agreement not to compound interest for six months would save the farmer $1,000. Now in reality, if you run it through a simple calculator, it saves you $300. And governments are continually criticizing the farmers for not doing their books properly!

Our original proposal to them was that they pay a percentage of interest or rebate on the interest paid in 1981. The farmers who were having the most difficulty were the ones who were paying the most interest. The whole program could have been carried out in two weeks. You could calculate how much interest you paid last year, and the rebate of five percent (or whatever) could then be calculated. The farmer could receive a cheque and use the money to get things squared away again. The way they did it, paying the interest subsidy on next year's expenses, amounted to little more than the compounding of last year's interest. Farmers were forced to continue their current operations and maybe even expand them, trying to keep up the cash flow enough to qualify. Whereas if they had had the money in their pockets, they could have used it to pay off the loans, and perhaps to cut back their operations. It would have gone right to the fellows who needed it, the ones who suffered the hardship.

I dwell on the details of this guarantee program because similar schemes have been used in other countries, notably Denmark, with the same effect — the government bails out the banks. Our plan would have put an influx of cash into the farm economy, and that is what it's all about. When the farmer has money to spend, he keeps the machinery dealers in business, they keep the factories in business and so on. If the government had put that money into farm communities, it would have saved that money seven times over on unemployment insurance. But they still weren't convinced of the severity of the situation. The Banker's Association was saying that only a tenth-of-one-percent of the farmers were in trouble, and Lorne Henderson was simply repeating this.

A year later, when both Massey Ferguson and International Harvestor went broke, and White's had already gone by the boards, then and only then did the government admit that a possible 15% of farmers were in trouble — an increase of 15,000%! By that time it was way above that.

It was just total ignorance, almost a desire to see no evil, hear no evil. They didn't want to admit that it was there, that we were right. It was a very frustrating period for me because I was running into a brick wall, trying to explain things to people who thought they knew all about it.

The thing is, the government was relying for information on the banks and on the University of Guelph. These are two of the things that got agriculture in Ontario into trouble. The professors at Guelph, or whoever the powers may be down there, were saying that the next crop out of Guelph would be able to replace these inefficient operators. Of course nothing is further from the truth; anybody who knows anything knows that experience is the greatest teacher. And there is no amount of science or business sense that can overcome 24.75% interest rates or $1.70 per bushel corn.

My biggest argument on the efficiency question is that pure efficiency will come when we all live in the same apartment building, when we all eat in the same kitchen, all ride the same bus and wear the same clothes. These are models of efficiency, but there goes the quality of life, right out the window.

The Ontario government was not relying on grassroots people, and the problem was magnified by the farmers themselves. When we got Dennis Trimble out to speak to farmers in the community, the meeting was set up by members of the Conservative Party, who had chosen the farmers he was to speak to. These farmers cleaned up their buildings; one fellow even went to the point of getting his name printed on the side of his barns, trying to impress people. We should have been showing them the empty barns, the human tragedies, the actual books of people going broke. But instead of that, the Conservative Party chose who they were going to see and politicians went around saying, "Well, things aren't that bad! Everything's okay."

This happens every time. We criticize the Premier and his staff but, everywhere they go, people are wearing three-piece suits and ties. Everybody's drinking champagne and eating caviar and we wonder why they don't realize there's a problem. If farmers would expose the real problems instead of putting on a front, something might be accomplished.

That was one of the main tasks of the Survival Association; to make it socially acceptable to be broke. To get people to admit it in public. I still have a hard time when the press wants to talk to farmers in trouble. I know hundreds and hundreds of cases but they won't go to the press — because they're in negotiations, or it might jeopardize their credit if the local suppliers found out that they were in trouble and they wouldn't be able to finance their fertilizer needs, or whatever. So an ongoing problem with us was getting people to admit it, to talk about it, to say, "I'm involved."

Many people support us but not openly. They give money under the table but don't want a membership. Their mere presence at our meetings shakes up the government, but they are afraid to be seen. But then fear has been a problem in organizing farmers from the beginning of time. The banks of course played on this with threats and rumours. One reporter covered one meeting with "the most courageous group of people he had encountered." Many who support us visibly are not in trouble but are smart enough to look ahead.

The banks were continually talking about failure, and the farmer felt guilty enough as it was. It finally got to the point where farmers realized their failure was a result of deliberate policy; that they'd gone broke, not because government policies failed, but because government policies *had* worked. If you've read *The Challenge of Abundance,* an Ontario government study of farm problems done twenty years ago, you will know that the government believes there are too many farmers and that they have to get them out of agriculture and into the factories. They want to change rural poverty for urban poverty, instead of addressing its causes. Their goal is more "efficiency," but what they really mean is controllable, larger farms.

There is also good documentation in the United States of definite government policies to lower prices, to get rid of some of these "excess farmers," or "resources" as they refer to them. In his book, *The Loss of our Family Farms,* co-published by the U.S. Farmers Association, Mark Ritchie comments that Paul Samuelson, "Mr. Economics" from M.I.T., set out the strategy in 1945 that has been the force behind U.S. farm policy since that time.

"Resources" (farmers) should be both forced and attracted out of farming. The only solution was to thin out the population of farmers so that "commercial" farmers will feel the pressure to become more efficient (capital intensive, and in debt) and the remaining farmers will find their incomes so low that they would go into industry or find part-time jobs off the farm. The really poor farmers will receive welfare.

Ritchie also quotes Kenneth Boulding, the influential agricultural economist at the University of Michigan:

> The only way I know to get toothpaste out of a tube is to squeeze, and the only way to get people out of agriculture is likewise to squeeze

agriculture. If the toothpaste is thin, you don't have to squeeze very hard, on the other hand, if the toothpaste is thick, you have to put real pressure on it. If you can't get people out of agriculture easily, you are going to have to do farmers severe injustice in order to solve the problem of allocation.

Ritchie also exposes The Committee for Economic Development, which is composed of 200 leading businessmen and educators, and which bases its business and public policy recommendations on corporate interests. It has been the major exponent and lobby group for the destruction of the family farm in the United States.

Mark especially quotes Gerald Meier and Robert Baldwin's textbook, *Economic Development:*

Every specific principle of economic change should be considered alongside a specific principle of cultural change. For instance, the economic criteria of investment are alone not sufficient guide for investment policy: they must be supplemented by non-economic criteria. For illustrative purposes, some non-economic criteria for investment might be as follows; . . . invest in projects that break up village life by drawing people to centers of employment away from the village because, by preventing impersonal relations, village life is a major source of opposition to change. Such non-economic considerations may reinforce or contradict economic considerations, but they constitute an essential part in any assessment of the requirements for development (p. 357)

. . . Where there are religious obstacles to modern economic progress, the religion may have to be taken less seriously or its character altered. (p. 356)

Ritchie points out, in his section entitled ''Underlying Motivations,'' that the CED warns that the possibility of ''A recurrence of agricultural instability'' must be kept in mind so as to maintain ''an atmosphere relatively free of the political pressures from farmers experienced in the past.''

Suddenly, the picture becomes much clearer. The real target of the CED appears to be the political strength of the farmers, and they acknowledge that their tactic of enforcing below parity prices and providing income subsidies has successfully minimized farmers' ability to exercise political power.

The minimizing of farmers' power was crucial to the corporations for several reasons:

Farmers had historically aligned themselves with trade unions and urban workers, including the formation of Farmer-Labor Parties which held political power in a dozen mid-west and southwest states. These parties were committed to the restriction and control of corporations, such as the state-owned bank and grain trading enterprises in North Dakota, and the ban on corporate farming in several mid-west states.

The political strength of farmers was displayed in their ability to lobby for and win favorable farm policies. These policies helped strengthen their economic, thus political power, making it difficult for corporations to dominate agriculture as they were attempting to control other industries.

The United Farmers of Ontario put candidates in the electorial process and formed a minority government supported by labour in the 1920's. The Ontario government has worked very hard to assure that this will never happen again. The elimination of large numbers of farmers is very necessary to their goal.

The government, it seemed, was simply getting its information from the wrong sources, and we were as much at fault as anyone for not getting the point across and not standing up for our rights.

There weren't proper lobby efforts by farm organizations, particularly in Ottawa (and in Washington until the formation of the American Agriculture Movement). No one was riding herd over these things. The Banker's Association is a lobby group, paid to do public relations. The oil companies have paid lobbyists and, in Washington, political action committees are big business.

This is one area where farmers have really fallen down. A true farmer wants to be on the land; he doesn't want to sit in Ottawa or Queen's Park. Most of our best organizers and thinkers are farming — they're not sitting in on the political process. If you take a good person off the farm and send him down to Ottawa, after five years he's so far removed from what's going on in the countryside he has to go back.

I thought it would be good for everybody if, as they used to do it in Communist China, people at the top had to go to the bottom and dig the ditches, that sort of thing, so they got back into the groove of how the country is run. I think a lot of government officials could benefit from that policy.

Fighting the Banks
for Our Farms 6

*From Antigone through Martin Luther to Martin Luther
King, the issue of liberty has turned on the existence of a higher
law that of the state.*

The actual name "Farmers' Survival" came out of a meeting
in a little hall in Kilsyth on December 8, 1981 when the Grey-
Bruce Farmers' Survival Association was officially formed. The
place was very well chosen, I thought. In an old township hall
on a dark night, down in the basement, about thirty local farmers
got together and discussed the vigilantes, which was of course
the big news. They discussed the fact that there had to be a
legitimate organization where people with problems could make
contact for help. We had to have a telephone number so they
could get hold of us and we needed people with time to help
with financial counselling.

We also needed a leader. The general feeling was that
because George Bothwell and I had been very visible, very militant, we might scare some of the conservative farmers
away. Carl Spencer was elected president of the Grey-Bruce
Farmers' Survival Association. He wasn't in financial difficulties and thus, was not subject to charges that the organization was only for people who were desperate. Carl has a good
booming voice and speaks well.

A story in our local paper a short time later outlined our aims
as we understood them at that time:

*. . . The purpose of the association is to unite the Canadian farming
community across the country to demand government action now, before
violence breaks out in the fields and in the streets.*

The goals of the association are:
(1) To lower interest rates;
(2) To negotiate just and reasonable settlements between farmers and the banks;
(3) To provide a legal and financial counselling service to farmers.
This organization of farmers is growing hourly with telephone calls coming in from across Canada. The Head Office of the C.F.S.A. is located in Tara, Ontario. The Grey-Bruce Chapter is spearheading the growing number of Canadian farmers in demanding:
- Immediate one-year moratorium on bank payments to avoid further farm bankruptcies and receiverships;
- Reduction of the banks' interest rates to below 10% per annum retroactive to January 31, 1980;
- To re-instate a law against usury to put a lid on interest rates of 6%;
The Canadian Farmers' Survival Association is seeking to align itself with other concerned Canadian pressure groups, such as the Small Businessmen's Association, the Canadian Labour Congress (C.L.C.) and others.
The farmers intend to exert such pressure as is necessary to alleviate the untold anxiety among Canadian farm families. The organization will accept donations and letters of support from any concerned citizen who supports our goals.

The newspaper also quoted advice for farmers negotiating with the banks.

"Keep the line of negotiations open," I was quoted as saying. "Always have a proposal on their desk. If they have a proposal they'll have to pass it on. If the bank manager says he won't pass it on, go over his head or call us."

We also advised farmers to submit realistic cash flow proposals to the bank and always to negotiate from strength, refusing to liquidate stock or other assets, until a deal could be struck. Farmers with co-signers on loans should get the co-signer's name struck before making any payments.

"There are all kinds of possible negotiations," the article finished off, "but the bottom line is don't take no for an answer. Come to us."

There was a lot of fun in the initial start up. On one trip to Toronto to meet the Minister of Agriculture six of us met in Chatsworth. But the only roadworthy vehicle was my one ton truck with no license plates. So we decided to try to rent a car. The first dealership was bankrupt — Chrysler Credit Corp. had charged 35% interest. The second lent us a car free of charge when they found out who we were. But when we tried to get gas, the first gas station was bankrupt and we barely made it to the second. "Some day you'll have to write a book, Wilford," said farmer Bill Davis.

The first unified, direct action in our area, however, wasn't as the Survival Association and was prior to the vigilante picture. We organized a parade of a hundred tractors and implements into the city of Owen Sound on October 7, 1981. We went in at seven o'clock in the morning, gathering outside town at three depot points. This gave us a good opportunity to organize as we didn't have any idea how many would come. This is the frustrating thing with farmers; when you set something like this up you don't know how many are going to back out at the last moment, or how many are going to come in at the last moment.

Farmers are very leery about doing something that might be construed as illegal, and that is why governments quake when we are pushed that far. There was a lot of needless worry over whether we could be on downtown streets with tractors without safety chains, and we decided not to notify the police, as we wanted a complete surprise attack. The press came along with the television crews and we got good national coverage as it was the first farm demonstration for quite a while.

When we climbed the hill to enter Owen Sound at seven o'clock in the morning, we found the police were there waiting for us. They were very helpful and cooperative, particularly as they didn't ticket anyone for not putting money in the meters. They helped direct traffic, that sort of thing. They had been tipped off because Global Television pulled in at two a.m. to set up its equipment. If Global was in downtown Owen Sound at two in the morning there had to be something going on, and so they called all their men in. The local press heard about it on the police radio, or were tipped off by the police. They were all out there waiting as well. We had left them till the last moment, because we didn't want word to get around.

We had a very effective demonstration, with about one hundred tractors pulling implements behind. Some fellows just brought pick-up trucks. Others had driven for an hour to an hour-and-a-half in the rain without cabs in their tractors. The determination of these people! If you've ever driven a tractor

*Owen Sound. First organized demonstrations by Grey-Bruce farmers which led to for-
mation of Canadian Farmers' Survival Association.*

in the rain with the water and mud slopping up the front wheels,
not to mention the cold, you can appreciate what they went
through to make sure they were at the depot the night before
and that everything was arranged.

We zeroed in on the intersection where there are four banks,
one at each corner. George Bothwell is a great organizer and
he had all his stuff set up. We even had a P.A. truck, with
some people lined up to speak at the mike. Tom Clark ended
up doing a lot of the talking. We had some good responses,
because we had some inside information as to how many bad
cases there were at the local Bank of Montreal. We brought
these out. The bank's head office was saying that the problem
was confined to one or two. I think the branch had something
like 140 accounts, and 130 of them were in trouble.

We were contacted that evening by Eugene Whelan, the
federal Minister of Agriculture, to see if we could verify
that. Eugene hasn't always been very effective but he seems
to mean well. Two people in Whelan's office who helped ex-
tensively were Ezio Di Emmanuel and Peter Christian. They
could move mountains with F.C.C. and the banks, but eventually the banks resisted their involvement.

They did however take a lot of pressure off in dealing with
the financial emergencies. I was quoted in the *Sun*

Times: "Eugene is very good. He is doing the best he can. He's fighting the banks, he's fighting McEachen; he can't fight Trudeau because he can't find him."

We got some good coverage out of it, as we went from bank to bank. One of the valuable lessons I learned about dealing with the press is that they like excitement, something controversial. (The best way to get on camera is to curse a little bit.)

We asked the managers of the banks to come out. They refused. The main thing we were protesting was their lack of compliance with the Small Business Development Bond (SBDB) program. The federal government, in order to try and help, set up with the banks, through the tax laws, a bond whereby a farmer in trouble could borrow long-term money at a reduced rate. The interest the bank earned on that money was non-taxable. The banks theoretically are in a 50% tax bracket, so that every fifty cents they earned non-taxable from an SBDB was the equivalent of a dollar taxable. Effectively the bank could cut the interest rate in half for the small businessman and still get its same rate of return.

To show how banks "help," they were supposed to charge one-half of prime plus 1%. In some of the distress cases they charged one-half of prime plus three, or the equivalent of prime plus six — just to help farmers "out."

Now the SBDB, (later a Small Business Bond, SBB) was a good move by the federal government. The provincial government picked up some of the tab through lost revenues as well. But the banks didn't comply. I applied at the Royal Bank and they stalled. Instead of saying okay, let's go with this thing — we need it so let's work with it, we'll iron out the difficulties later — they said no, we're not going to get involved in that.

The thing had kicked around for six months. The Grey-Bruce area was the first and hardest hit. Not one of 400 farmers at one meeting in the area had been able to get an SBDB. So that was the issue as we climbed into the tractors that cold morning. We wanted these bonds and we wanted them now. It was months after that that the banks finally started utilizing them and they utilized them strictly to get security, or gain accounts. If the bank had a mortgage on your property already, your chances of getting an SBDB (later an SBB) were very slim. If they didn't have a mortgage and they wanted one, then you could get a bond, no matter if you could pay it off or not. One of the worst abuses and uses of it was to extract parents' guarantees. In other words, if a parent came in and guaranteed — as I mentioned before, these were expandable guarantees — put their name on the line, you could get a Small Business Bond. John Otto's case was one of these. The bank would only give an SBB if his parents guaranteed it. Then they pulled the plug!

The banks didn't care. I saw one case of a bond where the first payment was set out as $30,000, and yet the bank wouldn't give the man operating money. He only had thirty cows left. If he had sold all his livestock, he couldn't have made the first payment. But they gave him that bond providing they got a mortgage on his property.

Once the banks realized they could use the SBB as a tool to get securities, they started implementing the bonds. If used as intended right from the first, they would have brought effective interest rates down. Extended over a long term, the program could have helped a lot of farmers. As it was the banks dragged their heels. In some cases where they did set up the bond it would be five months before they implemented it. In that four or five months, the added interest could be another $40,000-50,000, and then they would turn around and ask why the farmer hadn't bought enough cattle. Well, he was short $50,000 before he started his projections.

When the bank managers wouldn't come out that day and explain their position on the SBDBs, we went in. Bear in mind these same banks were scouring the courntryside less than a year earlier in special loan mobiles so that farmers wouldn't have to stop work to borrow money. The first two banks were kind of quiet and the thing started to die. I could see the media were losing interest, and so were a lot of the farmers. So in the Toronto-Dominion Bank, I worked my way to the front, slammed my fist down on the desk and hollered that the banks were yellow bastards. Now what I meant was that they were scared to implement these things, hiding behind the bureaucracy. They didn't have the guts to go ahead and put them in, and worry about the consequences later. Why didn't they try and help these farmers when the help was here, instead of sitting on the fence and letting everything go to hell! It's the same with the government — when in doubt don't do anything.

That little incident got me national press coverage and onto television. My first realization of how the press works was that

Owen Sound. At an early demonstration, signs state farm position.

you have to say something notable and get your point across as briefly as possible, because a lot of issues are condensed down to a minute or less for the evening news. It has to be something new or you will never even get into print.

The president of the Bank of Montreal, Bill Bradford, later contacted us, saying he wanted to speak with us, so it was a good start.

Our first demonstration, after the Survival Association was formalized as a group, was in Port Elgin, December 8, 1981. This demonstration was to back up a farmer whose equipment the Bank of Commerce had seized. I guess the bank was terrified that the vigilantes were going to step in and stop them because they left half the equipment in the initial seizure. The farmer didn't object, didn't do anything as he didn't want any publicity. One of our directors knew the man quite well and was very angry at the way the bank had treated him. We got involved in it, deciding to demonstrate, not on behalf of the farmer personally, but strictly against interest rate policies and against the local manager, who had been quoted as saying that farmers were stupid. He blamed farmers' bad management, and didn't accept any blame on the bank's part at all. One farmer said he was the only bank manager whom he'd ever avoided. When he saw him coming on the street, he crossed the road for fear he might kill him.

However, we went in. There were about 250 farmers. There was a big manure tank — "the slurry spreader" we called it — parked right in front of the doors. This made for a good media event; George as usual had organized a rousing demonstration. I was introduced to a lawyer who came over, offering his free services. One of the fellows said, you pay peanuts, you get monkeys. We, again in our innocence, believed that because he was a lawyer he had to know what he was doing. But that's another whole story.

Basically it was a very successful demonstration. It put on a lot of pressure, and taught us quite a bit about organizing. The bank agreed in writing to return the equipment. Again there was very good press coverage. By this time the movement had gained momentum and everything we did was newsworthy. I can remember going out and announcing over the speaker that we'd won and the equipment was coming back. I had to do it about four different times for different television crews because they hadn't caught it. The co-op had

Tractors block Port Elgin Main Street. Sign in tractor shows farmers mean business, "Fight the Bastards."

Port Elgin farmers picketing local Bank of Commerce, to force the return of impounded farm equipment.

donated doughnuts for our meeting in the arena afterwards and we had donations from other businesses. It was very good community action. A group came up from the UAW Training Camp in Port Elgin and gave us a big boost. They sang unity songs — *"Old MacDonald had a farm, but the banker's got it now"* — and opened and closed accounts.

The night before, December 7, we had been approached by a group from Eastern Ontario who had heard of what we were doing and wanted to take part. Jean Lipton runs a beef feed lot with help of her sons in St. Bernadin in Prescott County. Independently of us, she got together with a group of about fifty red-meat producers who faced the same problems we did in Grey-Bruce. She contacted us about linking up our two groups and from then on, they put up farm survival signs at their actions. (Jean Lipton has remained a prominent organizer in the area and has been part of many of our lobbying attempts.) They phoned us while we were having a general meeting, and so we decided to change our organization from the Grey-Bruce Survival Association to the Grey-Bruce Chapter of the Canadian Farmers' Survival Association. This thing was growing by leaps and bounds, so we decided to go from Grey-Bruce, not just to Ontario, but to the whole of Canada.

It was important that the movement grew out of farmers' own initiatives. Problems were soon to arise over the man who came in to help, lawyer John Gorman. He wanted to be an organizer, to get us going, as he did see our problems as a national thing. He had a lot of drive but the big problem was, as the saying goes, the general shouldn't get too far ahead of the troops. It would have been better if he'd stayed more in the background, letting our members take the initiative as they saw fit, but when he started leading faster than the members were following then he got cut off. He didn't comprehend the farm mentality, or allow for the growing pains we had to go through. The idea of the association spread like wild fire but, as an organization, our growth was very slow. Farmers are very conservative, they are very cautious, so you can't just jump up and say let's get at it, and have everyone follow. There came a rift, and the lawyer was told that we were running the group, not him.

The people from Eastern Ontario followed up with quite a large demonstration on Highway 417, Tuesday, January 19, 1982, near St. Isidore in Prescott County. There were about

250 farmers or so on 70 placard-bearing tractors and manure spreaders. They were set to go out on the highway, but the police told them they couldn't go. They went down the side roads, cut the fences, and shut down the highway anyway, for about eight hours, with the police detouring the traffic around.

There was a bit of an exciting incident with a busload of people. Traffic couldn't get through. The bus tried to pass them and almost rolled over. Some of the farmers then apparently flattened the tires on one side to level the bus back up, or something to that effect. There also was a lot of press about a tank of hypo-acid that was supposedly going to blow up if they didn't let it through. Of course no one ever thought of turning the truck around, or backing it up, it just had to go through. But again there was good media coverage, and another group was on its way, which gave us the good feeling in Grey-Bruce that we weren't alone. We certainly appreciated their involvement.

After the highway blockade, the demonstrators closed down the section of St. Isidore's main street housing branches of the Bank of Montreal and the Bank of Nova Scotia. According to *Farm and County:* "After driving the front wheels of their large tractors against the windows and walls of the banks, the farmers demanded an explanation of the delays surrounding the SBDB program. Bank employees refused to talk to what had, at this point, become an angry mob."

Most of the farmers in that area were pork producers who were purchasing grain, usually from Western Canada. The price of grain was high relative to pork and, with interest rates putting the icing on the cake, there were very severe financial problems down there.

Another action in Eastern Ontario in the early spring of 1982 was at the farm of Robert Gibb, again put together by Jean Lipton and some of the other Survival members. Robert Gibb stated: "A lot of people told me survival groups could only delay things. I was told they couldn't really solve anything. Now I'm set up with new loans of about $55,000 from Farm Credit Corporation and a small business bond." He stated that heavy pressure was the only thing that made the two lenders change their mind.

We had actions at the same time in Quebec. A group of Anglophone beef producers in western Quebec, called the Western Quebec Feedlot Association, with 150 local farmers

and representatives from the Ontario Farmers' Survival Association, gathered in front of the Bank of Montreal in Quyon, in
Pontiac County, Quebec. There were also representatives of
the UPA (Quebec farmers' union) there. They had called a
demonstration in response to recent court action against two
local farmers, Fred Muro and Kurt Hos, by the Bank of Montreal. They had been given 48 hours to come up with
$165,000. The Association felt that the bank's position was
unreasonable.

Representatives of the demonstrators went into the bank, asking for an immediate stop to court action against Fred and Kurt,
a reopening of negotiations on both cases, and a 90-day
moratorium to either work out a new agreement or allow time
to refinance. They got the 90 days. Also, the bank agreed to
an immediate halt in court proceedings against the pair.

A survival group started in southern Quebec, in the Sher-
brooke area. Marcel Talbot remains the president with Jean
Claude Bouche my bilingual contact. There has been a lot of
good action by these people. A real problem in Canada is that
because of the language barrier the English press doesn't pick
up a lot of the stories that go on in Quebec. And that works
both ways. The hunger strike and penny auction, for example, weren't well covered by the French-language press. So
we're constantly fighting to get the news around, to give each
other encouragement.

The people in Quebec had a lot of demonstrations at farm
sales. Farmers had been evicted, and their farms were sitting
empty. The Quebec Survivalists said that this was ridiculous,
and started putting these people back in their homes. Because
of the activities of the Association, a lot of farmers were back
on their land, although still in a bankrupt situation. The banks,
and particularly the Quebec government, were a big problem. But they knew that if they tried to evict these people the
publicity would not be good.

It's been a holding action. A lot of the problem is getting
the Quebec government to take responsibility for its
policies. Prior to the referendum Rene Levesque wanted to encourage self-sufficiency for Quebec agriculture, and really went
out to these farmers saying expand, here's the money. The PQ
doled out grants, low-interest guaranteed loans. The fellows
who had farmed for years with small operations were encouraged
to expand, being told it was an act of (Québec) patriotism. It's

the same old garbage, "There's a starving world out there and you have to feed it." And then when the prices fell and interest rates rolled upwards, the farmers were abandoned. (The price of pork plummeted following the U.S. boycott of grain sales to the Soviet Union in 1978 as American farmers diversified into livestock.

In July of '82 I was invited by Richard Ratti of the Manitoba Agriculture Movement to a meeting with the American Agricultural Movement, at the Peace Gardens, on the Canada-U.S. border. The AAM has as its main program parity prices for agricultural products.

In the fall I was again invited out to speak, and through a series of meetings, the Manitoba Survival Association was formed.

John Jago, from Reston, is the president of the Manitoba Survival Association. One of their first actions stemmed from a meeting in a community faced with a recent suicide. The neighbours were concerned about a local bachelor in financial difficulty who was acting strangely. He had threatened to shoot the sheriff.

I encouraged some of the neighbours to visit the man and ask if he needed help. He sure did, and so did the local Credit Union manager — he was as frightened as anyone. They deeded some land to the Credit Union but left the farmer his equipment and some land. Everyone was happy. This initial success was great for morale.

The second incident, involving a stand-off of receivers, at Bruce Payne's farm in the spring of '82, ended in the farmer abandoning his farm. The situation had deteriorated badly before the Survival Association got involved. This new group did not have the skills to negotiate a settlement, and the odds were against them. The Manitoba government used the same ruse as the Ontario government in the Black case: setting up a review board to look at the case, then saying nothing could be done. This measure always fails, as far as the farmer is concerned, as the boards have absolutely no power, but for the government it is a great way of stalling for time, appearing to do something. Moreover, the people on these boards no matter how well-intentioned, view the cases they review as individual problems, rather than as symptoms of a social evil. They do not consider debt readjustment or any other structural changes possible solutions. But even with the loss, Bruce Payne felt the support of his fellow farmers and again pressure was put on the government.

In John Jago's own case, just days before he was to put his crop in, the Credit Union seized his equipment. His wife lay in front of a machine and the agent said, "Drive over her." John's neighbours finally put in the crop, but the Credit Union then figured that John's crop — which they had refused to allow to be planted — belonged to them. By seizing his equipment before seeding and not selling it for several months, they hoped to starve him out. If he couldn't plant, there was no prospect of repayment. So the Credit Union not only jeopardized the farmer's business but, in a vicious act of vengeance, tried to destroy him. By the time the receivers were done with the crop, only $7,000 was left out of 500 acres of grain to pay the neighbours for all the their inputs even though the neighbours had first security on the crop.

At Portage-La-Prairie, 16 RCMP officers swooped down to supervise the seizure of assets of a grain operation owned by Ron Painter and his son Robert. The Painter's only owed $293,000, and the crop in the field was worth $280,000 but by this time the Royal Bank had declared all out war on The Survival Association and so they appointed Coopers, Lybrand Limited as receivers, who sent the bailiff to add to the cost of trying to punish the Painters for being at the farm gate defence of Bruce Payne. The Royal Bank applied for and the Manitoba courts issued and ex-parti order against the Painters. This is a decision by the courts that one is guilty without a hearing or representation of any kind. As a matter of fact, one does not know that there is such a court action until the police are at the door. This was the second ex-parti order in Manitoba in one week. Anyone who believes that money does not talk within our judicial system is naive, and woe be to he who opposed the mighty Royal Bank.

Nancy Painter described what many farm families have experienced.

> Who can gauge the effect it has on a person
> to suddenly find strangers in his yard seizing his
> assets — the grain he worked himself ragged to
> grow; the machinery he maintains and repairs,
> curses and praises; and in some cases even the
> land itself, which for most farmers is more a part

of them than a possession. The effect can only be devastating, on the entire family.

Who can the farmer turn to? In our case there was much confusion as to the legality of some of the details of the seizure; even without those added questions, most farmers are not aware of their rights in such a situation. As we tried to sort things out, both in understanding the situation and in seeking help in resolving it, it seemed time and time again that the system was stacked against us, with it multiple levels of bureaucracy. Who are we to turn to when we feel an injustice has been done? Is there no avenue for us?

Saskatchewan is the only place in North America that did not experience in 1982 the drastic reductions in land prices. Their NDP government had declared a moratorium on foreclosures of homes & farms up to 164 acres. The moratorium was eventually circumnavigated by the lenders and the new PC government however, and forced sales escalated in 1983.

In the spring of 1983, after the hunger strike, the Canadian Agriculture Movement (an offshoot of the AAM) in Saskatchewan paid my expenses while I spoke on a swing through Saskatchewan. There was a bit of a conflict here as both organizations were trying to expand, although it was not too serious. They were paying my way, using me as a drawing card to get the farmers involved, and I was trying to get people to start up survival groups and use survival tactics. I didn't see the two in conflict, although there is only so much money to go around. I was trying to encourage the Agriculture Movement to get involved in stopping foreclosures, and I was trying to get the various groups to fight together. We've got a good alliance out there now between the two and they work hand in hand.

I did a radio show in Saltcoats, Saskatchewan and the announcer, Jim Couslin, became the new head of the Canadian Agriculture Movement in Saskatchewan and has done a lot of work trying to organize farmers. He had over 200 farmers with financial difficulties call him because of his visibility on the radio show.

I received a call from Jim about a farmer who had the bailiff in the yard, loading cattle. I told him to check his papers and, if in doubt, call the RCMP. Now bailiffs very seldom have the correct papers, but people are so intimidated they let their stuff go. Well, this case was different. The RCMP made the bailiff and his men unload the cattle, then sent them home. The neighbours very quickly organized. When the banker met with that farmer, he wanted to deal.

Later, a bank agent posing as a receiver stole another farmer's equipment. Jim wasn't notified until two days after. By that time, the equipment had been moved 200 miles away. In September, Jim and other farmers stopped an eviction and Jim reiterated my statement, "I will be in jail before any farmer is evicted." The creditors got the message and backed off.

One of the more interesting people I met out there was Bob Stevenson. Bob has one of the largest bailiff firms in Saskatchewan. He is an ex-RCMP officer and one of his statements is "The law is the law, and the banks are not above the law." The banks were changing securities. Withsome types of securities when they made a seizure, they had to leave a tractor, a truck, certain pieces of equipment — the bailiff had the rules and regulations as to how much he had to leave the farmer. He couldn't clean the families out. But by switching papers and such, they could circumnavigate that law.

In two cases where they went to Bob to get him to do this, he said, "No, what you're trying to do is illegal." He was getting sick of the whole business. It's one thing to go and repossess a car that someone isn't making a payment on, but it's a totally different thing to go into a farm. You're destroying a family and a whole way of life. He was emotionally tied up with the farm thing. He spoke of one farm where he had finished a seizure and he was afraid to leave because the farmer was very suicidal.

I talked to a trucker once who had picked up some pigs. He went into the house and the farmer was standing, banging his head against the wall. The trucker went and unloaded the pigs, saying the banks could get them themselves. That was the kind of thing that Bob was getting into. He'd been faced with guns by farmers in desperation.

When he refused to do these seizures for the banks, because to his mind they were illegal, the banks called his notes, which totalled about $30,000. His friends and neighbours scurried around for about a month to raise the $30,000 to get him clear of the bank. He had quite a few assets but once he'd taken on the banks, as he said, he couldn't borrow a lead pencil. They simply blackballed him.

When I arrived in Saskatchewan the Royal Bank was ready for me with a big press statement that there was no problem in Saskatchewan. There were only six farmers in all of Saskatchewan in trouble, and the Royal Bank had only foreclosed on two in the last two years.

Bob proceeded at the meeting I was speaking at to name some of the towns in Saskatchewan, saying, "I wouldn't call the Royal Bank a liar, but I did a foreclosure for the Royal Bank in such and such a town, and another town and another and to my knowledge that is in Saskatchewan." This just blew their case apart, proving them to be the liars they were. Bob had done quite a few cases with the Royal Bank.

Bob Stevenson continues to talk and organize on our behalf, to tell farmers it's in their hands, they've got to do something. If you want a helping hand, look to the end of your arm. He's made them aware of some of their rights.

It was heartwarming to see such dedicated people. Bob has everything to lose and nothing to gain. His whole bailiff business depends on working for the banks. Yet his moral sense will no longer allow him to do these sort of things. He's a very good man. If we had more men of his calibre it would be a short fight.

Farm Gate Defenses 7

We can't make God-like decisions and decide who we can and who we can't help. This thing is bigger than that. We're going to help them all and let God make the judgement later on . . . . We all need help. My turn is coming. There is no man today who can continue to farm under the conditions we have now — Greg Stamme, an Illinois farmer.

The Survival Association set out to put a stop to the kind of ordeal the Black family faced. Our main tactic when negotiation failed, or to help negotiations come to a successful conclusion, was farm gate defense. We now had a long list of people who were prepared to stand in their own or other people's driveways and actually stop these seizures; hence, the name of this book. Communities can stand together and stop the bailiff or the sheriff from taking a family's livelihood and putting them out of their home.

Farm gate defense was devised to give the farmer some access to justice, to give him time; to meet the raw brute force of the chartered banks with the raw brute muscle power of the communities they are supposed to serve. The banks have all the papers signed, all the weight of authority on their side; and it is a credit to the Survival Association that I don't think we ever used overkill. We always met force with equal force. It was a matter of stopping injustice, but not hitting back too hard.

At this point in our organization, there was a lot of fun at nights — creative thinking. Equipment was moved around to make sure it was available for use later on by farmers who were afraid the banks were going to try to scoop it. People were reminded that bailiffs could be thrown off the property and charged with trespassing — only sheriffs have legal rights to be there. It was suggested that flattening their tires was preferable to taking a swing at them. When the receiver arrived with a truck he would find it very difficult to tow off equipment chained together or wagons with their tongues taken off. If a farmer mixed some of his neighbour's equipment with his own, and the bailiff grabbed it by mistake, the bailiff could be charged with theft. Farmers arriving after the bailiff or the sheriff at a seizure could block laneways and nearby roads by parking strategically and locking up their vehicles.

Very shortly after the Prescott County incident, in January 1982, we got involved in the Romanelli affair. This one got a lot of press, but a lot of misconceptions still exist. Cecil Romanelli had purebred Charolais cattle, and had a good reputation as a cattle breeder. But he had testified at a inquiry into organized crime in the dry wall business. This came out very quickly and we got all kinds of calls about Romanelli, saying he was involved with the Mafia. He was never convicted of anything. In our society you're supposed to be innocent until proven guilty, but that's never the way it is — as soon as you're charged, people figure you're guilty.

Very briefly, this is how the Romanelli thing happened. The gap between the interest rate and prices had spread and the bank had cut him off feed money to run and manage his herd. In all justice to Cecil, with the pressures, I don't think his mind was quite right most of the earlier time I knew him; later on he seemed to be a lot better. It was like a divorce. The cattle were literally starving to death because the bank wasn't putting the money up and Cecil was refusing to try other methods — saying that if you (the bank) are not going to give me the money to feed them then they *will* starve. Yet at the same time he was very torn: this herd was his creation and it was being destroyed. It's almost as if these animals are children, especially in the purebred business. There's quite an attachment to individual animals — they have names, and are treated like babies.

Cecil had not approached us. We'd been raising hell, and he actually stole some of our thunder because, on December 14, 1981, when we happened to be in Toronto, he dumped three dead cattle on the bank's doorstep which got a lot of sympathy and outrage from city folk — and attention from the media. But we knew right away that the farming community would not sympathize with cattle starving to death — and sure enough Cecil's actions had a very negative effect for our organization.

Personally I felt that if we took the approach that the man was under extreme emotional stress we certainly could win some sympathy for him, and negotiate some kind of a settlement. But my arguments didn't win the day. John Gorman, the lawyer who had offered to help us, went to Romanelli and started to organize. He called George Bothwell down. As I mentioned before, George is very involved with human beings and, knowing what he was going through, could sympathize with Cecil. We all did.

I was down at Cecil's farm on New Year's Eve. By that time the Humane Society had been in there for two weeks to take care of the cattle, turning the bills back to the bank and the receivers. While I was there a cow starved to death, just laid down and died. The place was in a shambles, the mangers were broken. Cattle were walking all over the hay that the receivers were feeding them, shitting all over it, with the other cattle trying to eat it. The little calves weren't getting anything. It was terrible hay — musty, mouldy, big brown rotten bales. These cattle, in their emaciated state in the middle of winter, needed some high-energy feed, some grain. It was just a total mess, and to think the Humane Society was in charge!

We raised quite a bit of hell that evening, chasing the bank people out of there, telling them we would take it over. We started to fix up the mangers, and took a lot of pictures of what was going on. During the next few days Survival members went down and finished cleaning out the yards, sorting the cattle, sending some to Guelph to be looked after. They donated some hay, so the cows could be properly fed.

The Survival Association, however, formally backed out of the situation. Some of Cecil's supporters attempted a blockade of his driveway when the Humane Society came to seize the cattle but it failed for lack of numbers. So the Humane Society came in and picked up Cecil's cattle. They charged a fantastic figure ($200,000) to look after a hundred and fifty head of cattle for six months. It worked out to about $1,000 a head. This was ridiculous when farmers in our neighbourhood were getting about $20 dollars in winter and $12 a month in summer to put a cow to good grass. They charged thousands of dollars for trucking when five hundred would have moved the cattle almost anywhere. In my opinion, receivers are the only thing lower than a snake's belly and one of the main points of the Farmers' Creditors Arrangement Act is to keep them out of these situations.

There are real abuses of the system where receivers rip off huge chunks of money and people gouge all over the place. Cecil Romanelli got caught in the middle and he was the one to suffer. Cecil became the scapegoat, and coincidentally or not, he died a year later. We also took a lot of criticism as people saw the dumping of the dead cattle as something we had done and others said we shouldn't be helping Cecil, but we tried to make the best out of a bad situation. If we could have made people understand what it meant for someone who had been showing prize cattle to be reduced to the point where he was letting his cattle starve to death, then they would understand the tremendous pressure and desperation these individuals were experiencing.

This wasn't the only case, although it was the only one which became public. There were lots of situations where farmers were so depressed they wouldn't go to the barn anymore. They didn't have the proper feed and they knew that every time they turned around they were losing money. Their whole life was going down the drain. An animal would die and they wouldn't even have the will power or the strength to dispose of it.

Conditions were especially bad in the hog operations, where feed was cut off. One farmer in Eastern Ontario had been feeding hay to pigs for seven days, in desperation. When the hydro was cut off, there would be no heat or water for the pigs for weeks at a time. The farmer would run around watering with pails, exhausted and depressed. These were horrible situations for good, hard-working, intelligent fellows who were good producers. It says in the Bible that one of the greatest gifts is understanding. Jesus said hate the sin but love the sinner.

The Romanelli incident brought to a head differences in the Association: George became inactive but Carl Spencer carried on as our president. The break with George Bothwell was very unfortunate, although he is now active again. I ended up on one side of the fence, with him on the other. George was undergoing a tremendous amount of pressure at that time and the more I saw its manifestations in my own case, the more I understood it. As a person approaches a zero equity position the pressure mounts. Your whole life's work is at stake and you're trying your best to salvage what's left: the government is doing everything in its power to defeat you with its interest rate policies; the bank is not helping at all.

Until the last moment you don't see how bad it is. You firmly believe you will survive. Once a farmer gets to zero and realizes that he's broke, it's a big relief. He can go one of two ways: pick up and start to fight back, working back up from nothing; or go into a state of depression, a complete withdrawal, give up.

Usually when a person hits that zero, if you can get talking to him at all, he begins to pick up. You have to get his pride working for him not against him. One man wrote a letter to the editor of a local paper about us, very critical of our Association, and six months later he was out of business. He wouldn't come out and ask for help after having criticized us, so he was gone.

Our primary task was to give hope to individuals in trouble, by making them aware that they weren't alone, that there were many of us in their situation, and that it wasn't our fault. We had no control over the price of our product — still the big thing — and we had no control over the interest rates. Fuel prices were rising every time we turned around. Farmers are large consumers of energy, whether it be hydro or diesel fuel or gasoline. We had absolutely no control over our fates, and yet everyone was blaming the victim.

Our next farm gate defense was a nice one because it was only over a $10,000 loan at the Bank of Montreal to a local Grey County purebred pork producer. The bank had cut off Bruce Kiel's operating money; Bruce had been living from hand to mouth, literally putting fuel in the tractor until it ran out, then stopping and going out to scrape up $5 to buy some more fuel. He would sell a pig to buy some feed and, when the feed ran out, sell another pig.

You can imagine the pressures and the futility people like him felt, fighting a losing battle with no help from anyone. Finally, in January in desperation, Bruce went to the bank and said "If you're not going to advance me the money to run this operation properly and buy the feed for my pigs, I quit. You can feed the pigs yourself." And with that, he walked out.

Of course, Bruce had too much feeling for the pigs; he went on feeding them anyway. The bank decided it had to move; the manager went with the bailiff to pick up the pigs.

We were supposed to have been out at Bruce's the night before it happened, but we were at another farmer's. Bruce didn't seem to really know whether he wanted help or not. Then, George Bothwell phoned me in the morning of January 23 (1982) and said the bank was going to pick up Bruce's pigs.

Six of us went in originally. We went over to observe and to let Bruce know help was available. By then he did want our help. Often people don't ask until they realize that their livestock or equipment actually is going to be removed. The bailiff and the bank manager sat in the car with a couple of our executive members. I was in Bruce's house, thinking none of our members had shown up, but they were already on their way. I tapped on the window, saying the office had called, and did we need to bring some troops in? The bailiff asked what I meant by troops, and one of the fellows said that within twenty minutes we could have about four hundred farmers here. The bank manager said he thought he'd better call head office. So we went back to Bruce's house to wait for the call. Head office didn't call back, and by this time about thirty farmers had come over.

We went down and occupied the Bank of Montreal branch. It was kind of funny because Carl, at that time the president of the Survival Association, sat down at the manager's desk. We couldn't find hide nor hair of the manager, so we just went in and kind of sat around. The phone rang and someone asked about the angry farmers. Carl said there weren't any angry farmers here. The conversation went on, until the woman at the other end asked who she was talking to. Carl replied, "The President of the Survival Association." She said "Oh, we support you," and then hung up. She was a woman from another bank, in another town, who had heard of the incident and was phoning over for some news.

We got Bruce a bit of a deal because of the publicity. The bank retired half the loan. One of the larger farmers around bought the pigs and gave Bruce a two-year job with the understanding that he'd get 24 pure bred pigs at the end of two years to get started again. So, in fact, we saved his blood lines and helped him get going, getting him a job to pay some bills. It was a good outcome, although the price of pigs continued to drop, and it was not a long-term solution by any means.

The bank was adamant that we had set them up. It made very good press because with a $10,000 loan, as one of our farmers said, no wonder he's in trouble; he didn't owe enough money. We had been accused of supporting the rich farmers — the press was critical of a farmer in Port Elgin whose wife owned an airplane. It is very frustrating for me. As I mentioned before, I've worked in factories and fellows had airplanes there, and the only thing they had invested in the job was a lunchpail.

This conflict stems from the farmer's double role in society, what I call the Uncle Tom syndrome. A farmer isn't supposed to have anything other than a straw hat and rubber boots, and he's expected to kind of look at the ground the whole time he is talking to you. He isn't supposed to have the luxuries of life. It's very frustrating to hear criticism of the farmers with air conditioning in their tractor cabs from people who work in office buildings or factories worth millions of dollars where the whole thing is air conditioned and filtered. Their soft-chair working conditions are one thing, but a cab on a tractor so a person is not exposed to the elements is a wasteful excess.

That's why Bruce Kiel's case was a good one. He was a "quaint," small farmer, with only the small chicken coops that he kept his pigs in — obviously there was no overextension here on machinery or anything like that.

We found, as time went on, that there was no rhyme or reason to the difficulties people found themselves in. It didn't matter if you were a large farmer with extensive equipment or a small farmer with no equipment, or whether you were young or old. It only depended on where you were when the gun went off — if you were in the process of building a new barn, or had a son who was trying to get started, or if you hadn't expanded and kept up with the demands of the cost of living. The ones who were first hit by the debt load were the younger farmers, but as the situation worsened it affected everyone.

The other good thing about Bruce Kiel's case was the fact that his Durok herd, possibly one of the best in Ontario, was saved. Bruce had reserve grand champions, and had won ribbons at the CNE. Later on someone in the Ontario government criticized the purebred business as being a rich man's hobby but it is a very important part of our industry. If we don't have top breeding stock, the big commercial operators are in trouble. Genetic improvements, such as rates of gain and conformation, are a very important part of modern agriculture. Also it's not necessarily a rich man's game because a small farmer like Bruce, with his capacity for twenty or thirty sows, could make a living because those pigs are worth two or three times what market pigs are. The purebred business means more dollars per animal. Having enough time for them is important — because they're a more expensive animal they justify more tender loving care. You don't want a boar worth $1000 dropping dead on you. Bruce had the time to devote to the animals, and to show them, which is necessary because if you don't have the ribbons to back them up, then you don't get a fair price.

I failed to mention that when the bank was going to liquidate Bruce, those pigs would have gone to a commercial sales barn. Once they're dumped into a commercial sales barn, the chances of them picking up disease are such that no one would buy them for breeding stock. So they'd be fattened and sold as pork chops.

As I look back on the activities of the Survival Association, and wonder about what impact we will have on the rest of society in years to come, I know that here is one Durok herd of top pigs whose genetic material definitely would have been lost, and it was preserved.

When I returned from my first U.S. trip in the spring of 1982 I got a call from Ross Fisher, a Lindsay-area farmer in trouble. He had given up but his wife Ada wanted help and a sale was scheduled for the next Saturday. I went down Wednesday night and spoke to quite a few of their neighbours. They were very supportive, picking the man up from his doldrums. We decided to whisk away the equipment. One rule of thumb we worked with quite frequently was that they cannot take what they cannot find. There happened to be a stool pigeon in the group — someone told the banker. The banker called the sheriff, who called the police. They went out en masse Friday night and Saturday morning first thing, using an airplane and actually found about six pieces of the equipment. Using a search warrant, which had been issued for the whole township, they went in with the sheriff and the police and two trucks. Imagine the cost of this operation, which had to be paid for by the T-D Bank and the tax-payers, because the farmer had no money left! How much cheaper and better for all concerned to negotiate a settlement? In the last minute negotiations on Friday, we were only $40,000 apart on a million-dollar deal. But the bank chose to flex their muscles and to proceed with the warrant and the sale on Saturday.

There were a few lessons to be learned from this particular sale. One was the difficulties when there is a lack of time for organizing resistence. We never got a chance to talk to large numbers of neighbours and get them to understand what we were doing. Also about twenty of us picketed at the sale gate, forewarning not only the auctioneer but the other people involved. Unfortunately the scavengers, the parasites who wanted to pick up this equipment cheaply, went through the picket line. Sympathetic farmers, the ones who wouldn't buy the equipment, tended to go away. So our force was weakened.

I had gone down there with just one other fellow, Al Lemke from Bruce County who was used to doing this kind of thing, to shout down the auctioneer with a completely green force of local farmers. I think it was my determination — I just wouldn't quit — that finally got the neighbours to gather around and put pressure on the auctioneer to stop.

Al and I led the singing, shouting and arguing. But the local farmers were very hesitant to take part. They hadn't seen success. Once these groups have seen victory they know they can go ahead. But the lack of leadership is the key thing. If I hadn't persevered the way I did, the thing would have fallen flat. One of the farmers who I reached out my hand to, saying come and join us, said no, but later phoned me and apologized, thanking me for what I had done. He's been very involved since.

From this we learned that to stop an auction you have to make use of surprise — everyone has to arrive in force just at the time the auction is about to start so the enemy is not forewarned. Also, if you start organizing too far in advance the rumour mill gets going — in this case an OPP officer said he'd heard rumours that 600 police were coming to the auction — and these sort of stories can scare people off. The picket line, which turned away potential supporters, was a bad idea and we didn't use it again.

Farm Credit: Too Little or
Too Late   8

*To put a man and his family out in the cold at this time
of year is no less than criminal.* — Ed England at Ed
Gorman's Farm Gate Defense.

In March of 1982 the action centred around the farm of Ed Gorman, who had been in what you'd call financial difficulty for
the last three or four years, but who wasn't in really serious
trouble. His big problem, and I've run into this time and time
again, was lack of proper financing. He thought he was too
old to get Farm Credit help. The Farm Credit Corporation,
a federal agency somewhat like CMHC, was then about the
only place you could get a decent mortgage on farm land. I
remember when I started out trying to buy a farm, the bank
said that if it had sewers hooked up to it, they would look at
it. They just weren't interested in farmland mortgages. Farm
Credit was the only alternative for mortgage money other than
a few of the finance companies, or private individuals.

If Ed Gorman had had decent Farm Credit financing — and
I can extend this to almost all the cases I've run across — with
long term fixed-rate money he wouldn't have been in trouble. Minister of Agriculture Eugene Whelan claims he wants
to expand the Farm Credit Corporation but the banks have said
no, this is free enterprise, this is our business and you stay out
of it.

They made a hell of a mess, putting farmers on floating
rates. The farmers built new barns on floating loans; they got
mortgages to buy farmland on floating rates. This meant that
every week when the Bank of Canada rate went up, the farm

loan rate went up. This was not like the city person, where every two or five years house mortgages are renewed. These floating rates make you renew every week — a horrendous way to finance a farm, because farming is not a lucrative, get-rich-quick business. You might have a particularly good or bad year, but the long-term is the thing.

Farm Credit never had the money. It was a common joke: you were either too rich or too poor for them to help you or, if they could help you, they didn't have the money. It has been almost an act of futility to go to a Farm Credit office for the last ten years. They helped me purchase my second farm. But they wouldn't help me on the first one because I didn't have any livestock or other assets, and they didn't help with the third, because I was starting to get too big. I had two hundred acres, which isn't a large farm by any means, but they didn't want to go for more because they needed to spread their sparce funds.

Ed Gorman was working on mortgages that were renewable every year, paying horrendous interest rates. Of course he eventually couldn't make the payments and the private creditor was foreclosing. When he came to me, I saw that he was in an adequate equity position, with a lot of net worth. But it was all tied up in land — you couldn't spend it and you couldn't pay bills with it. This was something that Marv Black always said: "People have to realize that equity does not pay bills." You can have all kinds of land, but if you can't make the mortgage payment you lose it. We got Ed Gorman refinanced, with Farm Credit doing the thing up in about a week. However the mortgage holder was intent on foreclosing and the lawyer wouldn't back off.

I often saw rip-off artists come in with mortgages, with lots of equity behind them, knowing full well the farmer couldn't make the payments. In one case they were charging prime plus nine percent.

The mortgage holder knew Ed had no hope of paying instantly; they knew if they foreclosed they could sell the farm and come out with quite a bit more money. And so, we had to put some men at the gate at the same time our lawyer was in the courts trying to get an injunction to stop the foreclosure. The judge gave us seven days. Our lawyer was sweating as he could hear the farm gate defense on the radio as the judge signed the papers. We got the Farm Credit money through, paid off the

Neighbours block driveway in typical farm gate defense fashion to prevent eviction of the Gorman family in Grey County.

mortgage and Ed Gorman is still in business. We got all his small creditors paid off as well.

Ed owed a lot of people around, but even people he owed money to were standing out in the laneway. They didn't think the debts justified a man with five children at home being evicted in the middle of the winter. There was no justice in that.

It was one of the first farm gate defenses in southern Grey County and the people there felt good about it; the Gorman family was very grateful to those who helped them. There was no problem getting people out to another farm gate defense when we called them.

In January, Jean Lipton, who had helped to organize the tractor demonstration on Highway 417, went into action again. Jacques Renaud came to the Prescott group for help. He had received a letter from the Bank of Montreal demanding payment of $40,000 on a demand loan within ten days. The committee had received a tip that a sudden foreclosure had been planned for an unidentified pork producer the following Monday.

By Sunday night, 450 people were prepared to gather on less than an hour's notice to obstruct what they believed was the imminent seizure of Renaud's equipment and livestock.

While Renaud negotiated with the bank, the Committee sent a three-man delegation plus a CTV crew to occupy the farm. In the resulting stand off, the bank admitted it had intended to foreclose at 2:00 p.m. that afternoon, backed off without taking anything and gave Jacques Renaud 60 days to refinance through Farm Credit.

When foreclosure started in Southwestern Ontario we had a good group start up in Middlesex County. The president of that group became our vice-president when I became the Canadian president.

Tom Shoebottom is a great asset to the organization and a lot of his neighbours were instrumental in keeping us going through that tough first year. We were still viewed as radicals or militants, over-exposed people who brought trouble on ourselves. As more and more people got into the act, they began to realize that trouble was here to stay and we had to do something about this depression. They began to appreciate what we were doing and came in to give us the added moral support that we definitely needed.

Peter Timmerman's farm gate defense in the early spring of 1982, in Dutton, Elgin County, really stands out. The press pictures of it are beautiful. I had been working with Peter for a while, trying to give him some ideas for dealing with his creditors. It seemed impossible to get them all together and to get some sanity to the thing.

He phoned on a Sunday night that the bailiffs were coming. They had notified him that they were going to pick up his pigs Monday morning. He was quite a ways from Tom Shoebottom's place but some of the Middlesex boys and some neighbours rallied around. Because of the short notice there weren't a great many people there, about thirty farmers, I think. This, as it turned out, was usually all we ever really needed.

They ran a tile drainage machine across the front of the property to make sure the trucks couldn't get in. One of the reporters called it a cat and mouse game, as the Survival advance scouts drove up and down the road, looking for the trucks. The trucks were playing hide and seek. The lawyers for the creditors were prowling around. It was quite a bit of fun really.

Finally it boiled down to the fact that when all the creditors had had enough attention drawn to them, they sat down at the table and worked out a deal. Peter is still in business, and an adamant supporter of the Association. It was another case of forcing these people into negotiating, into realizing that there is an alternative to liquidation. That's victory in round one.

Again, in the spring, George and Henry Blaucke of Listowel, Ontario, were given three days by the local CIBC to come up with $160,000 on their operating loan on their dairy farm. The Survival Association and others organized several dozen farmers to picket outside the bank while negotiations were going on and fifty farmers blocked the entrances to the farm to stop any bank officials who might try to enter the farm. The result was an extension and the Blaucke's were "back in business."

Some of our victories (temporary as they may turn out to be, if the government doesn't move) involved "stonewalling" the banks. A good example was Stu and Doreen (Teddy) Barfoot, a highly respected and well-liked couple in Elderslie Township, who had guaranteed their sons' loans to get them started in farming. The bank called the sons' notes and cut off Stu's line of credit, effectively putting them out of business. Because the Survival Association had been so effective in the area they didn't even try foreclosure and the Barfoots are still farming. This was a situation similar to many in the areas the Survival Association controls and these quiet successes are among our most important. At the time, Stu said that the pressures of dealing with these problems were worse than his war experiences in the Merchant Marine, including being one of five survivors of a torpedo attack off Gibraltar and being part of the invasion of Burma.

Farm gate defense is a fantastic organizational tool, getting people directly involved. We heard right from the start that people were sick and tired of going to meetings, discussing and cussing problems, with no one doing anything about it. But here was a spot where they could actually take some physical action, do something to help an individual in trouble. People who have gone to one of these farm gate defenses come home with a good feeling inside that they have accomplished something.

I think it's far superior to any other kind of demonstration. You put a demonstration together with tractors, or what have you, and the farmers feel good about doing it, but a day or two later, they ask, "What did we really accomplish? Did anybody listen to us? Did we make any gains from the government?" Of course the government is very reluctant to give in to a demonstration, so in terms of moving the thing ahead, there's no visible result. The next time you'd ask a farmer to take a day off, he'd ask, "What's the sense? We didn't get anything the last time."

But at a farm gate defense there was a tangible victory. You could drive by and say that man is still in his home today because I was there. It is a terrific organizational tool. Once you had the people out to one of these, the next time you called them they would come and bring their neighbours. They talked about it.

They also talked about other things. We found out very quickly that the rumour mill would work against the farmer for the first week or ten days. Right after we had a farm gate defense, the stories would fly fast and furious, that the man had sold a load of cattle under the table, or that he'd been in Hawaii for the last two winters — some of the stories were unbelievable.

One of the stories about Marvin Black was that someone had seen him with a 20-foot truck, loaded to the hilt with sides of beef, headed to Toronto for sale to the ethnic market. If anyone had stopped to think of the work necessary to kill and dress that much beef — in a normal abatoire, with all the facilities there, it's a fantastic job. The thought that someone would do it in their drive shed is just preposterous. The first sides would be rotting before you got near to the last ones. Marv laughed about it, saying he might be ambitious but he wasn't crazy. But that didn't stop the rumours.

While the negotiations were going on, one of the first things the bank asked us was to stop talking to the press. The press always wanted follow-up stories, which weren't always available because the farmer would try to work out a deal. We were particularly discouraged from doing more by the lawyers, who were trying to keep the best interest of their client at heart. I can't blame them for that, but we were fighting for a cause, and we needed these things exposed to the public.

So we got bad rumours, which I felt were deliberately started but there were good rumours as well.

The first settlements we were able to get were in the winter of 1981-82, when grain prices, although not good, were still relatively stable. You could pencil in some kind of a long-term plan. The banks were anxious to avoid the publicity so we could get settlements with them. In fact, in western Quebec the banks gave out hats to the Survival members when a case got solved.

As commodity prices continued to fall and land values began to plummet because so much land was being dumped on the market, it quickly became evident that there weren't solutions to these problems. You couldn't set a man up to grow corn to pay his debt when you know full well that he would lose $100 an acre on the corn. We couldn't project anything in the beef business because as long as that glut of corn was on the market we knew that it would drive down prices of chicken and pork, eventually affecting the beef market. These things go around and around in circles.

As it became increasingly difficult to get settlements, increasingly we became involved in holding actions to make sure the farmer wasn't moved out, that his equipment wasn't taken and his livestock wasn't seized, ensuring that he had grocery money and money for fuel, heat and hydro until the government did something.

We kept up a constant lobby effort in Ottawa and Queen's Park as well as the other provincial chapters doing their own provincial legislature. The statistics in 1981 were mind boggling. Canadian farmers paid a staggering $2,265 billion in interest alone on farm debts of some $17.4 billion, some $6.5 million per day. Ontario farmers owed $4.514 billion. Farm bankruptcies in 1982 totaled 410, an increase of 57% when compared with 1981.

When the Bank of Montreal manager brought the receivers to the farm of Clarence and Sharon Rounds they were surprised by a shed full of T.V. cameras and neighbours, some of whom had run combines 24 hours straight to remove all the crop the night before.

Exposure on the national news brought about implementation of existing government programs, but even this needed direct action, such as the one at Glencoe on January 25, 1983, where 150 farmers, under Dennis Chevalier, Colin Campbell and Don Want, attacked the Bank of Montreal for their unwillingness to aid farmers under the Ontario Farm Adjustment Assistance Program.

The positive results of direct action were born out by the fact that nearly 200 applications were processed in that area in the next two weeks. One farmer stated that driving his tractor to town had gained him $2,000 in interest assistance. The willingness of farmers to travel to help other farmers was one of the fantastic organizataion builders. Don Lucier brought farmers from Lampton, Don Conliffe brought farmers from Kent, and Robert King brought farmers from Elgin County where they had just successfully held off the Bank of Commerce from the supply store of John Slatts.

Farm gate defense had a very good effect on government because it rocked it to its very foundations. The grassroots people were starting to rise up. Now instead of losing a farmer every day, we had all these farmers on hold — with no solution in sight. The pressure was building. These people were under a lot of stress, not knowing from one day to the next how bad it was going to be. The banks commenced legal action, and we were constantly blocking them. We could stop them from literally seizing stuff but we couldn't stop some of the legal actions they were taking to secure their positions and to put pressure on farmers, in order to try and get settlements.

One of the few avenues open to us was to put a great deal of pressure on the Farm Credit Corporation to try to get them thinking of buy-out situations. Farm Credit would look at some of these cases and say there's simply too much debt. You had to start them asking how much is this operation worth, what can that farmer carry, what cash-flow does he need? Fifty, or sixty thousand, or whatever? They could then take that figure to the creditors and say, okay, the most you're going to get out of that place if you liquidate it is $60,000; Farm Credit is willing to come up with that $60,000 if you accept it as full payment, and give the man a clean start.

And it began to work. Quite a bit of it was educating Farm Credit that it could be done. It was very frustrating, however, when they would do a lot of work on these cases and the banks would refuse to negotiate — out of plain stupidity. They would say, no, we want to liquidate this man, we want to dump more assets on a weak market, drive everything down even more. We want to punish this individual because he has sinned.

In one case very early on, John Mayes, the Bank of Commerce representative said, "I don't care if it costs us $100,000, I'm going to see you to the side of the road." A Bank of Montreal spokesperson said, "We're not going to acknowledge any of these losses, we're not going to do it until you are standing at the mailbox." (Until you leave the farm, in other words.) They used threats and intimidation, refusing to admit reality and to be businesslike about it. They kept screaming that we weren't being businessmen, that the proper approach was bankruptcy. All of a sudden, the farmer *was* starting to be a businessman, saying, let's stick in this thing — for the dollar. And the Survival Association gave him the support to stop the banks.

The Farm Credit Corporation, while at first quite helpful, gradually turned into a major problem. It was increasingly very difficult, because of red tape, to get them to realize losses and sell back to the original owner. They had now done this for several farmers but the time required to change their attitude in each and every case still means that more farmers give up and walk away, dumping more land and devaluating equity.

But the real atrocities perpetrated by FCC are the mortgages locked in at 16.75% for 20 years. Why would a farmer sign that? Why wouldn't he refinance elsewhere? Simple. The banks were charging 25% and there was no other viable source of farm mortgages. I tried to explain to Sonny Anderson, the head of the FCC, that they would be better to address this, problem for no farmer can pay these rates. The farmers simply cannabalises the farm until it collapses and *then* FCC will have to do something! We in Canada need a tremendous change in our farm credit system!

Ontario Food Terminal Blockade

9

Ten years ago the deficit on my farm was about a hundred dollars; but by well-designed capital expenditures, by drainage and by greater attention to details, I have got it into the thousands. — Stephen Leacock 1869-1944

One of the direct actions we took in April 1982 was a blockade of the Ontario Food Terminal. It started out quite innocently. We were getting rumblings from our members that something had to be done. The government wasn't acting.

We were looking forward to putting in our crops in May. The survey we did indicated that 25% of the people we surveyed wouldn't be able to finance their crops that year, and in fact wouldn't be able to plant at all. This is the death knell to the farmer. There is only one month in the year when you can put your crop in and it doesn't do you any good if you get the finances three or four months later.

So there was a call for drastic action. We held a meeting in Chesley on April 15, 1982, and discussed a few pros and cons. It was decided that we should move to shut down the Ontario Food Terminal in Toronto. It handles about 80% of the produce in Ontario. The produce is brought into the depot there, the purchasers buy it and ship it to supermarkets across the province.

It seemed like a good spot to start, because if we blockaded the stockyards there would be two or three weeks of frozen product around, giving lots of time to react. But produce is perishable. It's shipped and sold on a daily basis, so if we could shut it off, the effect would be instantaneous. The supply of produce in Toronto would not last two days. People don't realize how fragile their food supply is. In North America there is only a two-week supply of food in the pipe line, so if transportation is stopped cold we could face a tremendous calamity.

We knew it was a large undertaking, but I didn't realize it was so large until after the meeting. We decided okay, we'll do it next week. There were a few dissenting voices: one fellow thought that the old age pensioners would starve to death. Some of the conservative people weren't ready for that kind of action, and these concerns tended to weaken our forces. Nevertheless, we decided something had to be done and this was it.

After we made the big announcement, I did a bit of research, contacting some people in the labour movement about how to run strikes. I was told we could picket off the property, that we had to keep a rotating picket, and that we wouldn't effectively stop anything but we would get our point across. (The Teamsters had tried three times and had failed to shut the terminal down.) A representative of the Ontario Federation of Labour said they would come down at seven o'clock and support us.

We didn't share their caution — we fully intended to shut the thing down. We'd been doing farm gate defenses where vehicles were very effective in setting up blockades. This is something that organized labour is missing. People have been killed trying to block trucks on picket lines. But a hundred parked vehicles can block anything for some time! We organized it very quietly, because we'd let the cat out of the bag and they knew we were coming some time next week. We had to be very secretive as to the actual day. So we phoned around to our contacts in the different areas, lining up a potential 300 farmers to go down. In actual fact, 150 showed up that night.

We met at Orangeville (on Fead Street, which despite the spelling I took to be a good omen) at 1:00 in the morning. None of us got any sleep, as we were organizing all night. We had a bit of a pep rally. Carl Spencer, the president at that time, didn't want to go with 150 people. Looking back on it, I think this was a turning point for Carl. He figured we were a failure because we had only come up with 150 people. I was quite impressed that we had 150 men who were willing to go, because the action we were about to undertake was a very strong measure. We didn't know what problems we would run into with the police. There would very likely be arrests. For 150 farmers to say "The hell with it, we need help and we're going to get something done right away" was, I thought, a major step, a very positive thing.

We had set up a convoy radio system, with five CB radios. We sent one fellow out as a lead scout, to head out twenty minutes before the rest to see if there were any police waiting for us and what was going on, then radio back. We told everyone to go out to their vehicles and wait while we made some phone calls to the press to notify them, as we had kept everything under wraps.

When we got outside the parking lot was empty. The lead car with the radio had started down and the rest of the people were so excited and keen to go that they followed right hot on its tail. The lead truck was driving fast to try and get ahead to keep the distance, and the followers were going like hell trying to catch up. And here were the leaders of the organization twenty minutes behind everyone else! We could hear what was going on over the CB's.

Coming in from behind, it was quite a procession to watch. We caught up to it closer to Toronto. At three o'clock in the morning you're bringing up the rear behind a long convoy of vehicles, with not much else on the road. The red tail lights made quite a sight. The CB's were radioing back and forth. We had ironic CB handles: hog caller, coyote, and such. The police later told us they monitored the calls coming down and they heard us laughing through the red lights, and a lot of the joking going on. But they didn't know who we were or where we were headed.

We arrived at the depot at 3:00 a.m. We later learned that if we had gotten there at six o'clock the police would have been ready for us. They never anticipated us hitting at 3:00 a.m. It was no trouble for farmers, as we are used to working odd hours, day and night. As trucks started to roll in and out of the Food Terminal by four we knew we had to be in there before four. That was crucial to our success: we hit them by surprise, and blockaded them with our vehicles.

When Duncan MacDonald from the OFL came down at seven o'clock he had to walk a little over a mile to get there, because we had backed up over 350 trucks, blocking the four-lane Queensway and starting to back up the Gardiner Expressway. He remarked, "What do you do for an encore?"

Farm gate Offense.   Survival Association members shut down Toronto's Food Terminal to make a point.

Farmers' trucks block exit and entry of food transports.

It was actually too successful. The first trucks in had blocked *us* in. They went across in front of us in support. We were asking at that time for a moratorium on foreclosures, and the truckers said it was good to see somebody blockading who had a just cause.

The first police officers on the scene, when they found out who we were, just turned around and said, "Well, it's a bunch of farmers — we'll be over in our cruisers but we're going to take the day off." And they went and sat and watched. We took them coffees.

The truck drivers were very good. We took them coffees too and they donated baskets of apples. At the Ontario Federation of Agriculture directors' meeting that afternoon one of our boys brought in a couple of boxes of bananas that the truckers has given to us. Some of our fellows, who were also directors of the OFA, got a standing ovation at the meeting because of what we'd done.

Duncan Allen, the Deputy Minister of Agriculture, came down at seven o'clock in the morning to talk to us. We gave him quite a razz. Duncan is quite an outspoken person and a lot of fun to debate with. He's quite a character, but unfortunately hasn't comprehended the severity of the situation or its solution.

The trucks were backing up onto the Gardiner Expressway. We had to make a decision very quickly. We were holding the key, as all the trucks were faced in toward us. If we didn't move, nobody else went. Looking back, perhaps we should have held on 'til noon. Our hope was that city people would wake up and realize that the Food Terminal was shut down, start panic buying and clean out the stores. We'd like them just once to see empty shelves in the supermarket, to drive that point home. But because of the rush hour cars backing up the Gardiner Expressway, and because the police had been so cooperative, we were afraid there would be an accident, with someone hurt and bad publicity. Everything had gone so smoothly.

So we called it off about eight-thirty in the morning. On hindsight it was the wrong thing. We should have held on for a few more hours. Apparently the Toronto Stock Exchange didn't report that day because of the commotion we caused.

We got a meeting with the Deputy Minister of Agriculture, which was no big deal. We meet with him lots of times anyway. But we got the point across that we *could* do it, and that the farmers were angry enough *to* do it. Again, there was a lot of talk, a lot of reaction from the government, but no solutions. They still didn't believe it was a bad enough problem, still thinking it affected only a minority.

I had the quote of the week in the *Toronto Star*. I said, "The government is a bit like a mule — you have to hit it between the eyes with a two-by-four to get its attention."

To underscore some of our difficulties at that time: the government continually asked for facts and figures. The Concerned Farm Wives did a survey, with the help of the University of Guelph, on the stress on farm women and their actual financial situation. It was quite a while coming to print, but it revealed that in the summer of '82, 17%, or one in six, of the farmers in the Grey-Bruce area figured on losing their farms that year. It also showed that 45% were paying abnormally high interest rates in relation to their net incomes. They were indeed in financial difficulty, and that's nearly half the farmers in Grey-Bruce.

This 17% figure, expanded as a percentage of the 80,000 farmers in Ontario, means losing more than 1,000 farms per month — as bad as North Dakota, which had two years of drought.

Eugene Forbes and the Police 10

Every citizen has a moral obligation to object to bad laws.
— Wayne Crytz

At eight o'clock in the morning, Saturday, November 27, 1982, the phone rang. I'd been in Ottawa the last three days, and up late the night before. I debated whether or not to answer, and finally got out of bed. The message was short and sweet: "Sheriff and a lot of police are in front of Eugene Forbes'." The caller hung up. I didn't know if it was an authentic call or a joke.

I looked up Eugene's number and phoned him, "Gene I hear the sheriff and police are at your place."

"True, they sure are."

"Do you need any help?"

"I sure do."

I made the key phone calls — two to the local radio stations — and headed down.

Gene and his lawyer were there, along with at least twenty OPP officers. It was going to be the most dramatic farm gate defense so far. It actually started the day before when the sheriff and the receivers, acting for the Royal Bank, had moved in to seize Eugene Forbes' 20 standardbred racehorses as security on a loan.

Eugene had been a big operator in the Walkerton area with three, perhaps five, thousand head. As the beef business had been going to hell, he had been selling down the cattle and moving more into racehorses, because it seemed that they were the ones who were making the money. It used to be that if you had enough cattle you could afford a racehorse. Now it seems that if you have enough racehorses you can afford to keep a cow — a reflection on our society's priorities!

In May 1982, Gene had been forced into receivership and arrangements had been made to allow him to retain the horses on behalf of the Royal Bank, racing them in the summer of '82 and paying the proceeds (about $1 million) to the bank. Now that the racing season was over, the bank was moving to liquidate Gene's stable without even paying the summer expenses. When the sheriff's deputy came in on Friday, Eugene and his lawyer, Herbert Mosser, had some bills for the keep of the horses they thought should be paid before they would let the horses go. The bank, of course, didn't want to pay the bills. The deputy-sheriff went to the OPP for assistance. To their credit, the OPP refused to help the sheriff. This probably added to the problem the next day. The deputy-sheriff immediately went to Toronto, to a Supreme Court judge, and got a court order ordering the OPP to back him up. The receivers lied to the judge, telling him some horses were missing.

The sheriff, Aubrey Minard, deliberately stayed away. He was at the farm at 9:00 a.m. Saturday morning and returned at 3:00 p.m., but at the height of the altercation he stayed out of sight, apparently keeping in touch with the deputy-sheriff, giving orders. Considering that this was the biggest action a sheriff in Bruce County was ever likely to see, I found it very interesting that he stayed out of sight. Perhaps he suspected what was going on was illegal, and set up the deputy to take all the flak.

The next morning, Saturday, trucks, the sheriff and the police arrived in force. The fact that it was Saturday was the basis of their strategy and the crux of our problem. The deputy-sheriff's nose was out of joint. He was angry at the OPP and when I got there he was angry at me. He was bound and determined that there would be a confrontation and he didn't give a damn who got hurt.

Gene first found the police there when he came back from another barn where he'd been choring; the yard was full of cruisers and horsetrucks. He thought he had gotten rid of them the day before, but here they were back again, this time in force. He ran the front-end loader of the tractor up to the first cruiser and threatened to push it off the road.

The OPP said afterwards that there were some pretty tense moments. It took quite a bit of sweet-talking to get Gene cool-

Gary Gurbin, PC Member of Parliament for Grey-Bruce, talks to police at the Forbes farm.

Stand-off at Forbes Cattle Company. OPP arrive to assist the sheriff in seizing prize standardbreds.

ed down enough to back up. Then the OPP pulled all of their forces back across the road.

I have often wondered if the first call I got was from the police themselves, hoping that someone would come to cool off the situation. That was one of the ideas behind our farm gate defense: an individual who is alone, with his back up against the wall, has a terrific potential for violence. Gene later admitted that he had thought seriously of grabbing his gun, just before I phoned. When a man is under tremendous strain, a couple hundred of his friends and neighbours standing with him defuses the potential for violence. No one needs to get hurt.

We moved in. Very shortly there were a hundred men in there, blocking the driveway with their vehicles. Because it was a Saturday — and I made sure this was the last time they moved on a weekend — I couldn't get an injunction and I couldn't contact anyone at the Royal Bank. They all have unlisted numbers, and the ones I knew were all away. I couldn't reach anyone in government circles, not having weekend numbers. It had never occurred to me that they would try this kind of trick on a weekend. But I should have known better because the sheriff working for the T-D bank had previously moved illegally on a Friday night, after the sheriff's office and courts had closed, to Ross Fisher's farm, seizing the equipment Friday evening for a sale on Saturday.

My only hope was our MP Gary Gurbin. Gary, bless his heart, came down right away. He put calls through to all his contacts, but it wasn't until 1:30 p.m. that he was able to get through to the Royal Bank. By this time the sheriff was getting impatient. I suggested that we all go for lunch and that, by the time we got back, perhaps the Bank would have replied. The deputy-sheriff said, "No, I'm going to move," and at 2:00 the police surrounded the horse barn.

The police blocked the road back about half a mile both ways. Farmers went out in the fields to join us, but eventually gathered in small groups and walked through the roadblocks. We had some quick executive meetings and decided we had to stand firm.

Normally we would have let the horses go so that they couldn't catch them. But the horses had a virus and we didn't really want to let them out. There was a real danger that a neighbour, Bud Fritz, and others who also had horses boarded in there, would have their horses taken too. Racehorses are very highstrung animals, and if you start moving them into a strange barn with strange people, particularly when they're in a weakened condition, there is a real potential for harm. Eugene's troubles had started when his best horse, Daylon Thunder, had an operation on his foot and died from the anesthetic and they hadn't let up. In August, a fire had destroyed his trainer's barn and 14 horses.

I wasn't worried about the eventual outcome because I knew the bank would back down and that it was just a matter of getting through to them. However, when the OPP surrounded the horsebarn, we were faced with a dilemma. Taking on the OPP wasn't the same as chasing off a trustee. The easiest way to defuse the situation (and we no longer had a choice) was to let the horses go. Everyone could have a lot of fun catching them (it's a hell of a job at the best of times). We got into a pushing and shoving match with the police at the barn door, trying to hold the doors open to let the horses out.

While all this was going on — I was in the barn and I didn't get out to the road until after — they had backed a tow truck in to clear out our blockade. We had earlier watched them bring in about four different tow trucks. But the drivers were local people and, with a few words from us, they simply went away. One had stayed. He was very sympathetic, saying he would do his best to keep things at a slow pace. Our fellows, though, were not prepared to let them hook onto even one vehicle.

He backed up to the first truck. Our farmers surrounded it and wouldn't let the police around to the back, some of them threatening the driver. The OPP, to their credit, didn't come on strong; whoever was leading them was very level-headed. The fellows at the front of the police line were older or smaller men. If they had come in with riot helmets and clubs, there would have been bloodshed.

The farmers had nowhere to back down to. This was their own backyard. One fellow said that if they cleaned out Eugene Forbes no one would be able to sleep again. Jim Barfoot said he finally understood what his father had tried to express about the war. He felt absolutely no fear. He walked through police like they weren't there. There was a job to do and nothing else mattered. The police were in an awkward position — being

Eugene Forbes and myself taking a coffee break. (The sheriff was upset that we didn't invite him to join us.)

With the standardbreds safe in the paddock, the departure of the police tow-truck inspires applause. (Survivalists are always willing to give a hand to anyone.)

seen fighting farmers on national television is bad for their image. But if they had turned and walked away, they might as well have taken their uniforms off. It was a no-win situation for everyone.

I got very angry because I could feel the tenseness of our farmers; I knew they weren't going to back down. There was a real potential for trouble, and I knew it didn't need to be. All we had to do was hang on for that damn phone call. The deputy-sheriff was on a power trip and wasn't going to wait. He could have moved on his seizure warrant any time over the next two weeks. He didn't have to do it at 2:00 p.m. and he didn't have to do it on Saturday.

The phone call finally came through. Eugene would have two more weeks to work out a payment schedule with the bank. The bank had backed off, but even at that point the sheriff wouldn't. "Did we think we were above the law?" and so on. I tried to explain to him that the law is the people. If you get that many people in an area who don't think a law is right, then it's not right; it goes back to the jury system. However, he was determined, I suppose, not to have his reputation ruined. He also argued strongly with our MP who, as an elected representative, is the supreme representative in our county. But when he got back outside, the horsetrucks had already gone home, so he called it off.

But it was very tense when the sheriff heaped verbal abuse upon me and I had to bite my tongue. He'd been looking for me for a month-and-a-half, to serve me with a summons issued by the Royal Bank. He was mad that I would show up when I wasn't wanted, and that he couldn't find me when he did want me.

It was just after 4:00 p.m. by the time it was over. We had stood off forty OPP officers for about eight hours, just using moral authority. Apart from the little bit of shoving and pushing at the horse barn, there was absolutely no violence. Just a hell of a group of guys. I thought afterwards that there were enough of us to have three farmers to a policeman, and simply carry them away. But that would have created more troubles than it solved.

As a result of this action I was charged with verbally threatening the deputy-sheriff and obstructing a police officer. I had told him if there was any bloodshed I would kill him. We had called an emergency meeting and decided that we had no choice but to go again if called upon.

Our conversations with individual policemen were important: they didn't like to be doing what they were doing. They had showed that the day before when they refused to back up the sheriff. These are working men, sympathetic to farmers. They knew the impact of the interest rates. They realized that the banks aren't as lily white clean as they claim to be. There was very good crowd control — no night sticks or weapons of any kind. Quiet, soft-spoken policemen kept the lid on the thing.

Down at the Ross Fisher sale in Lindsay there had been only one uniformed officer. I'd been talking to the Ontario Provincial Police the night before about what we were going to do. If they had come in with five or six policemen in Lindsay, it would only have increased the tension.

Afterwards the OPP complimented me on the peaceful action, saying that we could yell and shout all we wanted as long as there was no violence. That should be the true role of the policeman — just to keep peace.

The funny part of that sale was the two undercover officers, and their impression of farmers. They wore pants two inches above the tops of black workboots, an old shirt and hat, and sunglasses. I can't recall ever seeing a farmer wearing sunglasses. But their most obvious mistake was not talking to each other or to other farmers. Most farmers go to sales as social events, to discuss prices and crops and so on. So these two lonely souls might as well have had their badges on.

Later on, the Jack Underwood case in the Chatham area was just the opposite. I thought I'd gotten Jack's problem solved at the Bank of Montreal, regional level, but I just didn't trust Ernie Morell, the regional manager: he hemmed and hawed, finally saying at 9:00 a.m., "Well, I tried to get to the sheriff, to call him off, but he's gone anyway, I missed him." I knew he was just trying us out. I had arranged for about a dozen farmers to be at Jack's place. I didn't anticipate any trouble, figuring we had stopped it through negotiation, but we had to be there for Jack's moral support.

The sheriff moved in. There were five black and whites (OPP cars), plus a station wagon, and four unmarked cruisers. They literally had a police car for every farmer there. I complained very bitterly the next day to the provincial Attorney-General and the Solicitor-General, and I finally got talking to someone at the OPP Commissioner's office. He checked it out and fervently denied any such thing. "There was only one black and white, only three uniformed officers — you don't know what you're talking about."

Well, I spoke to six of the farmers there in separate conversations, and got the same story from each and every one of them. There's no doubt in my mind that there were five black and whites, four unmarked cars, and the one station wagon — plus the sheriff's car and interested bystanders.

But I thought to myself, if the Commissioner's office of the OPP starts lying to you maybe you've got them shook up. They didn't know what they were doing, and were overreacting. With this sort of thing, there is a real potential for trouble. Whoever was responsible for the Underwood thing certainly shouldn't be in a position of authority.

The RCMP were a different story. Shortly after the vigilante picture, RCMP officers with guns, handcuffs, and two back-up units went into the home of Bill Wolfe, one of our local farmers who was very well respected in the community, to seize all his records and photograph literally all of his home — even taking several pictures of an old pile of magazines sitting on a chair. Their intent, to my mind, was strictly to terrorize; Bill's wife was still waking up over a year later with nightmares of police and sheriffs.

Bill was charged with fraud, and at the preliminary hearing, the RCMP officer testified that the Bank of Montreal had proceeded in a very unusual way toward its customers. As evidence, Bill's lawyer had a letter dated September 9, 1981 (more than a month before the Survival Association started), to the bank's regional credit manager T. F. Sullivan, from George Shaw, vice-president of Touche Ross and Co.

The letter advised the bank not to appoint Touche Ross as agents until the RCMP executed a search warrant for Wolfe's farming files.

"Such action by the RCMP," the letter said, "should have significant effect on the political climate and public attitude toward the bank's decision to realize its security as well as probably promoting a cooperative attitude on the part of Mr. Wolfe."

Also in evidence was a letter to the bank from its lawyer, warning it "could be guilty of extortion if it used the criminal process" to help itself in proceeding against Wolfe in a civil suit.

At Bill's preliminary hearing the judge ruled that there had been an abuse of power; in other words, the bank had been using the police to collect a debt.

At the Painter farm in Manitoba, the Royal Bank asked for and got an ex-parti order — or, in layperson's terms, the court only heard the bank's side of the argument and the farmer never even knew they were prosecuting. The reason given was that Painter was a member of the Survival Association. They seized his equipment for a $293,000 debt while he had $280,000 worth of crop growing in his fields. To me, the Constitution guarantees freedom of association, but in the Manitoba courts you are guilty of heinous crimes just because you belong to a group of farmers whose one principal is to force the banks to go through the courts rather than run around stealing things!

Bill Wolfe was one of three local Ontario farmers whose houses were searched by the RCMP for the Bank of Montreal, but he was the only one against whom any charges were laid.

The police also laid a charge against Ross Fisher for failing to provide the equipment the neighbours had in storage, knowing full well that we had publicly stated that we were holding it until the Farmers' Creditors Act came through.

To conclude our story, Eugene Forbes stayed in business. And as a result of the Survival Association saving his racehorses, he received in the neighbourhood of $1 million in earnings in 1983, with great horses, such as Annie Ivy, J.B. Surge, Rosie Dawn, Carol's Omaha, and Trudy Omaha. These horses, saved by the Survival Association, are some of the top harness horses in Ontario, if not Canada. Bud Fritz, one of the owners of some of the horses in the barn and one of Eugene's drivers, was the top driver in Ontario, winning the Ontario Sire Stakes in 1983, and is one of the top drivers in North America, driving the horses we helped save.

The last word on the Forbes stand-off has yet to be heard a year later. On my trial in December of 1983 I was convicted of verbally threatening Deputy-sheriff Peter Carter in the lawful execution of his duty. When I am sentenced, I will most likely appeal. But Judge W. Cochrane decided that the sheriff was acting illegally by moving on a Saturday, when the office "shall be closed" according to the Sheriff's Act.

It also came out at the trial that neither the receivers nor the sheriff, nor the OPP, had a list or a description of which horses were to be taken, or how many. They were going to take every single one regardless of who it belonged to. They came in with four horse trailers, with a capacity of perhaps 48 horses; 78 according to the deputy-sheriff. In order to have taken even 48 horses they would have had to have taken eight other people's horses. There were only 19 horses in the barn at that time that could be considered to the Forbes'.

In his "Reasons for Judgement," Judge Cochrane stated:

> . . . he (Carter) was prepared to carry out the order by simply seizing all of the horses in the Forbes' barn that appeared, I guess, to belong to Mr. Forbes and he did say that he had some person there from the Canadian Standardbred Association or some such organization who would identify the horses, but there was also evidence that there were apparently many horses there that did not belong to Forbes and would not be the subject of the order.

Mr. Carter did not make himself familiar, I guess with the terms of the security as to what animals he could recover and obviously he was going to make, for lack of a better word, a wholesale seizure of horses and then sort them out later. That to me would be in direct contravention of the court order, and as Mr. Donnelly has pointed out, there were certain rights given in the order and they must be clearly and strictly adhered to. Certainly that was not the intent at the time and so as a result of those various considerations, particularly the fact that it was on a Saturday — it could have been done the day before but something semed to have gone wrong with the order and it almost sounds like a clandestine arrangement between the Sheriff's office and the trustees and the bank. I'm not saying that it was, but that is the appearance it gives and as Mr. Donnelly has brought out in cross-examination, would the Sheriff's office do the same for you or me in general times, if we were in the same position. I'm sure the answer to that is no, they would not and so this is the kind of procedure which I can't accept as being proper or legal and I am quite satisfied really that any seizure that follows and flows from that kind of conduct for one thing is a direct breach of Mr. Forbes' rights under the Charter and a completely unreasonable seizure under all of those circumstances and for those reasons I find that Mr. Carter, on the the occasion in question was in fact a trespasser at the Forbes farm.

This business of grab everything and sort the mess out later was an intolerable attitude for a sheriff, or a police officer, whose role is to support and protect the innocent citizen, the judge ruled. He also found it "unusable" that six OPP cruisers would come in on a man while he and his children were feeding the livestock, and when there had been no previous trouble.

Soon after the incident, Gene learned that The OPP had sent a bill to the receivers, Coopers Lybrand, (who had taken over $40,000 out of Eugene Forbes' bank account for this bullshit) and were paid in excess of $20,000 for their part in the affair. That's right, our hallowed Provincial Police are little more than "rent a cops" for the Royal Bank! All the businessmen who've had any substantial dealings with Mr. Forbes subsequently had their loans called, even as far away as Alberta. The way the banks conspired together to attack members of our association should be a matter of an investigation by the RCMP, since they are definitely trying to deprive us of our rights of association, as guaranteed under the Charter of Rights.

Judge Cochrane also commented that:

> . . . substantial efforts were being made by people of substance, I may say, to have the matter at least temporarily resolved so that the trustees in bankruptcy would be satisfied if the proceedings were at least stayed for a short period of time and ultimately that is exactly what took place.

The lesson to be learned was that even though Eugene Forbes was right in defending his property, as were the others with their horses there, the existing law enforcement agencies, unless stopped by ordinary citizens, work for the power brokers — the bankers.

Usury

Worm or beetle — drought or tempest
On a farmer's land may fall.
Each is loaded, full of ruin,
But a mortgage beats 'em all!
— Will Carleton (1845-1912)

In my study of history, looking for causes and cures, I came to the oldest and best history book we've got, the Bible. In Leviticus 25 it speaks of a jubilee, and it says that every seventh year you lay the land fallow. And every fiftieth year — seven times seven is forty-nine — you declare a jubilee, and wipe out all debt. You give back to the people that which belongs to them. And it says to stop the practice of usury.

We got into quite a thing with the usury of the banks, whether their ability to create the money is evil, or whether just the fact that they practise usury is evil. Usury, in the strict sense, is the charging of any interest, whether it be one percent or a hundred percent. A lot of people take it just to be extreme interest. The Fifteenth Psalm asks who shall go to heaven and in the Fifth Verse it says not he who charges interest. There are a lot of quotations in the Bible on usury.

One of the more interesting is the story of the talent. One boy buried his talent, and it was taken from him. The master says why didn't you put it out to usury? The servant says I knew you were an unjust man. I knew you were evil, that you put out your money to usury, that you harvested but you did not sow. Usury is contrary to the teachings of Christ and to the laws of Mohammed of Islam. Margaret Thatcher and Ronald Reagan, Gerald Bouey or Pierre Trudeau, whomever you want to blame it on, are obviously not as intelligent as Christ or Mohammed.

Farmers are right in their perception of money as a medium of exchange. The problem of interest is based on the false premise that money is a real thing. People have to understand that money is only a method of keeping track of transactions, a medium of exchange. It, in itself, doesn't multiply. It doesn't grow. The only difference between a $1 bill and a $5 bill is the figure on the front of it. It is still only a piece of paper much like the bookkeeping entry in a company. It designates wealth but is of itself worthless. Try eating some for dinner, or offer it to a thirsty man! If money can be conceived as only a record of transactions, then it becomes understandable that changing the record does not change what actually happened. A car dealer with ten cars on his lot could write in his inventory 10 cars x 2 = 20 cars, but it does not mean that when he looks out, there are suddenly 10 more cars. Those cars have to be built before someone can say they exist. So it is with interest. Just because some bank teller writes $100 plus 10% equals $110 does not mean there is suddenly another $10 in Canada.

People say well, the money you borrow is tied up, and you're paying rent on it. You can rent a car or a truck, and you're actually wearing them out. They get older and are worth less. You are devaluating them. You don't devaluate money. Even if the bills get old, they are still worth face value.

Then there is the argument that interest compensates for inflation. Well in reality interest creates inflation. The only way to "pay" interest is repudiation or inflation, which is a form of repudiation.

Maybe usury is the real evil. Nehemiah came down from the mountains — Bible people are always up in the mountains — and saw that the people had their vineyards mortgaged, and their daughters and sons had been sold into slavery. He didn't tell the people that they were lazy and useless. He said you've been practising usury. Then he went to the owners and landlords, the rich men, and said tear up your mortgages, give back to these people what belongs to them, and let the practice of usury cease.

Every depression ended with debt re-adjustment, one way or the other to compensate for interest: the currency collapsed, the money wasn't in the banks and the depositors lost theirs, and debts were written off or lost in the foreclosure transactions. Sometimes the write-off was legislated. Quite often there were currency changes. On some occasions the assets of banks were seized. Historians are familiar with such events. The switch on and off the gold standard is really the same thing. You just re-evaluate the dollar, switch on the currency and off the gold standard, inflate the dollar and then switch back on to gold and deflate the dollar. Wipe out debt or add to it; whichever way they want to control the thing. Every once in a while you'll pick up a book on the need for hard money: "We have to go back on the gold standard." Look back through history: we've gone back on it, we've gone off it.

After the collapse of the populist movement, which was partially due to the split over the monetarizing of silver, Henry D. Lloyd wrote,

The free silver movement is a fake. Free silver is the cowbird of the reform movement. It waited until the nest had been built by the sacrifices and labours of others and then laid its eggs in it, pushing out the others which lie smashed on the ground.

The farm movements throughout recent history have blamed the banks for creating money through loans on fractional reserves. However, the creation of money is necessary for the economy to expand and grow with the population, increasing goods and services. The problem lies in the fact that instead of money being permanently created, it is only loaned out, therefore bearing interest charges.

It is interesting to look at Roman history. In 357 BC, Rome set the maximum interest rate at 8 1/3 percent, but in 342 BC, interest was abolished to favour debtors. In 96-90 BC, currency was devalued, and debts were scaled down 75 per cent. A few years later, loans were called in and that started the flight of gold out of the country until an embargo on gold exports was slapped on.

In the years 49-44 BC, Julius Caesar decided to use a "means" test to cut the number on relief rolls, and he did drop the number from 320,000 to 150,000 but by the year 2 BC, relief rolls were up to 320,000 again and Augustus cut it back to 200,000.

By the year 91 AD, there was an overproduction of wine, and Domitian set up a plan which wiped out half of the vineyards in order to check that overproduction.

By 274 AD, relief became hereditary, and bread along with pork, olive oil and salt were given out to the people. The size of the army and the vast number of public employees also added to the very high taxes.

Then Rome followed a policy of debasement of money, cutting the percent of silver in the coins. When Nero ruled in 54 AD, a coin was 94% silver. By the year 268 AD, the silver content was down to 0.02%.

In 201 AD, the ruler Diocletian came up with his famous "Edict" which spoke of "unprincipled greed" in the empire. And this edict "commanded cheapness." It put a ceiling on prices of about 800 goods, and a wage limit for teachers, writers, lawyers, doctors, bricklayers, tailors, and every other kind of worker. The law was strict, and the penalty was death.

But the edict failed. It was a bad time for the people, with a lot of bloodshed for trifling offences. The people simply quit taking any products to market because they couldn't get a reasonable price, and that caused such a shortage that many people died. There were laws too that forced men to remain in their trades and occupations, and to train their sons to succeed them. The peasants left the land and went to Rome, and that movement swelled the relief rolls. The Romans imported cheap grain from their conquests, destroying their family farms. They then set up huge corporate farms using slave labour. These workers did not care for the soil and the civilization started to die. Land was even offered free to anyone who would cultivate it. And the Roman Empire faded away.

Historians relate that ancient nations were strong and prosperous so long as the farmers owned the land they tilled. Whenever, through debt, interest and wars, land passed into the hands of the nobles, the nation would decline.

The Greeks had similar problems. The farmers were rapidly losing their land. When Solom came to power he cancelled all farm mortgages and limited the amount of land one person could own. Opposition from the nobles prevented him from redistributing the land.

Debt readjustment is necessary because the interest calculated does not exist. $100,000 debt turns into $200,000 debt in 40 months at 18% interest. One did not spend this money to buy assets, cattle, machinery, or plant crops, so these cannot be sold to pay the debt. It is nowhere in the system. You can't pay that money back because it never existed. You never actually had the money. It doesn't exist anywhere except on a little piece of paper that says the interest totals such and such. It's the only place in Canada where that $100,000 they want back exists. When you multiply the hundreds of thousands of people by the hundreds of thousands of dollars debt, you have an enormous, non-existent sum. It is this attempt to reclaim what doesn't exist which created the monetary shortage called a depression.

I like the story of the lumberjack in the 1930s. He was leaning against the tree with his axe at his feet. There was no sense in cutting the tree down because the lumber mills weren't working. The lumber mills weren't working because no one was building houses. No one was building houses because there was no money. So the lumberjack decided to go home, and he reaches down to pick up his axe, and there was an ant hill. The ants were busy building houses, completely unaware of the monetary crisis about them. And that's probably the best illustration of why it doesn't need to happen. The ants and the bees kept right on working. It is strictly man made monetary policy.

So how do we get this thing stopped? That was one of the big goals of the Canadian Farmers' Survival Association. Who could see this depression coming? It wasn't too hard to see that if the farmers were in trouble the rest of the economy would be too. The interest rates were destroying the whole thing. So how do you prevent this depression, this monetary collapse? The first step is to stop devaluation. Because when you're devaluating property values, asset values, you're changing the dollar value. This is what starts the panic. The run for the monies, the run on the banks.

I often thought that having a run on the banks might clear the thing, and so I came very close to trying to organize one. Much like what William Lyon Mackenzie did. The short term repercussions to society of this run on the banks could be devastating, but probably very beneficial in the long term.

The other alternative was to try to stop the banks from demanding payment. To stop the withdrawal of money out of the system, stop the devaluation. That's where we get into trying to help the individuals in trouble. Trying to get the banks to wake up and realize that by demanding all this payment all at once the thing would collapse. If they continued trying to collect this huge interest rate the thing would collapse. We tried to educate them, tried to stop their access to these assets, stop their ability to seize equipment and to foreclose on mortgages. Stop the panic situation. By withdrawing the credit (necessary without a profit the previous year) to put a crop in, they stop the purchase of fuel, machinery, parts, seed, etc. Factories close up and people are laid off. They foreclose on their mortgage and try to sell their house to someone who is worried about their future, and the spiral continues.

I truly believe that if the Survival Association hadn't gotten involved and slowed this thing down, we would be hell-bent for a total collapse very, very quickly. Because we were visible, because we were fighting the thing, we brought some pressure to bear on the five powerful chartered banks in Canada, who had to slow down. They backed off, took another little run at it, and backed off again. They started to realize the seriousness of the situation. It made them back up and think a bit, to take an overall look. Maybe listen to some of the things we were trying to tell them. By that we probably saved a major collapse. As it was, Ontario agricultural land values fell 20% in 1982, a drop of $3.6 billion.

When I mentioned the run on the banks I should explain that while there are only $9 billion in currency in Canada, the Royal Bank, for example, has something like $90 billion on deposit. If you go in and take the cash out there isn't nearly enough cash to go around. There's about $300 per person in Canada. Most of that is already in circulation. Very little is held within the banks' vaults. So these depositors, from my rough calculations, would get probably one and a half cents on the dollar if everyone went in and got out their money at the same time. Because physically it isn't there. This happened a lot in the Thirties, when people got scared. It happened to some of the trust companies in the 1980s that went broke — people started to run to them. The lineups started, and within hours some larger institution bought them out to stop the panic. The provincial government in Ontario put pressure on the federal government, raising the depositors' insurance from $20,000 to $60,000. Not that they wanted to give $40,000 away to each of these depositors, they just wanted to stop the people from running to the banks, to stop the panic. No one has explained to me where you cash the cheques from the depositors insurance after all the banks collapse. After all, once the depositors go in and try to take their money out, the first few would get their money and the rest wouldn't, and the thing collapses. Everyone takes what money they can get and goes home with it, and the banks sit empty, and broke. I would really like to see that; at times my anger at the banks is boundless — anger at what they do to individuals, their immense power built on faith, much like a religious thing. Strictly faith, no fact behind it. There are no volumes of gold in the bank, no piles of dollar bills. It is just all bullshit.

So that was what could have happened. In the United States it in fact did happen. They lost a lot of major banks. In 1983 there were 48 major bank failures in the United States. In one small bank five farmers were closed down and their losses broke the bank. Their assets were devaluated and thrown on the open market. The depressed market brought very little. The federal auditors reassess all the mortgages they hold. They claim that these assets aren't what you say they are, that you're broke, and they close you down. This was fine and dandy until they began to realize just how bad the thing was, and the federal auditors started to back off. In 1982 I used to say that I could predict the interest rate by just watching the bank collapses. Every time there was a major bank collapse reported in the *Wall Street Journal,* the interest rate dropped between one and two percent.

In Canada the banks aren't any less vulnerable, except that they're bigger. Instead of umpteen little ones, where one here and one there is lost, we've got five major ones. It's like an oak tree: it doesn't shake very much, but when it falls there's one hell of a crash.

The solution is not to create the currency necessary to the system through bank loans bearing interest. But rather to properly moneterize the new wealth coming into our system.

The Farmers' Creditors
Arrangement Act 12

More credit to agriculture is like more rope to a hanged man.
— Louis XIV

The Farmers' Creditors Arrangement Act was an act to ex-
pediate and facilitate bankruptcy, passed in 1935. Before I explain *what* it is, I better explain *why* it is.

When we go through periods of low farm income, we
substitute "credit" for "earned income." If you lose your job
you might borrow some money from a friend. Farmers can only
get that credit because inflation drives up our land values and
the value of our machinery — our assets. As the demand for
credit grows, interest rates rise. As I mentioned before in the
story about the marbles, interest is eventually impossible to
pay. It exists only on your particular debit sheet — nowhere
else in Canada. Most of the money in our system is made
available via loans from financial institutions. The cycle maintains itself as the bank keeps lending money to pay the interest
on ever-inflating equity.

A depression comes when the system starts to collapse. There
is a lack of money for financing production and for buying goods
because the interest is absorbing so much of it. Twenty percent of the money of the farming community in 1982 was going directly to the banks. It was not being spent in the hardware stores, not buying tractors and trucks and so on.

Now inflation on our land values has stopped so we can no
longer finance our farming through borrowing; operating
money has to come out of the marketplace, and when it doesn't,
there's no money to spend.

In our discussions among farmers about our plight, one of the older members explained the Farmers' Creditors Act and suggested that it be reinstated. It is an act of readjustment. The price of commodities and land values have fallen, and it is now necessary to drop the debt. When we investigated it we were quite thrilled to find the Act still on the books, but disappointed that it applied only to debt prior to 1935. In our lobby effort in Ottawa in January 1982, we requested updating it, pleading that if we did not get land prices stabilized everyone would go down. In April 1982, Liberal MP Ralph Ferguson introduced the bill as a Private Member's Bill. There it sat — despite my constant urging — until the hunger strike. If it had been made law in April 1982, the losses of all concerned would have been minimal at this time. Instead, there is now so much land and machinery on the market that losses are snowballing daily. And so, many whose spirit is broken will never go back, and the land will sit idle.

We're faced with a whole bunch of technically bankrupt farmers. What are their options? Traditionally, the belief has been that these are the ones who have done wrong or badly; they must be punished. So you liquidate them — evict them from their homes, seize their equipment and livestock, and sell everything on the market. This only works when there's someone there to buy. When the majority of people cannot buy, these assets are not saleable, or if they sell it is for half of what they're worth, maybe even a third.

This has a twofold effect: one, resistance. People can't get out with their heads above water so they fight. Farmers cannot be petitioned into bankruptcy and so the situation is often misconstrued by the press when they quote figures — only 400 farmers in 1982 as compared to 10,000 small businesses going bankrupt. A farmer normally will sell everything and then, if they still hound him, he declares *personal* bankruptcy, which goes into a different column. But for what it's worth as an indicator, farm bankruptcies were up 60% in 1982 from the 1981 figure. The interest paid by farmers equalled net farm income in North America in 1982. A banker remarked to me ten years ago that farmers don't go bankrupt, they just go broke. They simply have to sell off their assets, pay their bills, and start again with what's left. But when there's nothing left, you start to get resistance and you start to get human tragedies.

Two, "devaluation of property" machinery and everything else by dumping it onto the market. That's what's happening now, and with this devaluation the decline is hastened. As the banks see that the values of land and machinery values are falling, they reassess some of their accounts that are close to the wire. They soon realize that they're broke and so close in on them too. They get rid of them quickly, before their equity goes down further, and it gets to be a mad rush to see which bank can get rid of the assets the quickest before equity collapses even further. It doesn't take much imagination to see that this is a dead-end street with only one result — a bank collapse. The mortgages that the banks hold, the personal loan guarantees — that's the equity that the whole structure of the banking system is built on. It's not built on gold or the land itself, but on faith in paper, especially the mortgages which collapse very quickly as land values drop.

However in the 1930s they came up with a solution to it. They had debt readjustment — the Farmers' Creditors Arrangement Act. They said that instead of dumping all these assets on the market and further devaluating everything, let's be sensible about this. Let's acknowledge these losses for what they are. Because the losses are there. The assets have devaluated. In traditional bankruptcy you declare bankruptcy, assets are liquidated, and whatever debts aren't paid are wiped out. The bankrupt person is free and clear and can't be further harassed. The banks must write off this debt. They call it "retiring the loan."

So we're saying: how do we keep these assets off an already flooded market? Of course the best person to sell them back to is the original owner. This has a twofold effect. It used to be that when a person owed you money, he or she became your slave — an asset presumably. But remember debtors' prison. People in prison are liabilities. Today these people become welfare recipients, a liability to society. So the rich actually lose every time they dump someone on welfare, (providing they pay taxes) because it's tax dollars that support them. How much better it is to keep people as members of society, gainfully employed!

Of course the best place for a farmer to be re-employed is on his own farm. So let's readjust that debt. If there's $100,000 mortgage on a farm which is now worth $50,000 you might as well admit that it's only worth $50,000, and sell it back to the original farmer, and let him carry on as a productive member of society.

This would stop the destruction of our rural businesses — the hardware and grocery stores, the feed suppliers, and so on — and also keep their suppliers, the factory people, at work.

The important thing is that farmers have got to be left with viable operations, not farms half destroyed so that it's not just a matter of time before they die. You can go out to the pasture and take milk out of a cow every day for quite a while. But if you decide you're going to have a steak and cut off her leg, she dies and doesn't produce anything.

We had similar legislation in the 1880s, called the Creditors' Relief Act. One old man's grandfather had his mortgage postponed for twenty years. This is what we're talking about: an arrangement, or compromise. In other words you can't make the payments this year but maybe you can make them the next. You can't pay 20% interest — some of these farm loans are locked in at 20% — but you might be able to pay 5%. It's a lot better for a lender to get 5% than to get nothing.

Those that went along with the farmers in the late 1930s said okay if you can't make your mortgage payment, make half the payment, whatever you can make. We'll just wait until times get better and then you can pay me. Those people who waited got dollar for dollar when things turned around. Those people who didn't, and who forced liquidation, got pennies. Last time, the Act worked by having one person — usually from the Veteran Land Administration or what we might now call Farm Credit — to assess the situation. He talked it over with the farmer, and with the creditors. He made his proposal. If it didn't suit the farmer and the creditor and they came to an impasse, he would present it to a judge. The judge would hear all three stories and make a decision that was binding.

The farmers I spoke to said those judges' decisions were rather harsh the first couple of times in a county, but it facilitated honest negotiations from thereon in. If the judges cut the debt in half, from then on the creditors would be quite willing to work this thing out rather than go to court. They would back right off. This is in fact what happened. I've since talked to numerous people who've had their mortgages rearranged or held over, rather than having to go the whole Farmers' Creditors Arrangement route.

However, I visualize that if the Act is implemented and the courts don't have the necessary authority to write the debt down there's a danger; if they don't put enough teeth into the Act the creditors will tie everything up in the courts.

Many of the U.S. bankers I've spoken to *want* a moratorium because they are smaller and can see the overall picture and that these measures, while seeming harsh, will benefit the whole community in the long run.

The five big banks in Canada I liken to the dinosaur we learned about in public school — it was so large that it had a large nerve centre at the tip of its tail, a second brain to operate the back legs because they were too far from the head. The problem is, our banks don't have that brain in their tail — away from head office. They are trampling their own life support systems and don't even know it.

In 1934, moratorium legislation came through in several provinces. The problem was that the provinces didn't have the legal right to write off debt. A federal authority was necessary. So these laws were failures; the farmers were put on hold, lenders couldn't foreclose, and they couldn't write the debt down, get that farmer back into society. Rather they left him in a holding action much the same as the Farmers' Survival Association has been doing pending this legislation. We're not prepared to let anyone lose their farm, their means of livelihood, before the government finally does something.

In 1935 something happened that triggered the federal government. The Sun Life Insurance Company was facing bankruptcy. The Bankers' Association just loves to point out that the insurance companies never came back into farming after the Farmers' Creditors Act. The truth of the matter is that Sun Life was broke, long gone, before the Act. When the authorities examined Sun Life, which held a tremendous number of farm mortgages, they found that the reason it faced bankruptcy was that farm land values had dropped. They quickly realized that if they didn't get this land devaluation stopped, the banks would collapse as well. And so the Farmers' Creditors Arrangement Act was brought out, in 1935 to stop a bank collapse. They didn't give a hoot about the individual farmers, but the farmers of course benefited as the fear and insecurity was taken off their backs. It gave them an access to justice, to the courts.

I can't believe some of the resistance to this thing. All the farmers are asking for is someone to examine the situation and to make sure they have justice. They certainly don't under our present system. The banks have all the power. Government officials bow to their whims. They believe the banks can do no wrong. I've been quoted in the press as calling them "immoral bastards" and I have well-documented cases showing their indefensible practices.

But the Act that was introduced would throw open their practices for judicial examination, and so the banks' resistance. The Bankers' Association — which I think is probably the phoniest bunch I every met — don't want the banks examined because there *are* a lot of wrongdoings. They pretend to be a self-regulating body, there to ensure fair bank practices. But in reality they are just a lobby group to cover up bank atrocities, while pretending to help. One good example was at a cattlemen's meeting, when Al Droppo, a Bankers' Association representative, expressed shock at a complaint about farm improvement loans. He asked for the branch manager's name, pretending genuine concern. I asked who else had the same problem — over half the farmers there raised their hands. It has been a major complaint for years. The banks simply said farm improvement loans didn't exist because they are "forced" by the laws of Canada to lend money one percent below regular rates in exchange for a government guarantee.

But Droppo went through this phony show of shock and concern.

In the United States farmers are launching multi-million-dollar libel suits against banks and financial institutions. Our laws in Canada don't facilitate this, but we've got some going on now. The banks are clearly wrong, but it takes a lot of money and time to get justice. One of the reasons we have to resort to civil disobedience is the fact that justice is not available through our civil court system, particularly because our court systems are bogged down and the time element serves only those who have staying power which, roughly translated, means money. Of course the banks try their damnedest to make sure you're bankrupt and can't afford the lawyers.

But I don't see that there's any real justification for denying a farmer access to justice. If you want a divorce from your wife or husband, you have at least access to the courts to make sure it's a fair and just separation, that the assets are fairly divided. That's all the farmer is asking for. In fact, the Act will benefit the banks and all the other businesses that go with the farm community. I sometimes wonder if we wouldn't be better with a bank collapse. We have such a corrupt system set up there, so much power and wealth accumulated in so few hands.

A lot of the resistance we got to the Act — and I was surprised at some of the resistance in the testimony at the subcommittee hearings — was from people who had been hyped up by the banks. The Equipment Dealers' Association complained of the present devaluation of their assets, but at the same time they feared that the courts would have the authority to write off some of their receivables. Well if an equipment dealer has ten combines at $50,000 each on his lot, and there are three combines in the neighbourhood being forcibly sold by the banks, his are going to devaluate. And if ten of them each devaluates $5,000, he has effectively lost a combine. We saw machinery values drop to a third of what their value had been before. So the equipment dealer has nothing but to win if these farmers are kept in business. He's going to continue to sell them parts. The more that's dumped on the market, the lower all values will be and the lower the final bottom figure.

But the sad part is when the equipment dealer is going along with the farmer on the tractor — he's maybe making a partial payment — and the bank swoops in and steals the crop, or takes the livestock. There's no hope then for the farmer to make the equipment payment, and the equipment dealer ends up with another piece on his lot that he cannot sell.

There was also resistance from oldtimers whose fathers had held mortgages which were cut in half. But half is better than nothing, and if the dumping continues all mortgages will be worthless. I see lots of relatives who hold second mortgages get nothing because the bank shuts down the farmer. In Marvin Black's case, the CIBC threw a half-million dollar second mortgage into the waste basket because land values fell, making it worthless.

Small business is one of the most important potential benefactors of this Act. Just the other day I had a feed dealer who'd been dealing with a farmer for years. The farmer was going to pay him when he sold the cattle. He sold the cattle and of course the Bank of Montreal grabbed the whole cheque. There was no money to pay for the feed. The bank manager actually laughed at the feed company owner: "How could he be so naive as to think the bank was going to pay?" The unsecured creditors are being destroyed. Then the bank wonders why the suppliers can't pay their bills; they foreclose on them and dump more assets on the market.

Again, other small businesses — the Fertilizer Dealers' Association, and so on — spoke against the bill. It's not a question of whether or not they're going to collect these monies — they can't if the money isn't there. Where there is any chance at all of getting money back, they will get it, but not if the other creditors move in ahead and destroy an operation. Going back to the Marvin Black incident, the bank moved in and grabbed a crop, knowing full well that they had promised to pay for fertilizer. But the fertilizer dealer was unsecured and they had no intention of paying. In the last Farmers' Creditors Act the unsecured creditors received an average of 52 cents on the dollar. That's a fantastic rate, if you talk to anyone who's been unsecured in a recent bankruptcy. Usually in bankruptcy proceedings the unsecured creditors don't even bother going, because the receivers, the lawyers, the real estate and auction agents and so on take all the money that's there. The receiver literally works until all the money is gone. It's much like passing around an ice cube — it disappears but no one has it.

Small Businesses are key to the structure of our small communities. Some supply a farmer with fertilizer for years and years, and have gotten to be a very personal friend. Because of circumstances beyond his control — the bank has grabbed all his assets — the farmer can't pay the supplier. One local farmer was convicted of fraud and got two months in jail, because he paid his friends and neighbours ahead of the secured bank. Bankruptcy allows for reorganization or making a proposal. But it is conditional on all parties approval and of course, the secured creditor may not care as long as they are covered. The court does not have the authority to force a settlement. Judging from the resistance to this, we again see a deliberate policy to get rid of farmers.

In Ontario we have a tremendous amount of land being bought by "foreign absentee landlords." Our best land is being bought up as an investment for large corporations — and buildings are bulldozed down. In Blyth, Ontario, they talk of the stores stocking only one size of workboot — for soon there will be only one farmer. One foreign owner already has 8000 acres. Ontario Premier Bill Davis encourages this to get rid of those farm pressures! I only wish that the legions who fought to save this country for Canadians would realize that it is being sold away daily. With the current debt our farmers have no choice but to sell.

The banks use the threat of withdrawal. They say publicly that we were jeopardizing the chances of the *good* farmers. Other farmers who aren't in debt will have their credit withdrawn because of this Act. All the Act ensures is that if it is necessary to realize on security it will be done in a reasonable manner. You can cut trees in a bush lot, but we have laws that say it must be done in a reasonable manner so it won't destroy the bush lots for future generations. The truth is that banks aren't money lenders, but rather equity investors and as land values fall, equity disappears and so does credit. The banks, under questioning by the subcommittee specifically denied that they would withdraw credit. The newspaper hullabaloo and the scare tactics are simply the Bankers' Association trying to justify their existence.

Every time the farmers try to get more money into the Farm Credit Corporation — and this goes back the last ten years — the bankers holler "Keep the government out of lending. Free enterprise! Let us do it." The banks *have* to lend to the farmers. Eugene Whelan, the Minister of Agriculture, said he'd started getting telephone calls from farmers he hadn't met in twenty years. He caught on very quickly, saying, "You've been talking to your banker. Your banker said that if you don't speak against this Act, they would have to cut everyone's credit off." Well, it will be their own suicide. Banks invest in equity — they lend when the land value is there and when it falls they cut it off. The truth is, if we don't have the Act, we are going to have a tremendous withdrawal of credit from agriculture, and it is now underway.

What about the money lent out to foreign countries, which is totally exposed? Can you imagine the banks sending a receiver to Mexico to seize government buildings or vehicles? No, they simply defer the principal for years and make cuts in the interest rates as acts of charity and good neighbourliness.

To sum it up, the Farmers' Creditors Arrangement Act is an Act to force honest negotiations in these troubled times. Very few will have to use the Act, but just by virtue of the fact that the authority is there, it will stop the banks from using illegal and immoral actions by giving farmers access to justice, even though they aren't as large as Dome Petroleum or Massey.

If Massey Ferguson had collapsed it might have broken the Canadian Imperial Bank of Commerce. Everyone knows that if Dome Petroleum had gone down it might have taken all five chartered banks down with it. The government has recently made a move to nationalize fish processing in Newfoundland, because it would have broken the Bank of Nova Scotia.

We can't seem to get through to these governments and banks that agriculture is far larger and more important than all of these companies put together. One of the arguments is that the problem is not as great as it was in the 1930s. Of course the bankers won't admit this. A senior cabinet minister in the provincial government said that if the people had any comprehension of how bad a mess agriculture was in they would start a run on the banks.

We're looking now at product prices proportionately lower than in 1933. We're losing one percent of North American farmers every month, and one farmer per minute in Europe — half a million farmers a year. Land prices in Illinois fell more in 1982 than any year in recorded history, even in the depths of the Depression. Land values in the Netherlands are down 50%. In Denmark they're down 50%, and they've already had an act similar to the Farmers' Creditors Arrangement Act.

A leading insurance company executive reported that just one insurance company alone has repossessed over half a million acres in the Delta states of Louisiana, Mississippi, and Arkansas last year. The companies are either leasing the land out to other farmers, or hiring farm managers themselves. Another insurance executive reported that over 60% of the farm loans made by insurance companies were in serious trouble — either in bankruptcy or facing immediate foreclosure procedures in Louisiana, Mississippi, Arkansas, Texas and Alabama.

That is why the time is right for the Farmers' Creditors Act. That's why this depression is different from all the recessions we've have over the last three decades. I had hoped that by Canada setting this example of how to deal with it we could help our U.S. farmers. But they now have a moratorium on federal farm credit foreclosure, and we are still waiting!

Even the Bankers' Association's modest estimates of 15% means one in six farmers are in financial difficulty. Visualize every sixth farm burnt to the ground, with the families at the side of the road! If we don't get land prices stabilized, all, including the banks, go down. In reality, I think we are probably too late. In December, 1983, George Brinkman, an agricultural economist at the University of Guelph, commented on a paper published by *Agriculture Canada,* which documented a $3.6 billion drop in the value of Ontario farmland since 1982. Adjusted for inflation this is closer to $5 billion. If the farmers in Ontario who lost an average $70,000 in equity had been listening to us, and had donated only ten dollars for every million dollars lost, the resulting $36,000 could have kept me in Ottawa and we would have had the FCAA, and stopped this tremendous loss, which is continuing.

Debt readjustment may have to be done on an international scale. According to Statistics Canada, it took government spending equal to 38% of the whole gross national income to stimulate our way out of the Great Depression. It took government spending equal to a stunning 62% of all income to fight and win the Second World War. But those were exceptional circumstances, right? There were crises to solve, by whatever means. Well, right now total government spending in Canada equals an incredible 68% of national income, on its way to roughly 70% in 1990.

The national debt is impossible to pay. We have an admitted $160 billion — which is probably closer to $200 billion and going behind at $30 billion not including provincial, municipal or private debt — and the United States has a reported $1.4 trillion in national debt. People think that if inflation continues we can pay this off. They don't realize that inflation *is* debt readjustment. You're changing the dollar value. That's the only way you can pay the thing off, other than writing it off. For the next twenty years, the $200 billion Canadian debt, without interest, would be $10 billion a year, with interest $20 billion. This is an unbelievable amount; it would bankrupt our country. To pull that out of the economy without putting it back in would continue to lead to a depression of horrendous proportions. Our government cannot even operate now without huge annual deficits.

People ask who do we owe the money to — and that's the key — it goes to the international bankers or to the rich people in our own country. The large profits the banks are making are unbelievable. On $312 million of profit in the second quarter of 1983, the Royal Bank paid no income tax. In fact it got $28 million in tax credits and profits rose 26% at the next reporting.

The U.S. Connection   13

The bones, sinews, and nerves of modern civilization are coal,
steel, cotton and wheat. He who controls these is mightier
than the Lord. — B. Traven

One of the most important people I met during these early times
was Mark Ritchie. During a trip to St. Louis, Missouri, in
January 1982, I got to know him quite well and he has continued to have quite a bit of influence on me, and to be a good
friend. The author of *The Loss of our Family Farms: Inevitable*
Results or Conscious Policies?, Mark Ritchie is involved in and
works for the U.S. Farmers' Association, an organization which
broke off from the Farmers' Union back in the fifties. He also
runs a clipping service, for the whole farm movement, of farm
stories from newspapers. He does a good job of keeping abreast
of farm problems and is a terrific source of statistics and generally
what's going on.

Mark saw us in the news and phoned Bill Wolfe, who was
at that time our Secretary-Treasurer, and invited us to St. Louis
to meet members of the American Agriculture Movement at
its annual convention. He said he thought we covered a lot of
common ground. Our Association voted $200 to send Carl
Spencer, our president, down. Bill Wolfe and I took money
out of our own pockets and the three of us went. It was probably the best money I ever spent.

We not only met members of the American Agriculture
Movement, but also members of an organization called NORM
(National Organization for Raw Materials). Here we first
learned about raw material economics and the parity concept,
and were struck by the no-nonsense attitude of the American
farmer. The American Agriculture Movement is a fantastic

group of people, a grassroots farm organization set up in 1977 to promote the parity concept. They were fighting for a fair farm price (parity); the erosion of the U.S. parity program had led to high interest rates and farmers losing their farms.

I was very impressed with them. Everywhere I went, if I saw an American Ag hat, I knew there was a good, intelligent person underneath it — people such as David Muff and Corry Jones from Nebraska. They are particularly concerned about their country, and their fellow human beings. They had been pushing parity and raw material economics (the latter takes a bit of effort to understand, but is *the* solution to our problems), and they have a pretty impressive track record of direct action.

They organized farm strikes — withholding farm produce from livestock and grain dealers. In one series of incidents in Georgia they got their members to pack their tractors in their local high school football field to draw attention to the fact that the farmers weren't working and to make it clear which farmers weren't supporting the strike. Also in one area of Georgia they organized a one-day holiday for all local businesses sympathetic to farm problems. It was enforced on unsympathetic retailers by the threat of unloading a truckload of pigs into any store remaining open.

These actions culminated in a tractorcade on Washington in the winter of '77-78. Some farmers drove 800 miles in tractors capable of only 20 miles per hour. Their aim was to put pressure on Washington for parity and they were prepared for a long siege. Some of the stories we heard were humourous. Some farmers released chickens, goats and a donkey around the Capitol: the police tried to put a donkey into the back of a cruiser; a friendly billy goat butted a police officer down a flight of stairs, and while another officer drew his gun on the goat, one of the farmers reminded him that goats weren't particularly threatened by guns!

However, while lobbying was still going on, things took an unfortunate turn; the police surrounded the camp and wouldn't let the tractors out.

The police then clubbed demonstrating farmers. The farmers by this time had lost local media support and there seemed to be coordination between media helicopters and the police attacks: the only news coverage of the farmers' lobbying program was of clashes with police. In any other demonstration, when police attack with nightsticks there is public outrage. But this time, when the nation's food producers came to Washington for help, they were met with hostility from the media and police violence.

Ironically, later when a snowstorm paralyzed the city, farmers were asked to use their tractors for emergency calls for doctors and nurses but were given no credit by the media.

As I studied these and other actions I began to realize the much more powerful effect of specific defense actions for specific individuals. For the proper judge of a person is his peers and if his neighbours support him, then he must have a legitimate problem. The sympathy from the media and public, plus the added value of a personal interest story, were a much more powerful pressure tactic. The lobbying delegates then had the government's attention, whereas demonstrations at the seat of government have become normal events. If large enough to catch attention, the government takes a hard line.

One of the AAM members I met on that trip was Wayne Crytz, the hero of the "Ristine grain grab." There's a book out on Wayne: *One Man with Courage.* Wayne is a cash crop farmer in the "boot heel" of Missouri. He had stored a quarter of a million dollars of soybeans in an elevator and the elevator went bankrupt. The bankruptcy judge ordered that the beans belonged to the trustee in bankruptcy. Wayne said no, those beans belong to me, I only had them stored there. The elevators had been using a loophole in the bankruptcy law for some time. It was very coincidental that only elevators jam-packed with farmer's grain went bankrupt. If an elevator in trouble was empty, it didn't go bankrupt until it was full.

After six months of trying to get government help, Wayne gave the trustees thirty days to prove that the beans weren't his beans, or he was going to come and get them. They put guards on, sealed the doors and alerted FBI agents and federal marshals. Wayne got national publicity. He took in two thousand farmers and other supporters (three thousand others who had come to help had to be turned away). They cut a hole in the back of the elevator, loaded the beans, weighing them properly, and put them in another elevator. The judge reached over and seized them in the other elevator. Wayne's friends and neighbours came in and took the beans again. This time they took the beans and sold them, individually by the truckload, giving the money to Wayne, or so the court alleges.

Wayne ended up in jail for contempt of court. At the trial, he took the Fifth, refusing to incriminate himself, and when they put him on the stand to identify the other farmers who had helped, he refused. They charged him with contempt and he went to jail for some thirty days. The judge ruled the cased closed, dismissing himself from it. Wayne was released, then recharged with contempt and fined some $260,000, plus $1500 a day until he paid up. The case went on and on. He was tried for criminal contempt and found not guilty by a jury. The judge reprimanded the jury for its refusal to convict, but later apologized because his mother reprimanded him and he was quoted in the *New York Times* as saying, "When your mother is against you and the jury is against you, I guess you're wrong." Who had ever heard a federal judge apologize before?

Wayne's lawyer made an interesting summary: we have three levels of law: the legislature makes laws; the judiciary system interprets and enforces laws; but the jury, by refusing to convict on a bad law, can overrule the other two. Wayne is a courageous and intelligent man, constantly on the road now, organizing for the American Agriculture Movement. Last I heard he was fined $260,000 plus $1500 a day which he says works out to $1 a minute as you talk to him. I feel quite honoured to have worked with him.

Through the parity concept and raw material economics, I was exposed for the first time to the argument that the solution to the last Depression was not simply the Second World War. Wars give a false sense of prosperity because the government makes the people who fight the war finance it. They sell bonds and spend this money at home, creating a false prosperity. Then, when the soldiers come home, they must pay back the bonds. One of my childhood puzzles was how could a war which killed, destroyed and dumped millions of dollars of goods in the ocean create prosperity? It couldn't!

It was, in fact, the Steagall Amendment in 1941 which introduced parity pricing for farm product in the U.S. By parity, we mean a balance of purchasing power between agriculture and industry. During the War, the U.S. government raised and fixed the prices of agricultural products to guarantee farmers' incomes comparable to other segments of society.

When the farmer got a balanced payment he had money to spend through the economy. Everyone went to work, and prosperity returned. It was this prosperity that financed the War, paid for the Marshall Plan and raised the U.S.A. to the major world position.

In Canada, in 1939, they set the price of wheat at $1.50 per bushel, a barrel of oil at $1.50; and gold at $35 per ounce. Now gold is over $500 per ounce, oil is $30 per barrel, and wheat is $4 per bushel.

Mark Ritchie also filled me in on local problems. There had been drought conditions over the past two years in Georgia, North Dakota and Kansas, resulting in a thousand land transfers in the State of North Dakota alone every month.

Forging the Links 14

*The only thing necessary for the triumph of evil is for good
men to do nothing.*

In the summer of 1982, Mark and I used his clipping service
to put together a list of people who had been visible in the news
and talked about a U.S. tour that September.

I received a call on August 24, from Bob Smith, and Jim
Langman, members of the Minnesota American Agriculture
Movement. A farmer had asked for help and they wanted to
run a penny auction, and needed my advice. I gave him quite
a speech over the phone. He taped it and later played it for
the other farmers, to give them some encouragement. Basically,
I said that we were able to do such things up here and that it
could be done.

I pointed out a couple of things; one, that they had to identify their members. This was something we found to be very
important right from the start. If you try to stop an auction
it's important to know who's with and who's against you. They
decided to use the red bandana, the old farmer's hankey, and
it was to became the symbol of farm resistance across North
America. Now, when you see a red bandana, you think of a
farmer right away. The other thing I told him was that you
had to have neighbour support. We don't pretend to judge a
farmer's management ability after a couple of years of depression and no money to work with — it's nigh impossible. If a
farmer hasn't got the money for fertilizer or spray it's difficult,
when you look at the crop, to judge whether he's good or bad,
because the farmer hasn't had the resources to grow it properly.

So the proper judges of a person are his peers. As long as
his neighbours are willing to support him, that's good enough

for us. I told Bob that, and he phoned the farmer who lived some distance from him, about 150 miles.

To show you some of the isolation these people suffered: Wyman Hanson, the farmer, said he didn't have a friend in the world, all the neighbours were just waiting to buy him out. Bob called me back, and I said you've got to have the local neighbourhood behind you. So he phoned Wyman back and told him he would have to contact his neighbours, knowing that would be a very difficult thing for the man to do.

But Wyman Hanson did it. He was facing foreclosure, and he was desperate. He swallowed his pride and asked for help. He called Bob back and said a few of the neighbours would support him. Bob brought it up at the American Ag meeting and they said if the neighbourhood won't support him, then we can't. But they ended up deciding to go down with fifteen men to protest the sale, hand out some leaflets, and get what they could out of it for press.

They met in a community centre. Twenty-five of Wyman's neighbours showed up with red bandanas on. One old farmer, who had found out about it at nine o'clock in the morning, put over 100 miles on his pickup truck by eleven o'clock, going around telling people about it.

By the time they got to the sale there were seventy farmers with bandanas. By the time the sale got underway there were two hundred. They were tearing these bandanas in halves and quarters, little pieces to make them go around. It was a very moving experience — for the Hansons, of course, to see the support, and for the community, to feel that they were able to do something. At this sale one farmer stated that he had driven twenty miles to buy a grain wagon. One of our guys said that he had driven a hundred miles to make sure he didn't! The buyer went home.

I often thought in my travels, in my work in blockades and so on, that even if we failed, at least we showed that family that there are people out there who care. I think that's one of the most important pieces of our work — individuals in trouble have the support of other human beings, they're not isolated, they're not alone. And a great deal is owed to these brave individuals who stand to fight. They must withstand both public scrutiny and criticism from the ignorant. But as a group farmers are facing extinction and the action of these people who stand up goes a long way to change policy and buy time for the rest.

The Hanson action was very successful. It stopped the sale, and got a lot of press for being the first penny auction since the 1930s. There was a good article in the *Wall Street Journal* on the revival of the penny auction, and the parallels between the depressions.

> "Mr. Smith is gettting protest advice from visiting Canadian Farmer Allen Wilford, whose group, Canadian Farmers survival Association has protested foreclosures in Ontario. On five occasions when receivers were sent to reclaim a delinquent farmer's property, Mr. Wilford's group jammed the farmer's driveway with dozens of cars. 'The banks have since backed off' says Mr. Wilford 'They don't use any more strong-arm tactics with farmers, but have agreed to negotiate.' "

So as a result of that sale and the publicity surrounding it, I was invited to the Midwest to talk. My wife Wendy and I hadn't had a holiday — just five days in ten years, when we had taken a short trip to Ottawa with some friends — so we decided to blend business and pleasure and headed down.

Three days into our "holiday," Wendy didn't think it was much of a pleasure trip. I spoke morning, noon and night. Don Deichman, an American Agriculture Movement member, drove us around and gave us no rest whatsoever. I think we averaged two meals a day. We stayed with local farmers, and got a grassroots feeling of what was going on. I spoke to the farmers, heard and saw their problems. I ate with them and slept in their homes.

I spoke to local groups in Minnesota, Ohio, Nebraska and North Dakota. The results were very encouraging. There was the Minnesota COACT, a citizens' group that joined with the American Ag Movement. They were very good, having a lot of the organizational tools in place. They had an office, and knew how to do some of the negotiating. In the original negotiations on the Hanson sale, they used a conference call involving seven people, with a couple of reporters listening in. They knew what they were doing and were a big asset to the movement.

They started advertising their phone number as a Survival Hotline for farmers in trouble. That was the key point I was trying to get across. We didn't care what the organizations who were doing this direct action called themselves, but the Survival Hotline was something uniform tying them together — like the red bandana. This was good, because people in financial difficulty could call, and at times it is literally a matter of life and death.

I can remember the reaction of Gary Gurbin, our MP, after he came back from Minnesota.

He told me "You know, they have a survival hotline down there!" — it was the one I had organized. My trips to the United States have been some of my best educational experiences. I felt, maybe a bit egotistically, that I had a better picture of the economic activity of the world than perhaps anyone. Because I was farm-oriented, and I knew all economic activity is based on the top few inches of the soil, I went down through the United States — which is responsible for 65% of world trade in grain — to take a look at things at the grassroots level, not the statistics level, not the heads of corporations level, not the heads of farm organizations level, but right at the grass roots. I talked to the farmers themselves. They are the basis of this whole economy, it was dreadful, horrendous.

The statistics they give you in any particular year are made up of what happened last year or the year before. To see what's happening now, you have to be there. I travelled through and eventually spoke to farmers and helped organize in 13 States. I didn't get to all of the fifty, but I sure got a good view.

Within two hours of arrival in Minnesota I had talked to two farmers that had buried their neighbours, who had taken their own lives. Then, I talked to two more, one whose wife and another whose neighbour had attempted suicide. I was faced with the stark reality of farm suicides in the United States, when in every single meeting I spoke at, I had someone come up and recount the story of a suicide — a family member or a neighbour; one a man with ten children. These stories, more than anything, inspired me to keep up my work, to keep up the fight.

I felt that we'd been able to prevent suicides in Ontario because we had been visible and because we had given people hope. But when I came back to Canada and continued to be bombarded with the problem, with tears and desperation, I fought all the harder because there had been suicides and I knew the potential was there.

The picture of the vigilantes, quite often came up. People would draw it out six or eight months later and say this gave us a sign that somebody was doing something, somebody was fighting this system.

Some people, even in our own organization, were critical of my trips to the United States. They thought there were enough problems in Canada and we didn't need to go down there. But I went for the same reason we expanded out of Bruce County. These are people and I don't recognize borders, whether they be county, provincial or international borders. There are people in the United States, and in other countries, who all have the same problems, and they're all going through the same desperate times.

The advantage for me, besides the stimulation, was to get a sense of the magnitude of the problem. Once you get out of your own county, or province, or country, you begin to realize that you're not alone — that you're not going to be able to solve it in your own little county, because it's an international problem.

By the fall of '82 the U.S. had over a billion bushels of grain that they couldn't get in storage, and they started putting it in abandoned coal mines, old boxcars and just in piles on the ground. And with that kind of a surplus — the politicians and corporations call it surplus, the farmers call it inventory — there was nowhere for prices to go but down. They didn't need to go down, but that's the way our supply and go broke system works.

I knew that low prices create more surplus because farmers out of desperation grow more. They try to increase their production to pay their bills. And as they have less to spend on farm inputs, the rest of society cannot afford food. Seeing the American situation firsthand I came to a realization that we couldn't immediately stop this thing. Our only hope — and this I got from those inspiring people in the United States and Canada — was to be visible and to be right. The situation seemed so desperate that at the time we wondered — when the system collapses, how would we put it back together again? We were concerned with how we would communicate with one another after the collapse, if our efforts to bring about a solution failed. At that time the price crash seemed to be inevitable. But we hadn't given up the fight then and haven't now; hopefully this book will shake some more people up.

As 1984 begins we're still looking at a short respite, a short fake recovery, stimulated by government spending and huge government deficits. Governments persist in their policies to increase the supply of money through debt to keep the lid on the unemployment problem. But governments get shakier and shakier as the national debt soars. Another federal deficit of $30 billion is not a renewal of credit, but an additional $30 billion mortgaged on our future. Divided by an annual wage of $20,000 we realize that the governement borrowed and spent enough to create 1.5 million jobs which means that, with the reality of a balanced budget we would double unemployment. Panic buying on the stock market and increaases in the Dow Jones are, in fact, devaluations of the dollar. It's not that the stocks are worth more, it's not that gold is worth more, it's that the dollar is worth less. So to me these rapid increases in the stock market are not a healthy sign. Eventually there will be a day of reckoning and the thing will collapse.

I took a lot of inspiration from the heart-rending stories of the people in the United States, but also from some good people involved, and that's why I suppose I believe in victory. You get that quality of people fighting on the same side, fighting for the same thing, understanding the reasons and the cures, and we're going to win.

While in the United States I have helped in the attempt to unite groups. When I got there, there were alliances being set up between the National Farmers' Organization and the Farmers' Unions, and between different State groups. I thought Canada was split up into thousands of different farm organizations, but the United States is even worse — each State has its own branch of the various organizations: the U.S. Farmers' Association, The Farmers' Union, the NFO (National Farmers' Organization) and the American Agriculture Movement. The stopping of foreclosures turned out to be an excellent organizational tool: everyone can back them, even if they have different long-term solutions to the problems. And these actions put enough pressure on governments that they start to listen and communicate.

U.S. Farm Activism 15

The land is the source or matter from whence all wealth is produced. The labour of man is the form which produces it; and wealth in itself is nothing but the maintenance, conveniences and superfluities of life.
— Richard Cantillon (1725)

In North Dakota there is a movement called the Family Farm Foreclosure Legal Aid Protection. Sarah Vogal got a movement going through the courts which eventually won a moratorium on Farm Home Administration (FmHA) foreclosure across the U.S. It got a lot of attention.

A very good church group, Rural America, had started up in Iowa. There are two terrific fellows down there: Dave Ostendorf and Danny Levitas. They carried the ball very strongly. They didn't set up the survival hotline initially, they just started working with farmers. I spoke to small groups of farmers — at this time it was relatively new. These meetings would get five or ten people out, sometimes as high as fifty or a hundred. Some of the oldtimers were very inspiring. One of the important things I got out of my trip down there was through meeting members of the Farmer's Holiday Movement, the 1930s farm group that had originated the penny auction to stop the foreclosures. They were a tremendous inspiration, and they could go on and on with some of the stories they tell.

One big thing I learned was the importance of grassroots politics. The oldtimers said, "We tried blocking roads, strikes and so on but it didn't work. But when we went back to our own turf, to our farm gates, and stopped the evictions and the foreclosures and ran the penny auctions, then we started to win the thing." That's where we have an advantage — farm gate defense was a very effective tool to put pressure on government.

The Rural America group finally put out a telephone number, and were shocked by the number of calls they got. They couldn't believe that they were running at eight, ten a day.

Wendy and I returned home after ten days, tired and inspired, and very much better educated. A lot of our own people still criticized these American trips because they thought we should be at home solving the problems, but they gave us an education, and a break from some of the pressures at home — the individual farmer's cases at this point were starting to bear prettily heavily on me.

I was invited back to Minnesota in December 1982, to speak to some COACT groups from Ohio, Indiana, and Kentucky, which had branched off the Minnesota group.

The next time I travelled down through the southern states, speaking in Tennessee, Georgia, Missouri and Illinois. Again, there were a lot of good people. In Illinois an alliance had already been set up between the major farm groups. They were just looking for some inspiration. The U.S. Farmers' Association paid my airfare. But I was the expert — bear in mind the definition of an expert — "someone a long way from home." That I was. I had a scrapbook full of farm gate defenses and actions. I was just the burr under the saddle, the encouragement that let them go on. These people had the potential and were quite good. I just said, "You can do it. We've already done it."

I gave them a bit of a rundown of our initial successes to build up their confidence. And they were off. We had actions — occupations of Farmers' Home Administration offices, occupations of Production Credit offices — and won deferrals, renegotiations of loans. Initial success was very encouraging.

One of the difficult things in the United States for me to comprehend was that the actions of the federal government were a serious problem. In Canada, the Farm Credit Corporation had been trying to help wherever they could. In the United States the Farmer's Home Administration is a federal agency similar to Farm Credit. Set up after the '30s, it is a low equity lender of last resort. It took over a lot of bad loans from the banks three years ago, and has some good legislation.

The Reagan Administration had asked Farmer's Home to get rid of 30% of their farm problem cases. But instead of going to the bottom 30%, they put the pressure on everyone to see if they could make 30% fallout. It was just unbelievable what they were doing to some of these people. One pig farmer, in particular, was living on food stamps. All his pig sales were going to the Farmers Home Administration. When he hadn't been able to make the hydro payments, they shut off the hydro and sixty pigs died. The Farmers Home Administration couldn't have cared less. But three months later, when the counts were out two pigs because someone had made a mistake in the counting, they wasted three long-distance phone calls trying to locate those pigs. Can you imagine working at producing pork and at the same time having to live on welfare handouts?

Direct action brought a lot of attention to the issues and it changed a lot of Farmer's Home policies. The farmers won a moratorium on foreclosures in North Dakota and in Minnesota, and several other states. The thing spread quite rapidly. We tied all this together and formed the North American Farm Alliance. Twenty-six states were represented.

The biggest action — I wasn't involved but they were wearing the red bandanas — was the work of the American Ag Movement in Springfield, Colorado. Three to five hundred unarmed farmers gathered to stop the Federal Land Bank from selling the farm of Jerry Wright, one of the founders of the AAM. Three farmers were trying to get into the courthouse to bid. The *American Agriculture News* reported on January 11, 1983:

> "Deputies shoved them back out, but they got back in. Then the farmers outside saw deputies beating the farmers inside to the floor with clubs as other deputies were trying to close the doors . . . . Derrell Ringer from Quinter, Kansas, doggedly held the door open, at times almost alone, both eyes shut, with mace running off his face, screaming "No way, no way." Officers punched him and maced him repeatedly but he wouldn't let go of the door . . . . Farmers were mostly just standing in place, and things had quieted down considerably when someone threw three tear gas canisters from an upper floor window. Several people were overcome and fell to the ground."

To escape a police beating, Kinan Burk jumped through a window. Handcuffed and face bloodied, he remarked, "This is what you get for being Christian." (Auction of Jerry Wright's farm in Colorado.)

Kinan Burk jumped through a window handcuffed to escape the beating. His face covered in blood, he stated, "This is what you get for being a Christian." Two of the three farmers beaten were imprisoned for weeks.

It was unbelievable to me that the police would react in this manner. I can remember pictures of the '30s, the unemployed men in Vancouver occupying the museums and art galleries trying to bring attention to the fact that unemployed, single people could not get welfare. They were beaten most brutally by the police. And here we are in the 1980s with the police working over farmers with nightsticks, kicking them and beating them severely.

Carlos Welty, from the Missouri Agriculture Movement, later gave me hell. I hadn't told him about tear gas and he couldn't figure out what the funny tin can was. He also claimed to have worn two inches off his cowboy boots trying to back up.

The sheriff was later invited to speak to other law enforcement officers, behind closed doors, to teach them how to handle rioting farmers. That blood on the farmers' faces shook up the government. For a month and a half afterwards Reagan mentioned agriculture in almost every speech I heard. A few weeks after the incident in Springfield, he used Executive Order for the first time in history for agriculture. He implemented the PIK Program — Payment In Kind. The White House hadn't researched it very well because when they initially announced it, you could put soybeans on PIK ground, or in other words, grow soybeans and still get paid for the corn. The Payment in Kind program stemmed from the tremendous amounts of reserve grain that the government had been holding off the market. It boiled down to the fact that you could take 30% of your land out of production and the government would pay you a percentage of the grain you normally would have grown, in kind. In other words, they wouldn't pay you dollars, they would give you your grain back. It was done for political reasons, to make it look like there was a lot of money going back to the farmers — billions upon billions of dollars. In reality there wasn't any money at all: grain that the government already held in reserve was being simply put on the market. It was not intended to cost the Treasury anything, and saved them storage costs.

I watched the large grain companies go around and buy up the PIK grain, giving the farmers desperately needed cash. Then, with government help, these companies urged farmers to future contract their grain. They cornered the market, so when prices rose it didn't help the farmer but did help the grain merchants and cost the government a lot of money.

Roosevelt tried the same thing in the '30s. He shot pigs and cattle, and plowed down cotton. The best example to me was the old farmer driving the mule down the row, trying to plow down every other row of cotton. The mule had been trained his whole life to never step on a cotton plant. I don't know if you've ever had anything to do with horses or mules, but trying to get that mule to walk down the centre of a row of cotton must have been a very frustrating experience. And here's this man, struggling and fighting with this mule, trying to plow down this cotton . . . and he looks over at the clothes on his children's backs, that are rags, and there's no bedding on the bed. He thinks to himself, "The mule's got more sense than Roosevelt."

There seems to be a popular misconception (supply and demand) that if you short the supply you will get the price. It's a complete fallacy. All you're guaranteed is that more people will do without. They have to have the money to buy. There's no oversupply, there's a shortage of the ability to consume, because we farmers cannot buy their product. Our purchasing power has been destroyed, and they are unemployed.

The seeds of confidence that I'd been sowing through the United States grew rapidly. Thursday, October 14, 1982, *American Agriculture News* reported: "Sarah and Joe Nelmar took their case Wednesday to the Farmers Home Administration and they brought a hundred farmers and supporters with them. Farmers journeyed up to 200 miles, wearing red bandanas and carrying signs reading 'Save our farms.'" They marched into the office of Beckett County Farmers Home Administration supervisor James Johnson. They were accompanied by television cameras and vowed they would not leave until the case was decided.

The FmHA had been taking 60% of the Nelmars' milk cheque. The farmers applauded and hugged one another after Joe announced his agreement with the Farmer's Home officers. "Well," he said, "we got something done. I'm happy, I think I can help us get back on our feet." "If not," yelled one farmer, "we'll be back."

In Illinois I received a letter dated November 1, 1982:

> "Dear Allen, You were right. There were farmers right under our noses in financial trouble. We had a half dozen calls in the hotline already. We haven't done a big publicity drive yet. This past Thursday we moved against the Farmer's Home Administration in Anna, Illinois. A young fellow in dairy was behind in his payments and was getting squeezed by Farmers Home. They were taking 60% of his milk cheque. We occupied the Farmers Home office for nearly eight hours and won a two-year deferral. Farmer Jim Dutton attended the meeting in Carbondale and got hope from it. He's been feeling in the dumps but the meeting got him up and fighting again. Tonight we're planning a community meeting in the county just south of us." Signed, Larry Gallagher, from the Illinois Farm Alliance.

Gary Wright's sale in Colorado. Note red bandana. The red bandana, seen here on a U.S. farmer, became the symbol of the growing farm resistance movement in Canada and the U.S.

The *American Agriculture News,* Tuesday, October 26, 1982: "Fifty farmers protest Farmers Home sale in Betham, Missouri. Fifty farmers wearing red bandanas and holding signs proclaiming 'Save our farms' protested against the farm foreclosure sale."

An official from Rural America's Des Moines-based farm organization said the sale at the farm gate was illegal because of the pending suit. That was fundamental to the basis of the Farm Survival Association, to give people access to good legal advice, to let them know what their rights were.

The Wall Street Journal, Friday, November 19, 1982: "More than 100 farmers wearing red arm bands stopped an auction at Maycomb, Illinois. They stopped the sale of Ryan Carson's machinery. A group called the Illinois Farm Alliance."

Further to my trips through the United States, I spoke in Hartford City, Indiana. Jim and Barber Adams are two very dedicated instigators in Indiana. I went from there to Doug Dailey's sale in London, Ohio. Local farmers wearing red bandanas had occupied the local Production Credit Association on Doug's behalf to try and bring some sense to them.

Again I can't emphasize enough that these agencies — particularly Farmer's Home — had been set up in the '30s to help the farmer. The Production Credit Association were supposed to be organizations of local farmers helping each other, but what PCA turned into are organizations of the very rich farmers. This leads to tremendous abuses of power. The PCA foreclose on farms which are bought by relatives of its directors. In Doug's case, the PCA's lawyer bought one of the farms. This was deliberate corruption. But when Doug Dailey's supporters occupied the PCA, I guess the executive had been forewarned and had decided to try the hard line, refusing to negotiate. They proceeded with the sale on the courthouse steps. Again, to show you the power trip these people were on, they stood to get absolutely nothing out of the foreclosure of Doug Dailey's farm. The Federal Land Bank was in first position, holding a mortgage for more than the farm was worth, because these land prices had fallen so dramatically.

So Production Credit forced the foreclosure and would get absolutely nothing out of it. And that's the way the sale turned out. The only bidder, the Federal Land Bank, took the land back — just clearing the PCA off title.

All we were asking was for the PCA to stop the proceedings, because they were not going to get anything out of them. Doug would cooperate with the sale of the equipment. Otherwise, we would fight them all the way. They decided to fight.

We had about 800 farmers out to Doug Dailey's sale to shout down the auctioneer. I can still see the sheriff reading for twenty, thirty minutes the property description and so on, with farmers continually yelling, "No sale!" Helicopters from the press were drowning everything out. I thought, boy, the next time we want to shout down an auctioneer, bring in the helicopters — you can't even hear yourself shout. Unbeknownst to us, behind the other building, was a large contingency of police with quite a few attack dogs. We didn't see them until afterwards. It made me shudder that the police were reduced to this kind of thing, gestapo tactics. Doug stated, "We are in the forefront of a major battle for economic freedom. We will take a few hits. That doesn't mean this movement has given up this fight to save our farms. They can take me on but they sure can't take us all on."

The Federal Land Bank bought the farm back. The PCA got a court order ordering Doug to give over all his books,

Doug Dailey looks on as Federal Land Bank buys his farm.

Jerry Dailey joins Family Farm Movement (1800 strong) protesting auction of brother Doug's farm.

records, a list of his friends (that he refused), and his up-to-date income tax return within nine days. It was just physically impossible to do it. He couldn't get everything together, or the income tax filled out, so they arrested him for contempt.

Doug Dailey never even got to testify before the judge. He had never been in jail before, didn't drink or smoke, but because of the power of the PCA and the negative attitude some judges have towards farmers, he was jailed. On March 8, 1983, the *American Agriculture News* reported:

> A House Banking Subcommittee asked that Dailey be allowed to come to DC and testify before them, but Judge Robert D. Nichols refused. The Madison (Ohio) Press quoted Judge Nichols as saying "Dailey should not be conferred celebrity status for such disobedience . . . amplified by self-serving statements and encouraged by Congress, as it will only tend to justify like conduct by those similarly situated. Mass similar conduct coupled with liberal bankruptcy provisions will greatly destabilize our country's precarious system of credit. More importantly, our historical, legal and moral obligations to repay loan money will be undermined."

The Judge also said "It appears his conduct was calculated and intended to result in his incarceration so he could use it and public sentiment against the plaintiffs in exchange for forgiveness of a $400,000 debt."

Doug Dailey sat in jail for forty days, with no bail, no right to trial and no criminal charge. He had no possible way of doing the books, or getting his stuff together, because he was incarcerated. It was a complete dead end. He was in jail for not doing something, which he couldn't do because he was in jail.

Finally Doug declared bankruptcy, which seemed to cheer up the judge a little bit, and he released him to testify in Washington. This type of judge is unbelievable in this day and age. We associate this sort of tactic with Stalin's Russia, and Nazi Germany. But here in the 1980s we have it in the United States. Doug was a very intelligent, well-read person. He was very good on national television, when he spoke on the problem. He had a good comprehension of its causes and effects.

His own case came up after he and his brother complained at a PCA meeting and tried to get some of the directors removed for corruption. So they jumped on him. It was a case of someone taking a step for the benefit of humankind, at his own expense and at his own risk. He is a very brave individual. Again, it is very inspiring to work with people like Doug and his brothers, and the other people involved in the Family Farm Movement in Ohio.

In Michigan the only way the farmers in the American Agriculture Movement under Neil Rogers could get a Farmers Home Administration foreclosure stopped was by pointing to the city homes that the FmHA had foreclosed on. They had some 4,000, because they were also lending on urban buildings. It was costing them an average of $10,000 per home to fix these homes up and get them into saleable condition. Instead of leaving the people there until economic conditions turned around and they got their jobs back and could make their payments, they evicted them and then turned around and put in $10,000 of our tax money. The farmers said, "We object to you spending our tax money like that."

The pressure they brought to bear on the question of urban dwellings expanded over into the farm area. I saw a four-page list of farms for sale in one part of Michigan. There were two lines per farm. It listed the name of the farmer who had been foreclosed, a brief description of the property, and the amount of the claim the Farmer's Home had against the property. They would sell any of those properties for fifty cents on the dollar.

Now instead of turning to the original farmer — who had been there for perhaps his whole life and his father before him — who was hit by this economic crunch, and saying, "Okay, we're going to cut your debt in half, and leave you there," they had to punish these individuals who had sinned. They don't get into physical evictions too much, they just starve them out — there's no money and no crops. Their cattle gone, the people in desperation get up and leave.

Amongst the people I met who were involved in Illinois were P. L. Parr, and Larry Gallagher. On Thursday, November 18, 1982, the *American Agriculture News* reported: "One hundred and seventy-five farmers wearing red bandanas shouted down attempts by the Farmers Home Administration to auction off dairy farm equipment near Hennessey, Illinois, owned by Randall Carson. They were successful in getting the sale stopped. Involved in the penny auction were farmers from the Illinois Farm Alliance, the U.S. Farmers Survival Association, and the Canadian Farmers Survival Association.''

I saw pictures of the National Guard training with people dressed as farmers. A long time ago I had maintained that when farmers had to be put in jail, when the National Guard had to control them, we would have the thing won. We were winning.

Derrell Ringer of the AAM in Kansas told me of an incident that took place in Kansas, where the sheriff came to repossess some equipment from a farmer. Some of his neighbours came to help but he said, ''Let it go, it's not worth the fight. The equipment isn't worth it, and farming's bad anyway.'' But when the sheriff got to the gateway someone had stuck a sign up that said, ''If you are from the government and you're here to help, you're welcome. But if you're not, the survivors will be prosecuted.'' Now that sign, and that sign alone, turned the sheriff and his deputies from the gate, and held them off for about six months.

One day when the farmer wasn't there they came in with seventy-five men and seized the equipment. They took it, and two weeks later auctioned it off. At the auction sale, sixty farmers came out to protest. There were over 300 armed police officers. There were state troopers, sheriffs, sheriffs' deputies, out-of-county sheriffs, out-of-state police officers, the FBI, the Kansas Bureau of Investigation. You can imagine — 300 armed police officers to sell off a farmer's equipment!

One of the farmers had had a relative die and was trying to contact a young couple who were going on their honeymoon. He phoned the state troopers wondering if they could stop them on the road. The response was, ''There isn't a state trooper within 300 miles of here. They're all at some damn farmer's sale.''

The police force kept all the potential buyers away, and the farmer's father-in-law bought back all the equipment at a greatly reduced price. So here's another way to have a penny auction! Get enough fear out there and the police do the controlling of the bids by keeping buyers away. But at first I was repelled at the thought of that many policemen taking on the farm community. Then I thought, that's how we're going to win the thing. If they have to bring out three hundred armed policemen every time they want to sell out a farmer we've got the thing won.

Each of these incidences put further pressure on the American government to do something about the farm "problem." That's why they brought out the PIK Program. There's an article in the *American Agriculture News* that states:

> The PIK Program has worked beautifully. It has successfully stopped most demonstrations that were attracting national publicity, like that in Springfield, Colorado when Jerry Wright was sold out by Federal Land Bank, and the Doug Dailey case. It made it seem less urgent for farmers to join activist organizations. It gave farmers a grain of hope — just enough to make them wait and see if things would get better. Just enough to quiet them down and keep them working. It successfully gave the farmers another black eye to public and news media after the cost of the program was carefully leaked. Such an outrage — to pay farmers for not planting, and here they were still crying.

> It successfully snuffed out chances for decent farm legislation next year. After all, how much can the taxpayers be expected to give to the farmers? It successfully gave John Block and President Reagan ammunition to freeze and cut support prices, all in the name of the budget. It successfully put some money in the pockets of lenders, since most farmers had to spend their PIC money on debts. In short, the PIC Program was a total success for the government. It did what it was meant to do. It did not raise commodity prices. Unfortunately, farmers have lost another notch."

On July 28, George Shuman was sentenced to 14 days in jail on contempt, or until he signed a paper that he would not go back to his farm. His wife Diane was likewise jailed. She was released two days later. While George was in jail the John Hancock Insurance Company took bush hog disks to his farm and destroyed 300 acres of corn and soybeans. "In their prime, the best crop we ever had," said George.

Is this in memory of the scorched earth tactics of Stalin, where he went in and starved the farmers out? Can you imagine plowing down and destroying 300 acres of corn out of spite, just to make sure the farmer wouldn't go back to his home? They loaded up and literally stole registered Holstein dairy cows belonging to George, his two sons, and his brother over the protests of his sixteen-year-old son that some of the cows were his, and took them across the state line into Kentucky without health papers. "At no time were we ever notified by the Pedooka Bank of Trust. There was absolutely no litigation. The cows were stolen."

But here's the good part. George was released after about 25 farmers from Puxico, Missouri (the Wayne Cryts crowd), Nasyak and Union County, Illinois, invaded the courtroom August 2, 1983. According to farmer advocate Rick Elliott, "The judge got very nervous. They didn't know if the building would be torn apart. I'm sure that was the cause of some of the judge's stupid statements."

After Shulman's release he filed a law suit for $16 million. Elliott, who had been through a similar ordeal where he lost $400,000 worth of dairy cows in Colorado, went to court and recovered $1 million in damages.

As the farm problems bore heavily on the farmers of the U.S., it bore unbelievably hard on the Black farmers. Of the nearly one million Black farmers in 1920, only 50,000 are still in business today and it is predicted that only 10,000 will exist in 1990. FmHA comes under a lot of critism for racial attitudes. Blacks received only 2.5% of the total dollar amount loaned through FmHA's farm credit program.

There are some good organizations involved in litigation down there now. For some reason we don't have their counterpart — civil rights groups for lawyer's fees — in Canada. The class action suit kind of thing. The Farmer's and Rancher's Protection Association with Jake Latham and Chuck Perry, is very good at litigation. They're countersuing some of these creditors, and putting them in their place. But the sad part is the people the creditors break, people who don't know they have rights, that they can sue. Again, a main purpose of the Survival

Our American counterpart finds that, like anything else you want to sell, even problems can be marketed successfully. While not a profit making venture, these tools have expanded the awareness of agricultural issues into all walks of life. Note the red bandana. This has become the international symbol of farm resistance.

300 farmers and workers from several mid-western states protested the foreclosure sale of the farm owned by Ava and Bernard Bates (centre) in Hill City, Kansas, on October 3, 1983. Left: Derrell Ringer, Kansas American Agriculture Movement. Right: Merle Hanson, head of North American Farm Alliance.

Unity display at the November 1st farm-labor-community Solidarity Day on the Iron Ridge, Minnesota. Left to right: Ava Bates, farmer, Nicodenus, Kansas; Jim Daniels, president, United Steel Workers of America, Local 1938, Virginia, Minnesota; Tom Quinn, president, Wisconsin Farm Unity; Jim Krass, chief picket captain, Phelps Dodge Copper Strike in Arizona, United Steel Workers of America.

Association is to let people know their rights, to get them access to good legal advice.

On April 8, 1983, in Des Moines, the North American Farm Alliance was formed by 100 representatives from farmer, labour, church, and community organizations. It is made up of many of the people I had been working with and many many more who have been visible and active — a who's who in agriculture.

Building the Organization 16

We proceeded with meetings with the banks and the government. We still conceived it as a communications problem: communications had broken down between the farmer and local bank manager. A third party was needed to help them get talks started again. The banks always tell you, if you foresee trouble, let us know about it. Of course, what happens when you let them know about it is they call your loans while they still have equity. This is exactly what was happening. The banks wanted the talks, but as long as they were one way. They did what I called Soviet-style negotiating — they had absolute power, time was no element. The farmer of course had to make all the concessions.

We had good examples of their unscrupulousness. The farmer by this time was sick of figures and in a state of confusion. So the bank would do a cash flow that would include the sale of the land or machinery as income for the year, turn to the farmer and say, "See, you can make it, just sign the mortgage and we won't bother you unless you get into trouble again." Well, the trouble started the moment you had to sell the equipment, because the proceeds had to go to pay off capital loans, not for operating expenses. If an inexperienced person set this deal up, I could forgive them. But when special bank personnel for problem accounts do it, in my opinion, it is fraud.

We had very good meetings with the heads of the banks. But then I realized what their terms were.

I have nothing but contempt for a lot of the individuals in the banks. I've been criticized for the way I attack the banks. But I had helped put together good workable solutions to these things, spent time on them and got the farmer's hopes up only to have the banks turn them down flat. In my own case Lloyd Frazier, Kitchener regional manager of the Royal Bank, agreed that my first proposal was good for all parties but that three more farmers had come in on the same basis (I'd helped them make the proposals) and they didn't want to start a trend. He rejected all of the proposals on this ground. Later he did settle with the other farmers, essentially on the same terms, but so far he has refused to settle with me.

The banks again were not deciding on the purely commercial merits of a case but on an overall strategy of intimidation and maintaining the status quo in the financial system. They don't want to start a trend, or the head office doesn't want that policy, or they don't know what to do about it. In actual fact the last statement is true. They didn't know what to do. They sat for months and months on end and did nothing while the farms deteriorated because they didn't know how to address the problem and they are just now beginning to get a sense of its magnitude. In my opinion the worst bank to deal with was the Bank of Montreal. They had no common sense whatsoever — refusing to acknowledge losses and insisting on liquidating assets. Long after the other banks were making reasonable settlements they were still bent on self-destruction. But the Bank of Nova Scotia is the stupidest — no policy whatsoever.

The farmers who kept their crop or cattle monies could keep right on farming but those who cooperated by taking all their proceeds to the bank were faced with welfare, as there were very few jobs to go to, and no money for lawyers to protect their rights. We only recently got legal aid for farmers — a first.

The various governments were very receptive to our delegations. I think at a federal level they are beginning very slowly to understand the depth of the problem but not at the provincial level. The people who had set government policy for years believed what the economists had told them — that there were too many farmers and the real problem was what to do with the excess. The Bankers' Association said one tenth of one percent of the farmers are in trouble, and the provincial government mimicked it, saying one tenth of one percent are in trouble. It was amazing that twelve months later Massey Ferguson was bankrupt and International Harvester was in very serious trouble, facing bankruptcy.

White Motor Company, McKee, and the list goes on across North America. They must have been a damn powerful one tenth of one percent, if a year later they had broken nearly all the equipment dealers. Every farmer in Canada winced at the stupidity of bailing out Massey Ferguson, or should I say the Bank of Commerce, when the farmers could not buy its machinery because we were broke.

They wouldn't believe us when we told them. It's great, on hindsight, to be able to say a year or two later that we were right. Unfortunately, being right didn't solve the problem. It did give us a better track record, but they didn't listen any closer the next time.

Our meetings with government gave us a chance to show the National Organizations for Raw Materials' film "Prosperity the Simple Way," on raw material economics, explaining the importance of farm price to the provincial and federal governments. I don't think one exposure to it was enough, we should have been back again and again. It set up some dialogue with government. We met quite a few of the government people and began to sort out who was good and who wasn't. There's a real difference in people; I don't think there are any party lines on it, or a patent on sincerity — or stupidity. Time and again some of these members, whether they be provincial or federal, would come out with gangbusters on how they were going to help and a day later they would phone back and say well it didn't work, we can't do anything, but if you ever need help call me back.

We were very lucky to have in the Grey-Bruce area a very concerned, very good man, our Conservative MP Gary Gurbin. When rumours started to fly that active members of our association would have their "credit cut off for life," Gurbin brought it up in the House of Commons and Alan MacEachen, then Minister of Finance, said if we could prove it he would pull the bank's charter. In fact these things can't be proved but the banks did back off and we were very grateful to Gary. I don't know what Grey-Bruce would have been like without him. He's done a terrific job and is continuing to do so. Gary would come to the farm gate defenses.

In a case when a sheriff was going to evict a farmer, I asked one MPP if he could stop the sheriff and he said no, but that he would certainly like to help, and so on. I asked if he would come out and stand with us at the farm gate, and he said no. If the man had any sense at all he'd have been there. Commitment, involvement, standing beside your people, and visibility get votes. Most of them aren't even very good politicians. I came to have a great deal of contempt for our political system because of the power of the party line. Sixty percent of these politicians shake hands and kiss babies, trying not to do anything wrong, even if that means doing nothing at all.

I got a better response from the opposition parties — although they do have a freer hand, and their job is to criticize. But there were good men in all parties. I don't have any political leanings but if I were advising anyone how to vote I would say vote for the local person, because if we get enough good people involved in the parliamentary process then the leaders will go to them. If you don't have good people in there it doesn't matter who the Prime Minister is.

While we were meeting with the Members of Parliament and the banks, trying to help people, I got into doing most of the financial advice. We opened up an office in Tara, Ontario and widely publicized the telephone number. I manned the office and my wife Wendy started out as the receptionist. The more financial advice I gave, the more involved I became. Once you see so many tears and so much misery, you're in it right up to your neck. I often told people that if they could answer my phone for two days they wouldn't have any doubt that we were doing the right thing. Opening the office was one of the better moves we made because it exposed to us the depth of the problem and some of the solutions. And it gave us members, because these people got help.

Most of what I was doing was emotional counselling. They were in quite a state of shock when the pressures came on, and here was someone to talk to, someone who understood the problem and could give them some alternatives. I kept most everybody busy — with applications to Farm Credit and the Ontario Assistance Program, trying the different modes, ways to approach the bank — doing something to give a bit of hope here and there while we worked on the long-term solutions.

I don't know how much of the early advice succeeded, because many didn't get back to me. I soon realized that we had to start following these things up because when I didn't hear from people again I tended to think their problems were solved, but six months later they would call back, saying whatever it was hadn't worked and that they'd given up. We never did get time to contact all these people — I've been so busy looking after the new ones who are contacting me. I wish we had the financial resources to get more people involved and follow these things up. This is something we've encouraged in the other areas we've set up. As it has expanded a lot of pressure has been taken off me, although I'm still short on time for the organizing end of it.

Some other groups, such as the OFA and the Cattlemen's Association set up advisory groups which we welcomed. But, when they had not even asked us what we had been doing, we realized, as one government official said, they could do more harm than good and might set the thing back twelve months. In fact some of these self-righteous people do a lot of harm. In some cases they gave very bad advice, but then this was a totally new field. At least it might give others some idea of the extent of the problem. My heart went out to those that received bad advice for when they finally called us their situation was usually much worse than it needed to be.

I found it very frustrating arguing with DAFS (Dumb Ass Farmers) who think they are doing alright or are going to succeed. These individuals simply are not doing their book work. They don't know their true costs or realize that they are selling their equipment bearing by bearing and simply substituting credit for earned income. So, to the very rich, I tried to ask what kind of a community was going to be left to live in, and to point to the fact that with so many unemployed they would pay all the taxes. The devaluation of land values in 1982-83 cost the average Ontario farmer $70,000 and it did effect everyone. Selfishness and self-righteousness have been around for a long time, but stupidity seemed to be on the increase.

At this time we started to get calls, because of the publicity, from all around Ontario. Previously people had come mostly from surrounding areas, as the press had been local. Now we hit the road to organize. At first these meetings were very small — five or six farmers. We would get calls from people in trouble and put them in touch with each other, telling them to get some neighbours involved. There was still a lot of optimism among farmers that things would turn around. The government and the banks were still refusing to admit that the situation was serious but as we spread our organization and sorted out the good lawyers it got increasingly easy to settle some of these problems. We got lots of extensions, acknowledged losses and such, but a lot of farmers would not ask for help because they were not aware of our tremendous success rate or because they continued to believe bank propaganda. "Stay away from the Survivalists."

The people who got these initial meetings organized were very concerned and very good people. We organized in Wellington, Simcoe, and Middlesex counties. Looking back on it, I wasn't a particularly good public speaker to start with, but I learned a lot from experience. They were small meetings — I think of what Truman said, "A good night was when you passed the hat and got the hat back." We sometimes got ten dollars for gas, but most of the time we donated our time and services. By the December of 1982 the turnout for meetings was much larger. West Middlesex, Kent and Layston counties got organized with as many as 200 out to meetings. Of course, when a Survival group formed in a county, all the farmers benefited by a marked difference in bank attitude.

There were some things that kept coming up at these meetings. There was always the issue of bad farm managers. One of the things I stressed was that we had to stand united to help *everyone*. If you don't, those who are in trouble feel isolated, thinking it's their fault and that you won't support them. The banks will test you on every single case. We had to have a blanket policy of helping everyone, based on the Christian ethic that we are all brothers and sisters — everyone is a human being, deserving help in their hour of need.

I would tell the story of the two German brothers in the 1930s. They each inherited a million marks, and one invested it in stocks and in the banks. The other went out and drank it all, having a hell of a good time. The stock market collapsed and the banks went broke. The first brother lost everything, and the second had spent everything. They were sitting around the kitchen table, neither having any money. One fellow said, "You know, I have a cellar full of beer bottles." He went down, collected the bottles, took a case to the store and got some groceries. That went on for several months — beer bottles for groceries. That's a classic example of "good" management.

One of the strengths of the Survival Association is the quality of the people involved. The first people, particularly those who had financial difficulties, knew the isolation and the tremendous stress and strain on their families. They were able to overcome their own difficulties by helping others — their own problems were dwarfed in comparison to some of the ones they got involved in. They were doing this not out of any benefit to themselves, but from what I call Christian ethics. They wanted to help their fellow human beings. I had hoped that our visibility would encourage other farm organizations to advance the question of farm product price — I was wrong!

We're still a bit short on theory, so I hope this book will help to clarify the issues. A lot of people realize there's a problem and that it must be stopped, but most have a long way to go in order to understand what, and why. And the survival Association, together with the Canadian Agriculture Movement, will have to lead the fight for a fair product price.

History of Farm Movements 17

*The crash of '29 was spawned in the corn fields of Iowa
and the wheat fields of Kansas.* — Eliot Janeway

In the 1830s William Lyon Mackenzie, father of the farmers'
rebellion in Upper Canada, led a run on the banks, taking his
inspiration from England in 1832 when the radicals, in order
to force a bill through Parliament, threatened a run on the
banks. He was questioned on this: "Will the breaking of the
banks be an injury or a blessing to the country?"

Mackenzie's reply is classic, because I've seen this coming
through again and again:

> Perhaps there is no one subject in which the peo-
> ple of America have laboured under greater delu-
> sion, than that of banks, exchanges, and the in-
> strument of exchange — bank notes. *Labour is
> the true source of wealth.* The farmer produces
> wheat; the miller converts it into flour. The
> labourer breaks stone, macadamizes roads. And
> these roads, with the aid of steamers and boats,
> convey the flour to the place where it is to be us-
> ed. The owner of the flour receives his money,
> be it $1,000 or $10,000. This is wealth. It was
> wealth before paper money was in existence, and
> I hope it will be considered when paper curren-
> cy shall be no more.

In this chapter I'm going to try and cover the history of
depressions and the involvement of the farm movements. From
this history three things come through loud and clear: first,
depressions were farm-led and farm-fed, second, every fifty years

we have had a depression in North America preceded by high interest rates, (in 1780, 1830, 1880, 1930 and 1980) and third, every revolt or revolution has been led by agrarian workers — serfs, peasants, and farmers.

The 1780s brought the Whiskey Rebellion in the States. Basically the price of grain was so low that the farmers could not afford to ship it. (There's an old joke about sending the grain to market and getting a bill back, then sending a couple of turkeys to pay the bill. The station agent says, "There's still some money left from the turkeys," and the farmer says, "Keep it — I intend to sell some more grain.") The farmers, in their resourcefulness, converted the grain into whiskey. It was easier to transport and worth a lot more money. The government saw that revenue was being taken away from them, and put a tax on whiskey. The farmers said that's the last straw, and they started the Whiskey Rebellion.

William Lyon Mackenzie's rebellion in Canada in the 1830s was actually called the Farmers' Rebellion, and was the result of an economic depression. People with their bellies full, well-clothed and housed, don't pick up guns and try to overthrow the government. Mackenzie's attempt to organize a run on the banks failed but they collapsed two years later anyway. In a Nebraska museum I found that the banks in the 1830s had been creating money at the discretion of the directors. The banks were charging interest at 5% per month (60% per year) before everything collapsed. Local blacksmiths started making coins out of scrap metal and local stores issued stamps to be traded as currency because there was no money. I wonder what would happen today?

I've also read about the farmers revolt in Prince Edward Island, early on in the depression in the 1820s and 1830s. Most of the farmers were tenants and the tenants refused to pay the landlords. I guess the Canadian Farmers' Survival Association took a chapter out of their book without knowing. They would set up a hew and cry, with all the neighbours coming around, and chase the rent collectors away. They held what they called "liberated" or "secured" areas, which the landlords were afraid to go into, some for twenty years. People didn't pay exorbitant rents or face eviction because their neighbours stood together.

In the 1880s we had another depression. This was probably the worst as it lasted nearly thirty years. Again prices fell, interest rates soared and evictions were widespread. The U.S. farmers were forced West and the Populist Movement was born. Farmers and labour united and had a tremendous influence throughout the world.

The Great Depression of the 1930s is recent history and again the farmers led the fight — in the U.S. for the New Deal, and in Canada by forming the CCF (Cooperative Commonwealth Federation), the forerunner of the New Democratic Party. In Canada a lot of people do not associate farmers and socialists, but that's where it started and one of the main objects of the "farmers are businessmen" ideology has always been to separate us from labour; from the work farmers do, it's not hard to tell that we're very much akin to labour.

The thread that ran through all of these revolts boils down to farm product price. A low farm price runs on for about ten years before a depression is visible. People think that the dust bowl created the Depression, but it was the other way around. The farm problems of the '20s led to the collapse of '29 and the dust bowl of the '30s. Inflation was "adjusting the debt" and covering up the true cost. Inflation is not a new phenomenon in history.

The farmer is the basis of the economy. When he isn't receiving an adequate price for his product he is forced to substitute credit for income. When he's forced to borrow, so are his suppliers. The government as well eventually has to substitute credit for earned income, and the mountain of public and private debt is the result. Because the tax base is destroyed and the demand for credit skyrockets, interest rates soar until the whole thing collapses.

In 1830, 1880 and 1930, as the farm price fell, the farmer in desperation plowed fence row to fence row, breaking too much soil, cutting down trees, trying to maintain cash flow. Monoculture was rampant. There was very little thought of conservation and more thought to trying to get the mortgage paid. Today chemicals that are poisoning our environment are used because the farmer simply can't afford the labour to do it properly, or the initial slump in cash flow from rotating crops.

In all these depressions, farmers were losing their land. They were a hunted, chased people. In the 1880s they in turn chased the Indians off their land. The saddest book I've ever read is *Bury My Heart at Wounded Knee,* the story of how the Indians were robbed of their land. In the Louis Riel rebellion in the 1880s in Western Canada, the white men tried to take over the lands of the Indians and Metis. The Metis resisted, and fought. The population shifts caused by the depressions in Canada have had a profound effect on our native people.

All of these farm revolts involved the banks, and the banking system is a large part of our problem. For me, the monetary issue was a big conflict: did the poor farm price create the need to borrow money and pay interest, or did the banks, in their ability to create money and charge interest, actually cause the problem of the low farm price?

Arnold Paulson, a farm price crusader, has stated that in 1943, because we were getting a fair price for agricultural products, the banks could only lend out 17.5 cents for every dollar they had on deposit. And that they conspired to lower the farm price because they couldn't stand this prosperity. People didn't need to borrow money if they made it. They bought new equipment, improved their houses, and so on, out of their profits.

The lowering of the farm price keeps recurring — is this an act of conspiracy, or stupidity?

Throughout history the banks create money by putting your dollar deposit in as a secondary reserve. They can then issue loans, via cheques and bank drafts, etc., for 25 times that one single dollar, thereby creating huge mountains of money (or paper credit) — but only if someone has to borrow. In farming circles this is paramount to selling the same cow 25 times; it works as long as no one picks up the cow. The loans then put more paper in circulation. The trick here is that the banks take something that is worthless — the paper cheque — and charge interest on it. The interest, then, has no relation to what actually exists in our economy. But when the banks try to recoup this asset that doesn't exist, they take real assets. This is where the crime starts. They steal real land, real cattle, in exchange for something that is worthless. And the farmers get restless.

In the 1880s, the Populist Movement in the United States protested against government limiting of the money supply. The issue then was the "greenbacks," or the money the government spent on the Civil War.

In order to finance the war, the government went off the gold standard, rather than pay 26% interest. When the war ended, people who had lent money at inflated rates to the government by buying bonds suddenly wanted real money back. They wanted a return to the gold standard — to real gold instead of the paper money they had lent.

The government realized the bind it was in between the banks on the the the one hand and their creditors on the other. If they went back to the gold standard they'd be bankrupt. And the country couldn't stand much taxation after the hardships of the war. So in order to bring the thing back in line, they limited the money supply. (Does this sound familiar? Our government today creates the same effect by raising the interest rate.)

The population continued to grow, goods and services continued to grow, and the money supply remained limited. If there are ten farmers producing ten bushels of wheat — all the wheat in the country — and ten dollars is all the money in the country, then it's a dollar a bushel for wheat. But if you have twenty farmers producing twenty bushels of wheat, with still only ten dollars currency, then the wheat sells for fifty cents a bushel, since that's all the money available. So farm prices fall as the money supply shrinks.

Again, the money supply is limited by raising the interest rate, thereby cutting back the demand for loans and limiting the bank's ability to increase the money supply.

In the 1880s the farmers were being deprived of their land. They were having to borrow money from the suppliers in springtime to get the crop in, and then in the fall the crop sold at a reduced price. With the interest charges, they couldn't pay the debts back, and the merchants took their land. The merchants measured their wealth in plows because a plow could plow so many acres. Farmers became debt slaves because they couldn't pay the high interest. They were completely at the mercy of the landlords. Their bills at the company store always equalled their share of the crop. More than one farmer held back a bale of cotton until the accounts were settled and when he presented it for cash, was told, "Why did you do that, now I have to figure out your expenses again."

This is very common in the 1980s. If you have cash you get a 15% discount. If you don't have cash you not only lose that 15% discount, but you pay maybe 2.5 - 3% interest per month. Well the 15% discount, on say fertilizer or seed, which you're going to have in the ground for a third of the year, or four months, works out to 45% interest per annum, not taking into account the two or three percent a month. So these people are paying more than 50% interest. The same thing was done back in the 1880s. The actual rate of interest charged by suppliers added up to 300 or 400%.

In the 1880s in Canada we grew wheat continuously, trying to meet the interest payments. The worldwide price went to hell. They played around with British corn laws, trying to sell grain to England; they tried to bring it in from the U.S. Everyone was using grain as a lever.

Every one of these economic depressions turned into a war, as people were displaced or even driven out of their own country by economic conditions. Governments, in order to try and take the people's attention away from the terrible economic times, fight over trade privileges, blaming economic failures on loss of trading partners.

And people are encouraged to view war as a solution. Most soldiers in the Second World War would never have signed up if there had been good economic times. You'd have had to drag them overseas, except that they were so glad to get a job, to get away from this hell they called the Great Depression — ten lost years. They would literally line up for miles to serve, to get some excitement, to get away from terrible conditions. They got three meals a day.

Today we find it hard to believe that people in Canada actually starved to death. But in the last Depression many starved. Talk to someone who was in Vancouver in the '30s. Every morning that there was a cold snap there would be dead bodies lying in doorways. They simply died of exposure. People don't die of malnutrition — usually the flu, or pneumonia gets them. The simple truth though is that in reality they died of starvation. They didn't know that the farmer had cheap food not ten miles away. They didn't have the few pennies it would have taken to buy it anyway.

I read one story of a man who found a dollar and went out and bought 15 cents worth of eggs, and could hardly carry them. He bought a bunch of other goods out of the garden and still had some change left over. He went back to the hobo jungle and made the biggest omelette you ever saw.

One of the reasons I am fighting so hard to stop this depression is that with the dependence of most of today's farmers on fossil fuel energy — and the fact that 20% of farmers produce 80% of the food — the inability to purchase parts, diesel fuel or electricity in an economic collapse (not to mention the stoppage of transportation) could so disrupt our food supply that millions would starve.

Let us stop looking back into history and look sideways today — to the Third World — to see what is about to happen to us. Cheap imported grain has destroyed their farmers and forced them to move to towns, swelling the ranks of the unemployed. Their country borrows money to feed them. They are starving to death but *not* because of too many people. The Netherlands is the most densely populated country, and they are not starving. And it is *not* because of a scarcity of arable land — most so-called basket-case countries are exporting food. *Not* from lack of technology. Bangladesh produces more than enough to feed its people (the rich in Bangladesh eat several times the grain of the poor, and twice the protein) and one-third of the food is sold to India. The poor go hungry, no matter how much food there is, even in Canada and the U.S.A. I suggest everyone read *Food First* by Frances Moore Lappe and Joseph Collins.

There are mountains of surplus food in the world and millions of people are starving, because they don't have the money to buy the food. Herein lies the problem throughout history. Why don't they have the money? Because the farmers in their own countries have been displaced by cheap grain, driven off their land into bankruptcy, into town on welfare. And the economic activity stops. The land is sitting idle, and the topsoil is being washed or blown away. There is no incentive to grow grain if you only lose money, since they're going to dump in cheap grain from elsewhere. This is deliberately created starvation. It doesn't need to happen. If the farmer is paid a fair price, he can buy products — and society can buy his.

It's difficult to study the 1930s depression — people don't seem to like to write about depressions. But there are some significant parallels between the 1930s and the 1980s. Civilian detainment camps are being built, by an Order in Council of the federal government SI 81-76 *1305 *passed in 1981*. These are paralleled by the relief camps of the '30s, where single men were kept in remote areas so they wouldn't march on Ottawa. The Crow Rate was raised dramatically in the '30s, as it has been in the '80s. The spectacular rise in the stock market of 1982-83 was paralleled only in 1932-33.

The interesting thing about farmers in the 1930s was the Holiday movement. I have gotten a lot of inspiration from these people. Milo Reno was the head of the movement. I learned a lot of my strategy from them. Their idea was that the farmer "takes a day off," because there's no sense in producing food only to lose money on it. I also learned from their mistakes.

They started food strikes, or blockades. They said that no food was going from the farm to the city unless it went at a fair price. These incidents spread and violence erupted. They shut down whole cities, like Sioux City, for a month at a time, with no food going in unless it went in at a fair price. Companies hired trucks for convoys to try and run these blockades. With old belts off thrashing machines studded with nails, with railroad tracks, logs, etc., they blocked the roads. There was shooting and killing. Some governors were sympathetic and actually helped the farmers. Some governors were opposed and sent the state troopers out. A lot of bloodshed ensued. Milo Reno finally called the thing off, saying there was too much violence. They were losing the support of public opinion.

Media coverage was very poor — maybe it was controlled. The local press would print the local incidences, but they wouldn't cover it on a national scale. If they had had press coverage of what was going on in the different areas, letting the farmers realize how powerful they were, then probably nothing would have stopped them.

Today, the farm movement organizes actions in different provinces and states, but unless we work on the press to have them publicized, people are not aware of them. Part of our reason for joining the network with the North American Farm Alliance was to keep us aware of what was going on.

Violence in the 1930s was losing the battle, as violence always does. Milo Reno called off the blockade exactly fifty years to the day that I was organizing in Iowa. Farmers went back to the 1830s, Prince Edward Island tenant kind of action: protecting their own people, their own areas. With the penny auction and the stopping of foreclosures, the farmers started to win. It was a true grassroots style of politics — just the local people looking after their own. These were just neighbourhood people saying no, enough is enough, you're not going to move that person out. That man is a neighbour who doesn't deserve this, he has no control over what is happening to him and we won't let it happen.

And the government is really powerless because it's *the people* who have moral authority. On my speaking tours I stress moral authority. It was explained to me by one of the oldtimers of the Holiday Movement — there is a lot of inspiration in those fellows, many of whom are still around — who said moral authority was best expressed at a penny auction he was at. The sheriff came in and read something which stated this was a legal auction and anyone who interfered with it would get ten years in the pen. (One old farmer said that after farming the last few years it looked like a good idea.) However, they proceeded with the sale.

The first bid on the binder was a nickel, the second bid was six cents. The third bid was five dollars. The Farmers' Holiday leader walked over to the last man who bid and asked if he'd been authorized by the Farmer's Holiday Movement to bid at this sale. The fellow said no, and he pulled out a badge. The farm leader stood back, saying, "Well boys, what are we going to do?" There was a bit of a rustle in the crowd. The oldtimer who was telling me the story said the man beside him, who turned out to be the sheriff's deputy, drew a gun. The gun went off and there was a trickle of blood down the farm leader's face, and he fell. The oldtimer heard over his shoulder, "Hang the son-of-a-bitch!" He turned around. Now a lot of these farmers had been bringing lariettes and hangman's nooses and so on to these sales as an intimidation tactic. When he turned around they had a hangman's noose on that sheriff's deputy and they were dragging him to a tree.

The interesting thing (and this is where the moral authority comes in) was that there were up to twenty other sheriffs and deputies there, with legal authority and guns, and they didn't raise a finger to save that man's life. Now as it turned out the gun was loaded with only a teargas shell. The farm leader was just cut, he wasn't hurt seriously. The old guy said they took the rope off that sheriff's deputy and he didn't hit the ground for ten feet. The rest of the sheriffs and their deputies formed a semi-circle. One of the farmers said, "Where's the rest of those sons-of-bitches?" and, to a man, those twenty-some sheriffs and deputies all put their hands in the air. To a man. And that's the moral authority. No legal authority, no guns. Just moral authority.

Another example of moral authority was when a governor made it illegal to be a member of the Farmers' Holiday Movement, or for more than three people to meet in one spot, or for anyone to gather monies for the Farmers' Holiday. So a group of men went to the local mayor and asked to use the town hall for a meeting of the Movement. He said, "No, you can't do that, it's illegal." That evening they came back with 200 farmers. He gave them the Corn Palace for the meeting.

Another interesting incident involving the Farmers' Holiday Movement occurred when 26 federal marshals went out to conduct a sale. When they got there there were 26 gallows, and 8,000 farmers. The penny auction went through.

One reporter down in the Midwest told me that he was assigned to the last auction blocked by the Farmers' Holiday Movement. An insurance company was selling 1800 acres. On the day of the sale the sheriff went to the insurance company agent and said, "We've got 600 armed farmers out there. These are my friends and neighbours, they're not prone to violence, they're good hardworking people. But they're not prepared to let you sell their neighbour's land." The insurance agent said "I don't care, I have buyers out there who are going to buy it — the land is mine and I want it sold." The sheriff said "The other thing is, I was talking to the governor and he too asks you not to do this." The insurance agent replied, "I don't care, I want a sale to go through." The sheriff said, "The governor said something else. He said that according to the statutes I could take bids on whatever increments I want."

So by about one o'clock in the afternoon they were still bidding on the first farm; I don't know if he was taking increments of one cent or fifty cents. The sheriff turned to the insurance agent and said, "At the rate this is going we'll be here for two months." The insurance agent called the sale off. That was the last one the Holiday Movement had to block. The valuable lesson to be learnt here is the conquest of good over evil or of our right for freedom does not depend so much on our willingness to fight for our selves as it does on our willingness to stand up for the rights of others.

This story shows there was support from the local sheriff. There were a lot of good people who supported the farm element, and so they should. We discovered this with the Survival Association. A lot of the local police that know us, and know the farm community, are very supportive. They don't like to be pushed against us. It is very unfortunate, especially since they're not supposed to be put in a position of collecting civil debt. Their job is to keep the peace. But some sheriffs get power-hungry and request a court order for the police to back them up. The police know we're not prone to breaking the law. A lot of the farmers I've worked with have never even had a speeding ticket. Personally, I've never lost a point off my driver's license. And yet as a result of my activities over the past year or so, I face three criminal charges.

If you have read Orwell's *Nineteen Eighty Four* you will remember that the poor and starving offer no real threat to the ruling power. It is only the middle class that aspires to rule, has the education and the finances to struggle against tyranny. The farmers constitute the bulk of this middle class, we control assets that match or exceed all the other industries combined. As Orwell explains this middle class has to be destroyed for the rulers to be secure, as I read history I realized why. This is why government policies have for years tried not to help, but to destroy the farmers. And this will continue until it is resisted.

From history we learn that we, the farmers, hold the key to any real economic recovery, we have the story to tell and a populace to educate. Our job now as always is to raise ignorance from despair!

Economics

18

The purpose of studying economics is not to acquire a set of ready-made answers to economic questions, but to learn how to avoid being deceived by economists. — Joan Robinson

No book on agriculture can refrain from talking about economics, for economics is synonymous with soil. As I studied traditional economics, two things came out as their gospel. One, the government should intervene with the economy for the common good, by means of monetary policy, tariffs, grants, and tax incentives. But current government programs for agriculture have been counterproductive. In Canada, tariffs on manufactured goods range as high as 44%, whereas the average tariffs of primary products such as agricultural products average 4-5%. The other fact is, that goods should be produced where they can be produced the cheapest, and shipped to all other areas. This benefits mainly those controlling trade, often at the expense of producers, including agriculture.

It became very clear, through studying traditional economics and talking to the economists, that not only was economics a very imperfect science — witness the economic mess — but also that it was simply propaganda, perpetuated through our economic system to maintain those in positions of power and the wealth of the powerful, namely the large corporations. The simplest farmer knows more about economics than any of the professionals I met, namely, that if the farmers are prosperous, so is the country.

Keynsian economics taught that through deficit government spending you could actually borrow yourself rich. Cutting off one end of the blanket to sew onto the other. There are, of course, exceptional economists, such as John Kenneth

Galbraith, who was involved in setting prices in the parity program. He believes that because the farmers are small, independent operators with no influence on the market, there is no "law of supply and demand," and because the large corporations are so powerful, the government must intervene as a counterbalance.

But the one that impressed me the most was Carl Wilkens, who took economics from theory to fact, and is the father of "raw material economics" and the U.S. parity program. Carl Wilkens was an American farmer turned economist. When the depression started, he wondered why a country — with all its natural resources untouched by world war or natural calamity, and with all its skilled people — had to have a depression.

Since a depression is monetary shortage, one has to start with the elementary question, "Where does wealth come from?" Wilkens' work on the economic cycle brought him to the conclusion that the only new things that come in to fuel the economic fires are raw materials. These raw materials are literally free — sunlight converted to matter: fish, grain, timber . . . gifts that God has provided. Their only real value is the labour involved in harvesting them.

Once the hunter gatherer started to farm he could produce food surplus to his own needs. Others, who were not then required to produce food, were able to start secondary industry (pottery, shoes, etc.), producing goods to trade with the farmer for his produce. In areas of good climate and soil, enough labour was released to provide service industries. Today, two-thirds of our work force is in the "service industry." But servers of whom — who pays for the services? The answer now, as always, goes back to the primary industry, the raw material producers.

Wilkens found a direct relationship between farm product price and the whole economy. When farmers receive one-seventh of the Gross National Product the economy prospers, but when farm income falls below that ratio, debt spirals and hard times follow. Farm price is so important because gross farm income and gross industrial wage are equal. As gross farm income falls, the industrial wage must be reduced, either by wage cuts or unemployment. Of course the government can borrow money and spend it to create jobs and cover up the problems. Marvin Meek, past leader of the American Agriculture Movement, in testifying before Senate subcommitees in Washington in 1980, '81 and '82, actually predicted the federal deficit of the USA twelve months in advance, basing his work strictly on farm prices in the previous years.

Wilkens' work was based on the new wealth which comes into the system each year. He stated it, very simply, in the equation:

Raw material x price = New Wealth
eg. 1 million bushels of corn x $5 = $5 million of New Wealth
.5 million bushels of corn x $5 = only $2.5 million of New Wealth

We all know that if drought strikes and there is less "raw material," the whole nation has hard times, but we don't all realize that a drought on the price side of the equation gives the same result:

1 million bushels of corn x $2.5 = only $2.5 million of New Wealth

For example, tremendous prosperity results from a gold strike if gold is $400 per ounce. Whole cities spring up. But if the gold is priced at $1 per tonne, nobody benefits. But supporters of raw material economics realize that people must be able to purchase the products and suggest setting the minimum wage at the price of a bushel of corn to keep the economy in balance. Balance is both sides being equal.

Wilkens' formula of $1 in farm income = $1 of industrial wage = $7 of GNP, is called Wilkens' Law. The parity, which means balance, that results was implemented in the Steagall Amendment in 1941.

The United States had just entered the Second World War and was drafting legislation to finance the war. Wilkens presented the fact that the U.S. was bankrupt: it had just come through ten years of depression and would surely lose the war because of financial problems. But if parity was restored to agriculture the nation would experience prosperity, which would finance the war. This program was in effect from 1941-51, and it not only financed the war, but also the Marshall Plan, and brought the U.S. to a position of world power based on a balanced internal economy.

This prosperity was so real that by 1943 the banks could only lend out 17.5 cents on every dollar deposited. Now the banks had a depression — no one needed to borrow money if they were making a profit. So the banking powers, realizing that parity had to go, started pressure. They demanded repayment of the war debt, which of course came in the form of raw materials, and surpluses started to build. The resulting pressure broke the strength of the politicians in Washington, and parity was aborted to 90% of 90% of 90% and so on, until now again we are at 56% of parity. Our public and private debt threatens to destroy us all, because we've been trying to borrow prosperity.

I mentioned at the start of the book that government deficits are not a result of overspending, but rather of a lack of income. At 56% of parity, the total tax base is only 56% of what it should be.

According to Wilkens' law of 1:1:7, the first dollar of farm income generates the dollar for industrial payroll, and ultimately produces $7 of national income. This economic phenomenon is so consistent that Wilkens was able to project the national income of the U.S. with better than 98% accuracy for 14 years — six months prior to their official publication. This is not guess work! What we need in Canada today is an audit of our national income. The facts are there, they just have to be examined.

How did Wilkens' parity program work?

Quite simple. He took a period when the economy was in balance and we had prosperity. He projected farm prices at the same rate as the rest of society, much like economists index the cost of living. The basic idea is, if it took 1,000 bushels of wheat to buy a new car twenty years ago, then it should still take 1,000 bushels of wheat to buy a comparable car. That is, whenever one advances or declines, so must the other. It is sometimes argued that farmers are more efficient nowadays, but of course so are auto manufacturers.

Once the price was decided, then it was set as the standard for government support. If the price of a product fell to 90%, the U.S. government bought it off the market and put it in storage. If the price rose to 110% of parity, this stored product was sold onto the market, keeping an ever-normal grainery, to benefit farmer and consumer alike, and provide a necessary reserve in case of drought or famine. But the borders should have been regulated to ensure fair trade, not free trade. Also, the minimum wage has to be kept balanced with the price of corn to ensure the ability of workers to consume. Human need in the 1980s is desperate, and we can consume all that we produce, given the proper purchasing power.

Another one of the major influences on me was Arnold Paulson, one of Wilkens' disciples. Arnold Paulson got his start working for the Chamber of Commerce in Granite Falls, a small Midwestern town in the U.S., trying to attract industry to the sagging economy of a rural city. He did a tremendous job and attracted ten times what the other towns got.

But he realized that even with this success things were not rosy. He did an economic audit of his town, and found that with all the wages in the town in 1971 there was only $400 per person, or $1600 per family, and yet some made $40-60,000 a year. If he added more industry, he had to construct more buildings to house workers, more sewers, more police — with no net improvement in the per capita income.

Then he met Wilkens. He sat down and took the gross income of only the farmers who were on the mailing route in that town. He took their gross dollar income, because that's what the farmer spends in town, and the total, when he divided, worked out to $1600 per person, or $6400 per family. So then he looked at what farmers were receiving for their product and saw that they were underpaid. By adding 25% to the price of wheat he could do far more for his town than all the factories — with no new roads or sewers necessary.

Today there is less than five cents worth of wheat in $1 worth of bread, so if you doubled the cost of the wheat, you wouldn't hurt the buyer much but you could ensure that she or he had a job. If we doubled farm gate prices it would raise the cost of a food basket only 5%. My observations are that people could spend the same amount for food, if we were to cut down on the processing and the wrapping, and some of the frills that farmers view as luxuries. Processors and distributors can be prevented from increasing their prices every time the farm gate price increases. The increased tax base would reduce income taxes with a net income benefit.

Here lies our task. There is only one evil, ignorance; one good, knowledge. We must convince the consumer that higher farm gate prices are a benefit to society. We must convince the politicians in Sault Ste. Marie that their steelworkers are unemployed as a result of farm problems. We must make government economists do an economic audit of Canada, just as Paulson did of Granite Falls.

Wilkens' Parity Program was developed in the U.S. but, as all physical laws, his constants span borders. The importance of agriculture to the economy is the same everywhere. In Canada our Minister of Agriculture Eugene Whelan has been a step ahead, supporting the campaign for farmer-controlled boards to set the price for their products and control production in line with national requirements. Controls over imports must be included and can be implemented under GATT. Since the price of farm product is the wage for the farmers' work, legislation would be similar to minimum wage laws. Whelan tells of coal mines which have unlimited supply, but have contracts fifteen years ahead which guarantee the price. Coal is a storable, non-perishable commodity and they can easily regulate supply. Yet food is perishable and we are forced to sell a year's crop against a one-day demand, with no control in most areas over the amount of production. The commodities which have supply management and set price in Canada include eggs, poultry, and milk. They provide both the best buys for consumers and the best returns for farmers because of constant supply.

Do not confuse this with agencies such as the Pork Producers Marketing Board and the Wheat Board, which are centralized marketing agencies but do not control price or supply. The quota or license to produce so much product is the same as a license to run bus lines, taxis, etc. The government limits the number of taxis so that they don't over-compete and all go broke — one day too many taxis and the next day none. To think that we regulate taxis, but not food, again shows the priorities of society.

Our present Marketing Boards on some commodities have a flaw and it is just this — they are only on some commodities. We set the price of chicken in Canada, but the formula uses the market price of grain, not the full cost of production of that grain. Thus, if corn, which costs $3.50 to produce, is selling for $2.00, then a chicken producer feeding his own corn is losing money — so the smart thing is to run a chicken factory where one buys the grain (at the $2.00 price), for if the price does go up, it is taken care of in the pricing formula.

The escalating costs of the milk quota — about which everyone's heard — and the other quotas, are partly a result of red meat farmers, and other farmers, trying to get into milk or rather out of pigs and beef. But the biggest influence by far is the fact that as the groups which cannot set their prices go broke, the decrease in their purchasing power creates unemployment and less demand for butter, cheese, chicken, etc., forcing a cutback in quota. Remaining quota is thus more valuable.

As meat, eggs and milk are just ways of processing grain and grass, the most important thing is to set the price of grain properly. Quotas on some products and not others allows border controls to be circumnavigated; for example, cheap pork is imported to decrease demand for chicken and forces a cut in the chicken quota.

Equity of trade is very important to a solvent national and international economy. People still blame the last depression on protectionism. But we only have to look at the solutions put forward by our present economists: "We must export more and import less." Even the Third World is told that in order to pay off huge debts they must export more and import less. No one stops to think that if we are all successful we cannot all be successful. This beggar thy neighbour attitude has created the debt crisis that threatens to break us all and is exactly what happened the last time. The depression created trade barriers, not the other way around. As a farmer I don't put chickens in the same pen as cattle, for it is not in their mutual benefit. But a partition between them allows them to coexist in the same barn.

So it is with countries. On the world scene, free trade moves to lower price, but the consumer, in buying cheap imported beef, or cheap manufactured goods, is starting a process which will ultimately lower his or her own wages. Like the person standing up at a football game for a better view, the advantage is lost when all the people stand up. They get the same view that they all had sitting, except now they are more uncomfortable.

Free trade will reduce all labour to the lowest common denominator. This is recognized in most industries — I can't buy a car, nor a suit of clothes, in Detroit and sell it in Toronto, without duties and tariffs. Have you ever tried to buy a truckload of beer in Manitoba and sell it in Ontario? Or, have you tried to make and sell your own whiskey? You will soon find out about free markets. But you can go anywhere in North

America, buy a load of cattle, and slaughter them in Toronto with no interference other than veterinary certificates. The fact that we even import beef into Canada is, I feel, atrocious. The fact that we import 93% of our lamb means there is something basically wrong with our economy.

The arguments I constantly run into go something like this:

But if we raise the price of wheat we won't be able to export it — why do we want to export it at a loss? If the government wants foreign exchange then I suggest we increase our manufacturing industry which is only working at 70% of capacity and then export Ford cars at one thousand dollars a piece.

But farmers can produce far more than we can consume. This can be said of all our industries but why is agriculture the sacrificial lamb? In actual fact Ontario exports $1.4 billion in agricultural products but imports $2 billion, so we cannot even feed ourselves and we have a quarter of the farming potential in Canada.

But it is argued that if we raise our price the Third World won't be able to afford to buy food to feed their starving. The fact is that even Bangladesh produces ample to feed its population but it is exported because export is more profitable for those that run the country. Theirs is a political, and hence economic problem, not a supply or tecnhological problem.

If you raise the price it will benefit the larger farmer more than the small. Check the record — low prices throughout history have caused farm expansion. As smaller farmers are driven out, land is consolidated. But this is really a land reform question. Government programs, like ARDA, which encourage consolidation can be reversed. In many midwestern U.S. states there are laws against corporate ownership of land. P.E.I. has laws restricting land ownership to permanent residents. Other provinces have similar laws or taxes on foreign ownership. If we can restrict the foreign content of our TV shows, surely we should be concerned about foreign ownership of our food production. And there should be laws against absentee landlords.

Won't government intervention to set prices constrict our freedom? No more than the minimum wage law or a traffic light. But I find no freedom in poverty. The basis of all freedoms is economic freedom.

Won't higher commodity prices push up the price of land, negating any gain to the starting farmer? Again look at the record — land prices doubled and redoubled as overall commodities dropped. Farmers compete for land to solve cash flow problems by volume.

Farmers have been told for years that if enough go out of business conditions will get better for the remainder. We have lost millions of farmers over the years and still farmers have not improved their position compared to others in society. To me this is like a private praying for the total destruction of the rest of the army so that he can be the general!

We will have parity, or a balanced economy, but a balance can be brought about two ways: either adding to one side, or taking away from the other. With present government policies, we will all be at the balance — at the poverty level.

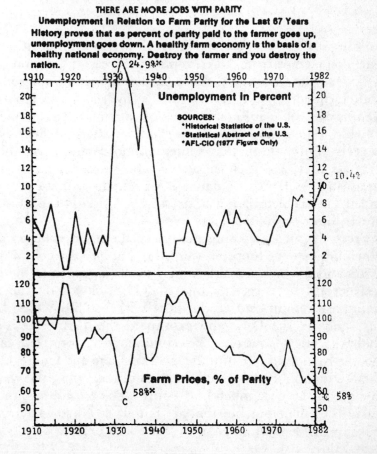

Rev. W. Milton Jacobson, Co-Chaplain, National Organization of Raw Materials. Reprint courtesy of NORM and ACRES, USA. (C = 50-year cycle).

Soil Conservation

19

*No man ever really owns the land; it belongs to itself and
a farmer should regard it with more humility than a sense
of ownership.* — Ronald Peden

Nothing clarifies soil conservation in my mind more than the
reaction of a man from America planting trees in Scotland. The
hills were plowed up and down, a definite no-no for soil erosion, but the soil did not erode. Why? Because it had an
organic content of 50% from years of pasture and a cold climate
which did not break down the organic matter. A healthy soil
consists of organic matter, minerals and bacteria and this in-
terrelation is absolutely necessary for continuing this living
organism. When this balance is upset, the soil starts to die,
and if the problem is not addressed, erosion is the final step
which removes the dead soil.

From the air, one cannot only see the light-coloured areas
which indicate the topsoil is thinning, but also the colour of the
rivers and the brown stains which reach far out into the lakes
and oceans. The recent abnormal U.S. floods on the river
plains are reminiscent of the floods in the '30s which killed
thousands in the U.S. and prompted the Tennessee Valley
Authority Flood Control. The economic conditions have caused
the destruction of our humus and this huge sponge gets to be
like a huge rubber raincoat: instead of absorbing the water it
sheds it, along with much of the soil. The erosion around the
world is tremendous but the fact is that in North America, it
is in a worse condition than in the 1930s despite our modern
knowledge.

The humus or dead plant matter is the key. It is the medium
which retains the water and is the home for the bacteria, whose

action breaks down the nutrients for plant use. The plant dies and becomes part of the humus and the cycle continues. Because of the addition of sunlight (energy) and water we can harvest a portion of this to feed and clothe ourselves. It is when in the name of efficiency we harvest too much or don't replace some of that which has been removed, that the deterioration starts. Our soils have a tremendous ability to absorb abuse, although some are much more durable than others.

Our prairie soils, which are a grassland base, will stand monoculture for nearly a century. But there are danger signs. I talked to an oldtimer who broke the prairie sod and raised 100 bushels of wheat, then plowed through the stubble and got 65 bushels, then once more for 45 bushels, and when they plowed, or turned the soil, they returned to 100 bushels per acre. Our average yield in the western provinces is now 27 bushels per acre, despite fertilizer and tremendous genetic improvements in our seed.

Our woodland soils, or that soil which was created by our forests, is much more fragile. If you have ever dug up nice, black, soft dirt from a bush or swamp for your flower pots, you will know what I mean. Very shortly it does not resemble what you dug up. It has aged rapidly. In Ontario our woodland soils will last only 30 years under monoculture, but in the hotter climates, the breakdown is much more rapid. In the Amazon Basin, when they remove the forests, the soil is good for only a very few years. The abandoned Inca city civilizations of Central America are now overgrown; this should serve as a warning. This destruction of our soils is not new and is a world-wide situation.

Tom Moller, a dairy man from Denmark, said, "We can see the same thing happening in Denmark. The very tight economic situation is pressing farmers to produce a bit more and some people have been growing barley on the same land for 25 to 30 years straight. They're using huge amounts of chemicals and fertilizers on the land. You can really see the erosion. They don't like destroying their own soil. If we can get farmers in a better economic situation, we can do something about it."

The causes of soil erosion are not necessarily bad farm practices but rather the economic conditions that force those practices. The mining of the soil — the expansion of farm size which removes the personal involvement with the soil — is determined by economic factors. The practices of monoculture are exemplified in the Third World. It is difficult to tell a man whose family can barely live off the failing production of his small acreage that he must rotate some of his land to an unknown new crop. Monoculture is a result of desperation on the part of the farmer or, in the case of a tenant, no concern for the future ability of that particular farm as he will soon be gone anyway.

This is the strong argument for the family farm. A family whose livelihood for future generations depends on the soil, moves to ensure the well-being of that soil which is a part of them through their mutual dependence. As farm size expands for economic reasons, this personal relationship is destroyed. It is perhaps impossible for a city person to understand the ties which a farmer has to his farm but it can best be illustrated by the Survival Association members and their devotion and dedication to keep that piece of land called a farm, no matter how humble the dwelling or how rocky the soil.

In the Third World, whole villages are massacred because they refuse to leave their land after the large corporations take over. This living organism called soil is more than a source of livelihood: it is a part of their whole being.

The personal involvement found only in the family farm is the best way that we as a civilization can ensure the care of our most important resource, the land itself, and thus our ultimate survival. For conservation is a grim synonym for survival. Conservation has not only been a concern in the 1980s, but throughout the history of agriculture in Ontario.

In the nineteenth century there was the repeated scenario of the people who came over because of economic conditions. The good, established farmers were able to stay in Europe. The people who came over were, for the most part, unemployed labourers, landless peasants, the downtrodden — not necessarily expert in the ways of agriculture. Having no capital and little expertise they literally mined the soil; they grew wheat and more wheat to pay for their farms. The land was judged strictly on its ability to produce wheat. They grew wheat until, by the 1880s, the soil literally couldn't grow any more wheat. Blight, a disease of wheat, began to infect it, finally destroying it all, in Mother Nature's desperate attempt to save the soil. The farmers in their desperation to pay taxes, the mortgage and the interest, to meet the grocery bill, used poor farming practices. They didn't have any alternative. This was a result of the depression of the farm produce prices in the 1870s in Ontario. It was quite obvious — they mined the soil to the point where it wouldn't grow any more. The economic crunch was both the cause and finally the result. In the 1880s these farmers were forced off their land, moved out and this is what really started the settlement of the West in the 1880s, early 1900. These people were pushed. The Northwest Rebellion resulted from the farmers moving in and taking the land from the Indians and Metis.

The second wave of farmers that came in from Europe were the sons of the good farmers. They moved into cleared farms that they could take over. Right away they knew you can't farm without animals. You have to return that manure to the soil. You have to have ruminant agriculture. The cow's ability is to consume grass and convert it to protein. What we have are two types of crops — soil-conserving and soil depleting. The latter are grain and row crops; they take away from the soil. The former is pasture and hay, the grasses and legumes that rebuild the soil. The other soil-conserving crop is the forest, the trees.

The strength of North American industry is literally built on 10,000 years of buffalo dung. The buffaloes ate young trees off. The only thing that grew was grass. They continued to consume the grass, returning the manure, and they built a fantastic rich soil. The European farmers have created an artificial soil the same way, with the ruminant agriculture and the grasses, the plow-downs. They had good management practices. They built a soil that is actually superior to natural soil, but today it too is being destroyed.

In Ontario in the early 1900s they realized they had to go back to grass, since they needed cattle to return manure. Even though the pig farmers are returning the manure to the soil, you still have to have that soil back in red clover, grass, or some soil-conserving, or humus-building, crops as well as the manure to keep the thing going properly. This is the case for ruminant agriculture. (Cattle, sheep, and goats are ruminant animals: they bring back up the food they have digested ("chewing their cud"), and in this way can digest cellulose.) If we don't have half our soil in soil-conserving crops, then we will not continue to farm because you can only deplete soil for so long. If you have half taking out and don't have half putting back in, soon you've depleted to the point where nothing grows. You have either to put the whole thing back to soil conserving or, if you do it wrong, Mother Nature destroys it — the soil doesn't have the ability to absorb rainwater, it runs off and takes the topsoil with it.

We now are losing an estimated five to nine tonnes per acre. The topsoil in Iowa has gone from 18 inches average to eight inches. We are losing one inch per decade. The rain washes it and the wind blows it. Farmers are forced to overgraze, to monoculture, literally mining the soil in order to pay the mortgage. They clear more land and expand their farm size until the whole thing collapses. One of the causes of the greenhouse effect or the heating of our world because of excess carbin dioxide is deforestation.

Farmers are plowing land that should never have been taken out of sod. Growing cash crops fence row to fence row, and not worrying about rotation, literally created the dust bowl.

The sun hits these soils, warms them up, and they stay warm at night, where grass doesn't. Grass absorbs the heat and turns the air cool by evaporation. But when the grass is gone the soil stays warm, and the hot air rises. So in the evening you get a high-pressure area and that brings clear skies — and eventually no rainfall. Cutting down a forest has the same effect as lowering altitude 620 feet, as far as rainfall is concerned. You can create deserts just by plowing. There's no such thing as a natural desert; they're always man-made.

In the 1930's the state of Oklahoma literally blew out to the Atlantic Ocean. They plowed the prairie, the topsoil dried out, and the wind came along and blew it away. Huge clouds of topsoil blew over the cities in the Eastern Seaboard and the ocean literally turned red with it.

We're facing the same thing again in Canada and the U.S. There are acres and acres of pastures plowed up, and a tremendous amount of forest and bush land is being cut down. Land is being cleared, even in these hard times, to try and make some more money out of it.

We've "turned it wrong side up," as the Indians say. I predicted another dust bowl when I travelled through the Midwest states. The fences were all gone and everything was plowed, even up hills I wouldn't drive — hence the drought of 1983. The only redeeming factor of the U.S. PIK program was the encouragement to return the land to forages (grass and hay).

The history of soil is really the history of civilization. Soil and economics are synonymous terms. History tells us how people treated their soils and the impact the soils had on those civilizations. One very good example was Greece. Because they had cut down all their forests and mined their soil, the soil had washed away. The only thing that could effectively grow were olive trees. The olive trees would live on the subsoils that were left and the harsh climate thus created. They would trade the olive oil they grew for the grain they ate. One of the impacts this had was on their pottery — world famous, made strictly to transport their oil. If they'd had a good agricultural base they never would have been in the pottery business. Because they had to trade this oil for food, they needed a merchant marine, and a navy to protect them. This made them a major world power. The lack of agricultural ability led to the need for aggression.

Another example is the Nile Valley, one of the first centres of civilization. The trees were being destroyed in the highlands to the south of present-day Egypt and every year the topsoil would wash down. So the soil in the Nile Valley would be annually replenished with the nutrients from upstream. The early Egyptians were mining one part of the country, unknown to them, and fertilizing their own. This created a great civilization. The ability of the land to produce meant that many people could direct their time to the arts, government, knowledge.

And, that's what North America is trading on now. Ten thousand years of buffalo dung have enabled us to free people from the farms, to create other things, to manufacture. We're at the point where we can afford "non-productive" people, just to philosophize, to write books and read them. Those people who, because our soil is so productive, aren't needed on the farm can enhance life. But a balance must be maintained.

A point made in *Soil and Civilization,* and I would recommend its reading to anyone — is that humans are a parasite on the soil. As with any parasite, they are not necessarily destructive as long as there's another host agent to keep them in check. But if there isn't anything to keep us in check, then we may kill the host.

Throughout history, civilizations have been destroyed when they destroy their own soil base. The history of humanity is the history of the movement of whole nations, people fleeing from their own land or expanding because of soil conditions. The history of Russia is a continual battle between the people who grass cattle and those who plow up the soil and grow crops, the eternal battle between the cattleman and the sod busters. In the days of the U.S. Wild West, the sod busters came in, breaking up pastures and ruining good grazing land. Genghis Khan, the famous cattle baron, even though he was more into horses, literally destroyed civilizations, killing every man, woman and child because he wanted the land for pasture and for his horses. He was able to do this because years of cropping without livestock had wrecked their soil and hence their civilization to the point where they were easily overrun. I make the case for cattle because the beef cow and the dairy cow have the most impact as converters of grass. I often wondered why in India the cow is considered sacred; somewhere back in time the people perhaps realized the importance of the cow to society, making it a crime to kill them. Unfortunately, instead of being utilized as converters of grass to human food they were worshipped and eating them was forbidden; good intentions gone astray.

I came upon this concept quite early, when I started to farm; it was one of the reasons I was in the beef business. I could only afford run-down farms and I needed to build them up, enrich the soils. Raising cattle was the way to do it — grow grass, feed hay to the cattle and put back the manure. Keep the fields in the alfalfas and clover, which are soil-conserving and help to build soil structure. Artificial nitrogen is used to break down humus or soil structure to make it more readily available to the plant, artificially aging the soil. It is probably the worst blight of humankind;

Governments don't admit the importance of the beef animal to the whole cycle. When the price of grain gets cheap enough, farmers take the cattle off the pastures, put them in the feedlots and feed them the cheap grain. Then they plow up the pastures and produce more grain, forcing the price down further. The large corporations don't make much money out of pasturing or other natural farming techniques. So by shorting the price, they force us to use their products.

These countries or provinces or ''experts'' who believe, with the banks, that beef is passe, and that from now on everyone's going to eat pork and chicken because they're better converters of cheap grain, burn me up — knowing that if we lose the beef business it's only a matter of time before we lose the rest. There will be no infinite supply of cheap grain. That is how they brought North American Indians to their knees. They destroyed all their buffalo and made them dependent on the whites for food and clothing. By destroying our beef industry, we are now dependent upon purchased fertilizers and chemicals.

In present-day Canada we have a direct pipeline taking the grain off the buffalo dung of the prairies, sending it east, and converting it into red meat. The eastern provinces get the manure out of it. The people eat the meat and bread, flush their manure down the sewer, and it goes out into the river and creates pollution. The problem is that all the nutrients go into the river, so it's there that all the plants, algae grow. If you magnify it over time — we're stealing the topsoil out of western Canada and dumping it into the St. Lawrence River, and eventually the ocean, causing pollution.

Every country does this nowadays. We have to get a balanced agriculture — get the red meat industry out where the grain is produced, put a lot of that soil back into grass, get the people out in the countryside, in smaller communities, so that we keep the ecological system balanced by returning the manure to the soil whence it came. And we can go on forever. Otherwise we're simply mining, stealing from ourselves, and destroying our heritage.

Since 1968, Canada has lost 1.4 million acres of farmland, an area twice the size of P.E.I., our smallest province. Because of urban sprawl, erosion, and waste, we are increasingly in danger of being a food-dependent country.

Our present economic policies are like the man who bought a horse to make deliveries in the city. When questioned about his decision, he responded that everything was fine except the part about buying hay, for it was expensive and hard to find. His friend, an economist, said he had read that horses were very intelligent and one could likely train them not to eat. So the man started to reduce the feed daily. A while later, his friend asked, "Did the horse learn to go without hay?" The man answered, "If he had lived two more days, I would have had him trained."

The International Farm
Crisis Summit

20

Because systems of mass communications can communicate
only officially acceptable levels of reality, no one can know
the extent of the secret unconscious life. No one in America
can know what will happen. — Allen Gimsbey

The international meeting in Ottawa, July 7-10, 1983, was a
major step forward in the education process. For most of the
organizational work I should give credit again to Mark Ritchie
of the U.S. Farmers' Association, member of the North
American Farm Alliance, and many other people who were involved in putting the thing together.

It started in Tennessee the year before when I met Arie van
dan Brand from the Netherlands. We were talking about farming, he realized we were having serious problems, and I was
first made aware that they were having a serious problem over
there. They had recently had an 80-year-old man evicted
because his grandson had gone broke. Arie copied my scrap-
books to take back because he didn't think people in Holland
would believe him. We started up a three-way communication
between us and Mark Ritchie. Arie did a lot of the coordinating
work in Europe, and the North American Farm Alliance, of
which the Canadian Farmers' Survival Association is a member,
sponsored the meeting.

Thanks to some friendly MPs, we ended up with an international meeting in a palatial conference room in the Canadian
House of Commons, with representatives from the Netherlands,
France, Germany, Greece, Denmark, Italy, Japan, the Philippines, Canada and the U.S. We got a lot of good press

coverage: one of our main objectives was to convince people in our various organizations that this thing is world-wide. They're still looking at their own little county, not see-ing the magnitude of the problem, not realizing how commodity prices are set. As I explained earlier, seven families control the world trade in grain and much of the infrastructure (the elevators, transportation, and so on) despite the activities of governments. For instance, the "Merchants of Grain" in-fluence the U.S. Congress to what the reserve price of grain shall be.

There were three billion bushels of grain on reserve in the United States in the fall of '82. The U.S. Congress sets a max-imum and a minimum price for grain, the "reserve price" and the "release price." If you're selling grain and the reserve price on corn, for example, is $2.50 and the market won't pay you $2.50, then you borrow $2.50 from the government. The corn stays on your farm; they put a seal on the bin, and they lend you the money — $2.50 per bushel. There is a third middle price, the "call price," for example $3.00, at which they call your loan and you have to start paying interest on your $2.50 loan. Of course, this is an incentive for you to sell the corn onto the market and thus keep the price down. The release price, at which the government can demand payment, was $3.25 for 1982 corn. When the market price hits the release price it generally triggers a release of grain reserves as the farmer must now find cash to pay off the loan and finance the crop out of his own resources if he wants to hold on for a better price. So in other words, when the price gets to $3.25, farmers dump billions of bushels of grain on the market, and the price rarely gets above $3.25.

This is a distortion of the original parity program. The parity price for corn today should be US$5.10. The parity program, which fixes minimum and maximum prices, was set up by the Steagall Amendment in 1941. It was intended to work just like a minimum wage program. The floor minimum was set at 90% of parity and the ceiling maximum at 110%. In other words, if the price dropped to 90% of what you should be getting, then the government bought it off the market. If the price got over 110% of what you should be getting, the government sold it back on the market. So it protected both the farmer and the consumer, and it kept a very valuable reserve in the face of crop failure or natural catastrophe.

Dutch farmer, Arie Van dan Brand. (International farm crisis meeting, Ottawa, July 1983.)

The deliberate policies to destroy this program started back in 1947; by 1952, "parity" went to 90% of 90%, of 90%. So effectively the ceiling was dropped — as I mentioned 1982 corn was at US$3.25, instead of US$5.10. This is the bottom line of the world problem, because the U.S. Congress is setting the price of grain at half of what it should be, and the United States controls 65% of world trade in grain. They're dumping this grain out there for political and economic reasons that have nothing to do with the health of the U.S. farm community, U.S. industry, or the world economy. They are, in fact, literally destroying the farmers around the world.

A lot of North American farmers think the farmers in the European Common Market who have a set price are in heaven. But the price over there is much the same as the U.S. price — not high enough — although a little better than North American standards. What they do there, with milk for example, is they set it just low enough that farmers have to produce

Jean Claude Bouche from Quebec.

a little more each year, to try and make a living. They dump the surplus on the world market, and then they tax the producer to make up the difference between the price the government is supporting and the world market price.

The producer is paying to get rid of his own milk, which his country is selling to get foreign exchange.

Another key is that Common Market farmers have no control over production, or supply management as we think of it. The European farmer is guaranteed so much for milk, and he can produce all he wants. However, that which is produced in excess of domestic requirements is exported and sold at a reduced price. In order to make up for this reduced international selling price, the farmer is taxed on the country's excess production.

Some very interesting things came out of the international meeting and we had some terrific people there. The fellows

Wayne Crytz (left) of the American Agriculture Movement and Merle Hansen of the North American Farmers' Association.

from France pointed out that they don't have a welfare system in France. And there are no bankruptcy laws as we know them, which could give them a release from debt. So creditors literally hound farmers the rest of their lives for the money they owe. Farmers in France have a lot more incentive to fight. When they see things getting tough, they're literally going to be beggars on the street if they lose their farms. They'd been recently getting 14-16,000 people out in Paris to demonstrate.

The mountain people in France, who traditionally raise dairy cows as in Switzerland, have land good for little more than pasture. If you plow it up it will wash away, so the cows pasture on the hillsides. With the importation of cheap (usually U.S.) grain, the dairy industry has moved from the mountainsides to the port cities. They've switched from traditional breeds to the Holstein milk machine, a cow bred strictly for production.

The fellow from Holland said that, literally, cows in his country now pasture on the banks of the Mississippi. The grain companies bring in the cheap grain and soybeans from the United States, feed them to the cows, and produce the milk. The mountain people are out of work and those Holstein cows are eating up foreign exchange.

Here we get to the heart of the agricultural problem in the European Common Market. American grain is being converted into European milk, and dumped onto the world market. If they weren't importing the grain they probably wouldn't have the surplus of milk. Buying that grain requires foreign (U.S.) currency, and they export cheese in order to get this foreign currency. This is something I emphasize again and again; we're all in this thing together. Grain is synonymous with cheese which is synonymous with chicken, beef and pork. All, even potatoes, are tied in together. International trade does not benefit farmers, but the traders and suppliers.

Arie van dan Brand made a very good presentation. He spoke for about 20 minutes, and when he was done he said that in the 20 minutes he had spoken, they'd lost 20 farmers out of Europe; losing one per minute, 500,000 families a year are displaced. The land values in the Netherlands had dropped an estimated 50%. Tom Miller from Denmark told the same story: land values had dropped by half. They'd had a Farmers' Creditors Act, or a debt readjustment, about six months previous.

Again the parallels were very interesting. Government guarantees had come in, similar to those introduced by our Ontario Ministry of Agriculture. The problem in Europe was that farmers couldn't get money — the banks had cut off their credit. So the governments are guaranteeing their loans, but doing nothing about the price problem. The loans come due, and the government is on the hook for great wads of guarantees. The Ontario plan cost $42 million. The money went straight to the banks, not the farmers. The taxpayers guaranteed the loans and then gave the money, principal and interest, to the banks. Government hoped the problem was small, temporary, and would go away. I called it the Bank Assistance Program.

Eugene Whelan said at this international conference that only 5% of Canadian farmers were in trouble. One reporter picked up on that and said one out of twenty, which sounded a little better, but in reality it's a lot worse and Whelan certainly knew better. But he used political b.s. — "six and five keeps us alive." I had asked him to speak on supply management, how price is the problem and how we might address it. But he got up saying people were starving in the world and we in Canada were doing well because of six and five, that the Liberal government had solved this problem, the recession was over, and so on, just garbage. To give him one word of credit, he was reading a speech that had been prepared for him, maybe he was overtired, I don't know.

The Japanese have lost a million and a half farmers in the last ten years. In Japan they had expropriated huge chunks of farmland to build an airport. The local farmers were fighting this; they had 14,000 farmers in one demonstration. Of course the United States is dumping cheap grain in there, fighting like hell to get the tariffs removed so they can dump in even more cheap grain. And the farmers don't look that important to the Japanese government — trade them off to export cars.

Japan had some very good farm policies. With tariffs (fair trade I would call it) they were bringing grain in at a fair price, tariffing wheat up to the Japanese cost of production. This has been an important element in Japan's success over the years.

In the Philippines it is a very sad story. You can see where we're going by looking at these Third World countries. The evils are magnified. The government was again expropriating land, evicting tenants, so the large corporations could set up huge farms. Little farmers who'd been farming three, four, five acres for generations were being removed. Hilarid Padilla, the Philippine representative, said their major crop was "rice to sell to the United States." Now can you imagine in a Third World country where people are going hungry — in Southeast Asia there's hunger — they're exporting rice to the United States. While I was in Missouri, a fellow lost his grain bins, full of rice. There was no sale for the rice and no storage. And here they are bringing rice in. Eleven Philippine families had recently been massacred because they were resisting eviction. This was very touching because resisting evictions, foreclosures, was just what we'd been doing.

About a quarter of the bananas the Philippines grow for export are culled, and dumped in the rivers. Because local people couldn't afford to buy them, they were dumped to the point where they blocked a river and flooded a town.

Their dependency on the large corporations is much like heroin addiction. The multi-nationals get them hooked on chemicals, equipment, fuel and so on, and they *have* to export bananas and rice in order to buy the fertilizers and fuel, etc. that they're hooked on. One farmer in Africa had thanked an American farmer for food aid for a drought year, ''but would they please stop sending cheap corn as he could not compete and was losing his farm.''

A cousin of mine from the Sudan told me about paving roads with molasses, as it was cheaper than asphalt, while at the same time people in the Sudan were starving. The large sugar plantations had thousands of acres of irrigated sugar cane for export but grew no food for the local populace.

We'd all gone through similar experiences; the big thing that came out of the conference was the need for self-sufficiency. You've got to become self-sufficient so you're not dependent on large corporations to buy your product, and to sell you the wherewithal to produce the product. For thousands of years the farmers in the Philippines had been self-sufficient; they survived without the United States.

Self-sufficiency is completely opposite to all the government solutions. In Toronto in October, 1983, the experts said the answer to the Third World debt problem is for them to export more and import less. The same for Europe, ditto for us. It's like calling for an above-average income for everyone.

Many people do not associate the lack of self-sufficiency with chemicals. I've been adverse to chemicals, and very supportive of regenerative farming. Chemicals allow the farmer to mine the soil very quickly. You put in the chemicals and get a large crop, but you deplete your soil. So you dump that large crop on the market in order to try and pay for the chemicals, creating a temporary surplus. All the nutrients in your soil are being immediately transformed into crops, you get wads of grain but the price goes to hell. It's like taking fuel out of a barrel with a little spigot, filling up a can. It gets a bit slow. So you grab a hammer and knock the spigot off. Of course the fuel flows all over you, and you fill up the can right away. But pretty soon you're knee-deep in oil and the tank is dry. That's what we're facing around the world. We're mining our soil at a tremendous rate. We're up to our knees in surplus but our soil

Delegates to the International Farm Crisis Meeting in Ottawa, July 1983. (left to right) Paul de Loire, France; Wolfgang Reimer, Germany; Bruno Buffaria, France; Jan Wone Errico, Italy; Allen Wilford, Canada; Tom Moller, Holland; Hilarid Padilla, Philippines; Merle Hansen, United States; Henk Hijink, Holland; Armand Chatellier, France; Arie Van dan Brand, Holland; and Neil Rogers, United States.

is being depleted and pretty soon there isn't going to be any there.

Organic, or regenerative, farming is in fact more efficient but, because with chemicals most of the labour is hidden in the cities and most of the true cost in soil depletion and environmental pollution are not visible (and ever-increasing amounts of chemicals are necessary to maintain production), it seems the opposite. Let's face it: the large corporations sell very little to an organic farmer, so they spend millions in our universities, promoting study of the wonders of chemicals. The so-called independent research has been defined by corruption and bribery. Can you imagine people putting money ahead of human lives and, indeed, the future of humankind? There is corruption in the Environmental Protection Agency in the States, with the deliberate removal of experts who did not tow the line. One bright point, research done at the University of Nebraska showed that organically grown corn could double the yield of chemical cropping at a fraction the cost.

I listened to an "expert" from the chemical industry speak on Dioxin. Dioxin, the poison in "Agent Orange," is an undesirable contaminate of a lot of our chemicals, notably 24D and 2-4-5T used for weed control. It is the most deadly poison known to humanity. He quoted, "Dioxin is destroyed by sunlight and is biodegradable." These are "facts" from Dow Paid Research, which are fifteen years old and contrary to all other evidence. In the Love Canal, Dioxin has lasted thirty years. It is sprayed on fields and ends up in our fish, yet both fields and water are exposed to sunlight. Running water with sunlight will kill bacteria, a living organism, but not chemicals. That chemical man said one part per billion is one grain of salt on ten thousand tons of potato chips. In reality, a strength of one part per trillion has been proven to cause cancer and birth defects. One person in five dies of cancer and soon it will be one in four. Wouldn't you sooner pay three cents more for a loaf of bread?

Another thing about the chemical industry in the Third World is the lack of education for the workers, causing death and destruction. It's going to be a long battle, and maybe someday, hopefully, potentially dangerous chemicals will be banned. Many communities have ground water supplies contaminated with agricultural chemicals. One third of the bottom feeders (suckers) from one of the Great Lakes have abnormal growths (cancer). Paraquat, or gremoxin, is an example of a chemical that can be used to stop soil erosion, a positive aspect. It kills and leaves the roughage, or dead material there, and you can plant through. But they don't know how to use it in the Third World — they're selling it in empty whiskey bottles. A major cause of death is drinking it by mistake. Paraquat penetrates your skin on contact, as all chemicals do. But Paraquat is deadly; if it enters your bloodstream through the skin you'll be dead in seven days. It destroys your lungs and your heart. Studies attribute 10,000 deaths a year to Paraquat. Pictures show people with a hand sprayer, in the Third World spraying fields, in their bare feet. There are no government regulations, and the sellers don't want to scare away their customers.

One of the most impressive books I read on the international scene was *The Merchants of Grain,* by Dan Morgan. It tells of the five immense and secretive companies controlled by seven families that control the world grain trade. Grain is at the root of all economic activity. As Socrates said, "No man should be a statesman who does not understand the problems of wheat." The grain trade is not based on free enterprise. It is most emphatically controlled — the price is set. Whole areas are blocked up by one organization.

If you begin to understand the magnitude of their control, you begin to realize that our current problems don't just happen, it's not coincidental cause and effect. These merchants use the grain just like a heroin pusher uses heroin. They dump cheap grain in the Third World countries, get them hooked on it, destroy their self-sufficiency, their traditional ways of growing tapioca, or some of the other root staples of their economies, such as potatoes. It has happened in the "developed" countries as well. In the Netherlands they tried to destroy a starch plant based on potatoes by introducing a starch plant based on cheap American corn. Even if they have to take initial losses, they get people hooked on white bread and hamburgers, hooked on grain. And then of course, they control the price.

This cheap grain policy, and the cheap raw materials they needed to enforce this control, are what caused our current problems. The grain companies had to stimulate production and keep prices down in the large grain-producing nations so that they could sell it cheap. They literally created the Third World. With the imperialism and the colonization they've been ripping off these countries for years. This was the final straw. You put in the cheap grain you destroy their farmers, the backbone of their industry. The farmers end up in the city on welfare, and the corporations get the land. Then the governments have to borrow the money from the international bankers to buy in the grain. Once they destroyed their own production they had to feed their people. The governments have to borrow the money from the banks because if they don't it would be open revolt. One bank representative argued that these governments *had* to pay when we criticized differences in policies on loans to the Third World in default, and loans to us in default. But the fact is they can't foreclose in these foreign countries, because they are terrified that the countries will just repudiate the debts and set off a world-wide economic collapse.

Why then were they foreclosing on our agriculture? Why didn't they give us the same breaks, the same deferrals of in-

Dennis McDermott, Allen Wilford, Merle Hansen (l to r). International farm crisis meeting, Ottawa, July 1983.

terest and principal that they give the countries that are in trouble? And he argued emphatically that those countries had to pay it back, or else we wouldn't sell them the food, the people would revolt and overthrow the government. So the government was in a position where they had to keep borrowing the money to feed their people. Either that or they would get shot. But sooner or later the countries will come to the position where they cannot squeeze any more — where they cannot pay it back, much like the farmers' position. It doesn't matter how much you need to or want to, you simply can't. And they couldn't conceive that.

The key points that came out of the international meeting, besides the push for self-sufficiency and the need for information exchange, were definite steps to recovery:

I. *Parity Prices* — All farm products will be priced at parity. For storable commodities, non-recourse loans at 90% of parity shall be available to producers.

II. *Supply Management* — Annual national production goals shall be determined, and marketing quotas shall be allocated to each producer based on the production history of each farm.

III. *Equity of Trade* — Import/Export laws shall be amended so as to assure freedom of trade based on a fair and equitable exchange between countries.

To explain equity of trade properly, think of putting chickens, pigs, and cattle all in the same pen. It doesn't work and could kill them all. Each is different with different diets and needs. The cost of production of any commodity varies from country to country but that cannot be the sole determining factor. Just because rice can be produced more cheaply in the Philippines does not mean that the U.S. should not grow rice, although that is the principal goal of world government thinkers. Each country has their own economy to think of, but some trade is desirable; some resources are plentiful in one country and completely lacking in others. Fair trade must ensue. The product should enter a country at that country's parity price and the necessary tariff money should be collected and not grabbed by governments for general revenues, but rather held in reserve, so that when exporting, the country can use it to purchase at parity prices, maintaining the balance or equity. Remember labour is the true source of wealth and whether we are talking wheat or television sets, it is the labour that we are trading. Present "free trade" moves production continually to low wage areas and therefore exploits labour.

Our international meeting of grassroots farmers was the first of its kind, and the contacts set up should have a lasting effect. If the funds can be raised, a similar meeting in the Third World will ensue.

Unity

21

You may burn down your cities but leave your farms and the cities will spring up again as if by magic. But destroy your farms and grass will grow in the streets of every city in the nation. — William Jennings Bryan

In October 1982 I ran for the presidency of the Canadian Farmers' Survival Association against Carl Spencer. We were divided in our philosophies. Carl saw organized labour as being to blame for high prices. Having been involved in the labour movement, and knowing the relationship of labour and prices, I knew it wasn't true. Only 13% of labour is organized. These were people who were simply trying to get a fair wage. And, as William Lyon Mackenzie said, ''The only true source of wealth is labour.''

The large corporate monopolies have been trying for years to get the farmer to consider himself a businessman. For if the farmer was in his own mind separated from labour, he would view organized labour as the enemy. In turn, organized labour would oppose the farmer as the ''rich businessman.''

But there is nothing to separate the farmer from labour, since they share the work ethic. Business ethics are a bit different. If you get away with robbing a bank you have a tremendous business profit. Society as a whole is no better or worse off — money has simply changed hands. Labour, however, changes raw material into something useful which moves through society, generating more economic activity.

My job then, was to get organized labour to realize that unemployment was directly related to low farm price, and to get the farmer to realize that if the city people don't have any money to spend, they can't buy our farm product. Farm labour and urban labour have a one-to-one relationship. United, we can control the government.

On Wednesday, November 17 Ted McCannel of the *Kitchener-Waterloo Record* covered the election. The following is excerpted from his article:

> When nearly 200 farmers met here Tuesday night for the first annual meeting, it was a stark contrast to the formative meeting one year ago. Most of those attending were still from Bruce and Grey, but they were there also from the counties of Perth, Huron, Wellington, York, Middlesex, and from Waterloo Region.
>
> Wilford can be credited for much of the association's expansion. He has travelled across the province and has toured several western states in the U.S. on the theme of helping farmers to ease their debt loads.
>
> When a farm is about to be taken over, he favors massing fellow farmers and their equipment at the farm gate and defying the banks.
>
> "The farm-gate stand is the only way," Wilford said. "A farmer on his own turf fights the best."

After I won the election one of the things I set out to do was to work to unify farmers with organized labour, and with the churches. We have tremendous support from the labour unions. I spoke at different labour functions, especially the unions for the unemployed. The Canadian Labour Congress, and President Dennis MacDermott, have been very supportive. When I was on the hunger strike there were many letters to Ottawa supporting the Farmers' Creditors Arrangement Act, standing in unity with us.

In the U.S. there is some very good labour involvement. The North American Farm Alliance, in particular, has made a real move to unite with labour. The United Auto Workers came to help block a farm sale, getting national coverage in the *New York Times*. They also came out and helped us at the Port Elgin demonstration.

All of society is in this thing together. A good example of this is Canada's fishing industry, whose problems parallel those of our farms.

From the international meeting in July, where I met Kirbey Nickerson and Philip Malone, I travelled to Nova Scotia to meet with the Pirates. This is a group of lobster fishermen who have been in the news for chasing two federal Department of Fisheries boats to harbour. They cut them loose, towed them out to sea and burned them. They sank one and rammed the other one which wouldn't sink. As a result they were charged with piracy and convicted of theft.

The first question that comes to mind is: Why would 200 honest hardworking fishermen chase government boats back to harbour and burn them? The underlying problems are that prices have remained the same or dropped, input costs have gone through the roof, and the fishermen need these quotas changed. They're facing a 350-trap quota, which was set 15 years ago and was supposed to have been reviewed regularly. It hasn't been reviewed at all. A lot of the fishermen have gone out of business. The ones who are left want to expand — they aren't asking for more traps, just a redistribution of existing quotas. These fellows had been requesting this in the usual way and had had a couple of demonstrations to bring attention to it. The government reacted by attacking.

The three ports that had started the protest were the ones hit by government inspectors. They went in with big boats, checking for lobster trap tags. They would pull up the trap and and if it didn't have a tag, bang it against the side of the boat. If it didn't smash immediately they would drop it back into the water in tangled piles. A single man in a rowboat was trying to sort out this mess. Lobster traps when wet weigh about a hundred pounds each.

As a result of the protest — and the fishermen were also complaining about not having enough tags — the government issued a new tag. It was just a plastic loop. A six-year-old could put his finger through it and break it off. The Fishery officials were pulling out these traps and anything without a tag — whether it had been lost or not — was being destroyed.

But the fishermen heard the Fishery guys over the CBs, talking about picking up a line of traps, some of which had tags and some didn't, saying seize them all. One fisherman had previously lost 140 traps, and these things are fairly expensive to make. So when the fishermen heard that, they went over to the Fishery boats and, sure enough, there were the traps with legal tags on them, seized. On the CBs, the fishermen started to tell everyone what was going on, and eventually about 65 boats gave chase. Some of these fellows didn't get into the fracas until the action was over — some of them put in five hours in order to get there. It was a community issue. They chased the Fishery officials to port, where they stood hurling abuse at the fishermen. The RCMP eventually asked the Fishery officials to leave the dock because they were causing trouble, inciting a riot. The fishermen cut the boats loose, towed them out and set fire to them.

In the week I was there, about eleven fish processors had closed down. Just prior to my arrival, processors were going broke in Newfoundland. They couldn't sell fish on the world market.

Spain and Portugal are probably the biggest buyers of Nova Scotian salt fish. While our dollar was being supported by high interest rates, it wasn't just being held up, it was being raised in relationship to the Portuguese currency, which was devaluated threefold in comparison to the Canadian dollar. So what was costing them a dollar before was now costing them $3.00 — they couldn't afford to buy the salt cod. Spain was right out of the picture.

The expansion of boat size, and the necessary substitution of credit for earned income, combined with the low price, were identical to problems on the farm front. The price problem is primary. So we're all in this thing together. When chickens in the United States are selling for 36 cents a pound on the supermarket shelf, our fishermen are not going to get a fair price for their fish, nor are we for our beef or pork. The government is cutting down fish quotas, trying to relieve some of this surplus. Yet all the canned seafood that I saw was imported.

I also made a move at this time to get the churches involved, because to me they certainly *should* be involved, as we are involved with human suffering and social problems. I was very disappointed, when the interest rates were at 18% and 20%, that the church wasn't taking a stand, as usury is contrary to the laws of Christ. I approached one of the church leaders, who said it had gotten to be socially acceptable. I thought, here comes murder and adultery. I was completely turned off.

Another member of our organization had gotten petitions signed in his church. He took it to the leaders, but they turned it down. One old fellow said he liked to collect big interest, and he thought it was okay. Another farmer, whose whole life had been wrapped around the church, was in financial difficulty and requested some church involvement. So the church gave out a questionnaire asking if they should get involved. Only about 15 people bothered to fill it out, with only three people wanting to do something. The man was devastated, in his hour of need they had turned their backs on him.

I like the line about the Christian being thrown to the lions: "Christianity never used to be a spectator sport."

I first got turned back to organized religion by the Rural America group in Iowa. I made some contacts with the Catholic and the United Church, and spoke to them about the human tragedies I had witnessed. There was very good support from the local clergy. Walter King is a controversial minister, and a good man. He was criticized by some of the elders in his church for getting involved with the "radical" Survival Association. Walter was a very deep person, having done personal counselling with people who had attempted suicide. If anyone phoned him with emotional problems he just dropped everything and came. He could see the tie between the financial and the emotional problems people were having. Phyllis Barnes of the United Church has also been very supportive. Father Mooney of the Catholic Rural Life in Ontario has done some very important work for our rural communities.

A lot of the people involved in the higher echelons of the church were very aware of Third World problems, as created by the large corporations and the use of cheap grain as an economic lever.

The churches *have* supported the Farmers' Creditors Arrangement Act, although I had hoped they would take on some of the financial and emotional counselling. They should provide more education about suicide prevention. It's important that the minister or priest be qualified to deal with the emotional problems which stem from the financial. There are danger signs to look for, one of which is an increase in a life insurance policy. I got a call from someone at an insurance company, who was concerned because I was mentioning farm suicides. He said he'd seen tremendous increases in life insurance policies, but farmers would refuse to let the company see their books. Other danger signs are: paying off small bills, cleaning up the farm yard, getting the house in order. Then comes the fatal car accident. The Survival Association doesn't have the financial or human resources to deal with this.

Even the old order Mennonites are losing their farms. These people certainly haven't overspent — they're still on horse and buggy power, with no hydro. Inflation has separated the generations. A father or uncle, as the traditional source of money, might have sold his farm to a family member for $10,000. But now he cannot help the son who buys a farm which costs $50,000. He has to finance it through F.C.C., or the banks. Although their inputs are reduced by their self-sufficiency, they must still buy kerosene, nails, etc. But they don't produce the volume of goods to cover even these modest purchases, not to mention large mortgage payments. One man with nine children had only one steer for his year's supply of beef, and he had to sell half of that. One woman couldn't eat the berries out of her own garden, as they had to be sold.

There are now divisions within the church, because the elders don't understand the modern financial problems, thinking the younger generation should have known better.

Old order Mennonites are not allowed to declare bankruptcy to clear these debts, nor collect welfare. With no marketable skills, they can't leave their communities.

I do not want to be critical of the Mennonite church as a whole, because I am impressed with their philosophy. And, they have good people involved in the farmer's movement. At John Otto's penny auction, his Mennonite neighbours held some of his equipment. Some church members were horrified at this, but the minister said, "You profess to love and want to help your fellow man, and that is what these people are doing."

The U.S. farmers have been making strong moves towards the peace movement, something which Canadian farmers must tap into. We all realize that world peace is paramount, as in this nuclear age we have no alternative. The message to the peace groups, put out by the World Council of Churches in Vancouver reads, "We cannot have peace without social justice and we cannot have social justice without economic justice." My message to the peace movement is that there is no hope of economic justice unless you start at the roots, and get a fair price for agricultural product.

The Penny Auction   22

*Those who profess to favor freedom and yet deprecate agita-
tion; are men who want crops without plowing up the
ground.*

*They want rain without thunder and lightning. They
want the ocean without the awful roar of the waters.*

*This struggle may be a moral one; or it may be both moral
and physical, but it must be a struggle.*

*Power concedes nothing without demand. It never did and
it never will.*

*Find out just what people will submit to, and you have
found out the exact amount of injustice and wrong which will
be imposed upon them; and these will continue until they
are resisted with either words or blows, or with both.*

*The limits of tyrants are prescribed by the endurance of
those whom they oppress.* — From *The Limits of Tyrants*
by Frederick Douglass, (1857)

The Farmer's Holiday Movement in the U.S. in the 1930s
pioneered the penny auction. I had been made aware of them
through talks with the American farmers. A famous one had
taken place at the Avery farm, near Petersburg,
Nebraska. Farmers marched to the farm 3,000 strong and
presented their demands. The sale was held at bargain prices
— cows bringing in 25 cents, three pieces of machinery selling
for a nickel each. The farmers had found the banker guilty of
trying to take advantage of the orphan sons of old man
Avery. So the banker was forced to be satisfied with $7.10 for
his note.

Four thousand farmers coming down into town at Plot Centre induced a banker to accept $1.98 for his $400 note; the
banker was about to take an old couple by the name of William-
son from their life-long home.

The action I particularly remembered hearing told was one where they told the banker that if he cooperated, he would get reimbursed for his advertising and auctioneering costs, and if he didn't he wouldn't get anything. So of course he cooperated. They had to sell the last piece of equipment for something like $7.00, which was more than it was worth, in order to get enough to cover those costs. In order to control the bids they sometimes took men to the barn and removed their clothes, or they put a bucket over their heads and everyone would hit them with a stick.

I had helped to organize in the U.S. Midwest in August 1982. There had been about seven penny auctions in the U.S. altogether. The frustrating thing was that the auctioneer would stop the sale, so it would not go through to a true penny auction where the equipment was sold for pennies. People kept the bidding down, or intimidated the auctioneer to the point where he called off the sale. We were helping the individual farmer, but we weren't getting enough press coverage out of it to get the idea around.

Then came the John Otto case. It was the T-D Bank, and they were a special target for me. In two other cases they had refused to negotiate in good faith. The frustrating thing about this case is that we're still waiting for the Farmers' Creditors Arrangement Act to come through. John had a very good case. John Otto has a 150-head beef operation on a 200-acre farm near Palmerston, 50 kilometres northwest of Kitchener, Ontario. He had originally borrowed $200,000 and interest rates had ballooned it up to $450,000. The T-D Bank had literally shafted him. They had set him up on a small business bond, knowing full well that he couldn't pay the principal. This came out in the subsequent court case. He knew, and I knew, that he could make the interest payments but not the first two principal payments. The T-D Bank had been willing to give him the bond, conditional on getting his parents' guarantee, getting another mortgage on the farm, and so on.

Three months later when the first principal payment of $30,000 came due, he was faced with selling off a big chunk of his breeding herd — which he was trying to make the money with — so of course the thing couldn't work. He balked, saying "this is a five-year deal, I can't make the principal payments for two years — you knew that when we set the thing up, and if you leave us alone we can pay the interest, and we will make it through.'' John's farm, equipment and cattle were worth more than his debts — but not if the bank simply moved to get the farm at auction.

The bank moved, however — they called in the receivers, Coopers Lybrand, in January 1983, when John refused to give them $200,000 more security. The receivers hadn't been properly appointed and the banks had not crystallized their security, and that's how I got into it, and why the first penny auction in Canada since the 1930s took place at John Otto's farm. John had never signed over the authority to the receivers and he complained repeatedly about the receivers to the T-D bank. He'd never authorized the auction — the bank just came in and did what it liked.

A lot of people who witnessed what happened — and even some of our own group who didn't realize what was involved — thought it was pretty easy. But it took a lot of background work, a lot of research to make sure that we were on good legal grounds.

We went in with 500 farmers. An amusing point is that the bank's auctioneer, Murry Gerber, was *very* angry, because when he saw the huge crowd arriving, dollar signs rolled in front of his eyes. A large crowd at a farm sale usually means that the bidding will be brisk. He didn't realize that 500 of the 550 people there were Farm Survivalists bent on saving the farm.

Just prior to the sale, Tom Shoebottom, our vice-president — and I should say auctioneer extraordinaire — went to the receivers. Trying to find out whether there were any loans against the equipment, he asked about a particular tractor, saying that if he bought it, were there any encumbrances going with it. The receiver said no and showed him a piece of paper. Tom took the piece of paper and put it in his pocket, proof positive that the equipment was free and clear of all encumbrances; there were no reserve bids from the bank. When the bank's auctioneer started the sale, he read off that there were no encumbrances, no reserve bids.

Then I literally took over. I had a hollow stomach for a few moments when I got there because I was leading the press contingent, and we had hoped Tom would have already taken over the sale by then. The lawnmower or something had been sold. Gerber was rather stubborn and reluctant to give up these

The penny auction. Hundreds of members of the Canadian Farmers' Survival Association gathered at a farm southwest of Palmerston, Ontario, Wednesday afternoon, to disrupt a bankruptcy auction of local farmer John Otto's assets. The official auctioneers were shouted down and replaced by Thomas Shoebottom of Lukan, Ontario, a vice-president of the Farmers' Association, who then sold $100,000 worth of equipment for $19.81.

big dollars he could see rolling. However when I got up on the wagon and told him he was out of business he didn't kick up much of a fuss. He turned to the receiver and said "What do we do now?" I announced that this was a service offered by the Survival Association to try and save John Otto some money — namely the auctioneer's fee — and to save the Toronto-Dominion Bank some money too. We would donate, free of charge, an auctioneer. Tom took over and the auction was on.

Unfortunately, since the auctioneer *was* free, and we were new at this game, the equipment didn't command too much. Some of the tractors went I think as high as a $1.50. A pick-up truck got carried away at $5.00. The cattle sold at something like six cents for 170 Herefords; the barnful of hay at seven or eight cents. Later the fellow who bought the hay complained because the cattle were eating up all his hay. When the police questioned one farmer's wife about a purchase he had made (17 cents) she hit the roof. "I told that son-of-a-bitch not to buy another piece of equipment." The poor police didn't realize her sense of humour and quickly left. One farmer started with a bid of fifty cents. It was hard to keep them restrained but Tom told him quite firmly that with the price of grain and livestock he simply could not afford that much, and then accepted a bid for two cents. The gross receipts were $19.81, they were put in a bag and offered to the receivers. (This was a good omen, as the Survival Association started in 1981.) The receivers refused it. John later took it down to the bank. In the later court proceedings, the banker swore up and down that he never even counted the money — he just took it and put it in the vault and refused to accept it. I don't know how he knew that there *wasn't* $400,000 and some there, and the debt was paid in full. There were about 20 reporters there and they had a heck of a good time.

Despite our tight security, the bank had been tipped off. The receiver phoned from John Otto's house just prior to our arrival and told somebody at the other end that everything was okay, going smoothly with no sign of any trouble. When we took over he came running back in to use the phone again, but unfortunately it didn't seem to be working properly. We have television footage of them running across a ten-acre field through the snow trying to hail a provincial police car that happened to be passing.

Sergeant Roy Anderson of the Listowel OPP came back after the sale, saying something to the effect that it was illegal. I questioned his ability to judge, asking him if he was a civil magistrate or lawyer, or what basis he was going on. He said, "We'd better discuss this in the car." John Otto and I got into the car and we talked to the officer for about twenty minutes. When we got out one of the press people asked, "What did he say?" I replied, "I think he wants the equipment to stay here." She said "It's a bit late." I looked up and the last piece of equipment was just going over the horizon. The neighbours and friends, including a person unknown in a black hood, had taken the equipment and it was gone.

The next day there was a blockade of the driveway. About 25 of us dumped a couple of truckloads of gravel in the laneway — John's lane needed gravelling anyway — to stop the seizure of the cattle. The bank came very quickly to the bargaining table. They were very adamant that the Survival Association not be involved. It didn't matter to me whether or not we were involved, as long as the negotiations were fair. I had a lot of

Kitchener, February 9, 1983.   Tom Shoebottom, auctioneer, sells John Otto's cultivator for 12 cents.

faith in John's knowledge and ability.   He picked some friends and neighbours.

They finally did hammer out a deal, the banks wrote off $300,000 because they were wrong, and John is still in business with his cattle and the equipment we saved.   Within a week of the sale the equipment was returned to John.   The whole idea of the sale was to tie the thing up in litigation.   The bank could either negotiate in good faith or they would have to go through the civil courts to decide who really did and didn't own the equipment.   By that time, we hoped the Farmers' Creditors Arrangement Act would have gone through.

The bank and the legal apparatus didn't let it go at that, however.   I was rather shocked at their stupidity.   When I watched the Susan Nelles case and realized that the Crown Attorney and Solicitor-General cannot be held liable for the costs of malicious prosecution, I began to see why they do these stupid actions.   They're not accountable to anyone.

They decided to charge myself, Tom Shoebottom, and Joe Fischer with theft over $200.   We hadn't bought anything.   We had not taken possession of any of the equipment and at that point all the equipment was, as far as I knew, back at John Otto's.   At the time, the arrests appeared to be strictly an intimidation tactic, to put pressure on John during negotiations with the bank.   Moreover, it is extortion to use criminal law to collect civil debt.

Tractor sells for 97 cents. (At these prices farming starts to make "cents.")

In my opinion, in order to attempt to intimidate us further, the Crown Attorney had asked for our physical arrest. According to Canadian police practice, they could have quite easily summoned us to court. I'd been charged in the Eugene Forbes incident at Walkerton with obstructing the police and verbal threatening and the police had simply handed me a summons. I was infuriated because we had run through the same thing with Marvin Black. They had physically arrested him in Saskatchewan at the feedlot, not even allowing him to tell his wife. But because of the Black incident I was forewarned. I had searched through the Constitution and knew that my arrest was unnecessary and quite clearly violated my civil liberties under The Bill of Rights and Freedoms.

Al Droppo, director of commercial lending for the Bankers' Association, denounced the auction as "self-defeating" and threatened that the banks would stop lending money to farmers! I must say, however, that the banks are still in the farm loan business, but they haven't given me another chance at running a penny auction!

The Hunger Strike   23

*If you want anything from government put their back to the
wall, put your hand to their throat and they will give you
all they have.* — Agnes McPhail, first Canadian
woman MP,1930s

I did a bit of thinking in the police car on the way to Walkerton
to be fingerprinted and photographed. I had two charges
against me already — verbal threatening and obstructing police
— and now a theft charge. I wasn't too worried about these
initial ones. But if every time I turned around I got charged
I could very easily spend the rest of my life fighting court cases
and trying to pay lawyers' bills. Sooner or later, if they did
get a conviction, I would then have a record. If they got two
or three convictions in a row I would likely go to jail.

It had to be nipped in the bud. If you've ever picked up a
hot frying pan and got halfway across the floor before realizing
it, when it's too hot to hang onto and you can't drop it because
you'd spill grease all over — you just don't know what to do
with it . . . . Well that's the position I wanted to put the government in. They had me, now what were they going to do?

I refused to sign a release, which consisted of a promise that
I would appear in court on such and such a date: no bond,
no restrictions. It was just further proof to me that they didn't
need to arrest me, that they could have just summoned me, since
they were going to let me out on my own recognizance anyway.
I said, "What if I don't sign?" They said they'd have to put
me in jail, and I said, "Well, do your worst."

I sat for two hours in the holding cell in Listowel. They arranged an appearance before a judge in court in Stratford. They
read the charge and the judge explained that there was no pro-

perty bail, that there were no conditions and all I had to do was sign the piece of paper. Again I refused. I was put in a holding cell in the Stratford court for probably an hour-and-a-half. Then they took me to the Stratford Jail.

I remember the police officer saying to the jailer as we went in, "This man can go as soon as he signs this release. There's absolutely no reason to hold him, if he just signs his name here he can go home." The jailer said, "Well, we can make him sign it. We'll make him want to sign it." Ten minutes later the same jailer came back and said, "Are you some kind of celebrity? That whole yard out there is covered with television cameras." I had phoned my wife and told her my intentions.

To end the need for further auctions and farm gate defenses we had to have the Farmers' Creditors Act reinstated. So, in the car ride I decided to do a hunger strike to focus attention on the problem and force movement on the bill by the House of Commons. I stated that I didn't intend to eat until the Farmers' Creditors Arrangement Act was brought through second reading.

We had got it through first reading as Ralph Ferguson's private member's bill almost a year ago. The government kept hemming and hawing. Of course, they were going to bring it through. Andre Ouillet was going to attach it to the bankruptcy revisions of Bill C12. They were always going to bring it forward, but it never happened. Both the Conservatives and the NDP said they were supporting it, and it was a Liberal bill! Why couldn't it be done? There wasn't House time. Well there was House time.

Looking back, Andre Ouillet was simply using us to try and get his bill, C12, through. It was a good bill which restricted the action of receivers and made them accountable. It also gave business with over $1 million in debt access to a court settlement. In the discussions, I urged that farmers and fishermen be included. I certainly agree we need the bankruptcy revisions to address the tremendous evils of receivership. This government bill has been sitting for two years and could have been introduced and passed if the Liberal Party wanted it. Members of the Conservative Party and the New Democratic Party were opposed to some aspects of C12. Because Saskatchewan had had the NDP moratorium, and land prices had not collapsed, there was western resistance to debt reduction. The truth was that the banks really controlled both the Liberals and the Conservatives. I asked the NDP about bank lobbies and they laughed. The banks don't even talk to them. Remember that, the next time you vote!

The thing went round and round and, to top it off, the week before I was arrested I had run into two suicides. One was a local 36-year-old man, and one was a young farmer a little further away, whose father had helped set him up in farming. He couldn't make the interest payments because of the commodity prices. Here were human beings losing their lives, families being destroyed with breakups. It was a very serious bloody mess, and this government was dragging its heels.

So I said, "All right, if you don't realize how serious this thing is, I won't eat until we put that thing through."

The time in jail was very interesting and very educational. I think maybe everyone should spend a week in jail just to see the other side of this world.

My daytime cell was a 10 by 30 foot room; a room about 4 by 8 feet, with two bunks, was my nighttime cell. One is locked in this small cell from 10:30 at night 'til six in the morning, when the radio blares on and wakes you up. When you come out of this cell you're locked out. You're allowed to take with you books for reading and one towel. There aren't any pillows or blankets. The rest of the day you sit confined in this communal 10 by 30 foot cell with a picnic table bolted to the floor, and radio that's on 'til 12:30 p.m. — just past the start of the TV news, which was very frustrating. The television comes on at 12:30 p.m. and stays on 'til 10:30 at night.

The comfort was minimal: we had nothing to lie on except the floor. There was nothing to cushion yourself except a towel. Two or three other prisoners would put three towels down as a mattress and take turns sleeping on it. I took my running shoes off to use as a pillow for my head. The floors were cold. It was very uncomfortable for an older prisoner there.

In order to open windows, you had to get the guards in pairs — one standing at the door and the other taking the screen off to open the window. So the windows were either opened or closed; it was either hot or cold. They would open other windows, and the breezes would blow through whether or not our windows were open.

The mattresses we slept on at night were about an inch-and-a-half thick, on steel beds with no springs. It's just like sleeping on a piece of rock. By the end of the week I was starting to get used to the mattress, but it would be a long time before you could enjoy a good night's sleep.

A new person in the room feels unwanted as no one wants to share a cell. Nothing to do with privacy, just that if you are alone you can use both mattresses. So the cry goes out, "Not in my cell." A newcomer feels like he has leprosy!

The prisoners were very supportive. They were all rebels, fighting the system. I met very interesting people in jail. Some were bored with life, others were frustrated. One young chap said that the first three months on unemployment weren't too bad, then it started to get to him — he wrote bum cheques for $18 or $20 at the local grocery store. He had a wife and a child. The pressures of unemployment, the humiliation of shortage of cash, the sense of failure, were too much for him. I would say that three of the six in the cell were there directly because of unemployment.

Also, a great many of the problems there were alcohol-related, made worse by the financial depression. One fellow had gotten drunk and broken into some cars. He decided he wanted to go for a joyride. Most of them in my cell had above-average intelligence. They were very clean, orderly, and generally considerate of each other. If there was a cigarette butt thrown on the floor everybody squawked until it was picked up. There were a lot of emotional outbursts — you can't cage people together without frustrations or strong feelings coming out. Probably the fact that I was there was a highlight of their stay. It gave them something to take their minds off their own troubles.

One fellow, Larry, was very supportive. About the third day, when my stomach pain was getting to me, he walked around with me and said he'd get me through if he had to carry me.

Larry was also the brains behind getting the signs out when the church service was going on outside. On the pretense of cleaning the cell, on Sunday morning, he picked up some brooms, mops, paper towels for windows, and a handful of toothpaste tubes. To clean the windows the guards removed the metal protection from the windows and we got the glass out before the crowd arrived. Then, after writing messages on the paper towels, my cellmates worked them outside the bars and glued them in place with the toothpaste. They toothpasted one sign on the top of a Monopoly game box, tied it to a broom handle with shoelaces, and stuck it straight out. Such genius is obviously going to waste in our jails. Of course, when Toronto saw the signs on TV, the jail keepers — "the keys" — caught hell.

I drank considerable amounts of water trying to kill the pain of hunger. When I first went in the other prisoners asked how long I was in for, and I said until I signed the release. They asked why I wouldn't sign the release and I told them I would go on a hunger strike until I got proper legislation from Parliament. One young boy — Red, we called him — said, "You're going to die!" One of the other fellows said, "I get his dessert." In an instant, my meals for the next three weeks were spoken for. Everyone had their pick; one fellow wanted the coffee, another fellow wanted the first course, and so on. I got to be very popular because they always seemed to be hungry; there wasn't anything else to do but eat.

On the second day the keys realized I wasn't eating, although the initial reports were that the trays were coming back empty. So now I had to send the trays back full, just to make sure the point got through. There wasn't any question about whether I wanted to eat; if I had the other inmates would have shared their food with me. But that wouldn't have accomplished anything.

I felt I wouldn't have the power to get any action in Ottawa until I landed up in the hospital, so I wanted to lose as much weight as quickly as possible, bring this thing to a head and get it over with. Initially I lost about seven pounds: then I started to gain back about half a pound a day, as I was retaining fluids. I was drinking tremendous amounts of water. One woman, who didn't give her name, brought a gallon of pure water because she didn't think I should be drinking the contaminated water of the city. I wished it could have gotten through (the jail guards wouldn't allow it); I detest city water — I can't stand the fluoride and chlorine in it. But at that point I had no choice.

I almost felt sorry for the superintendent. The whole world was watching his jail. Literally all I had to do was come out and criticize it and he would be in trouble. He didn't like the publicity. He brought me into his office twice a day to make sure everything was alright and going well.

The nurse checked me regularly. One of our people in Ottawa asked a government official if they knew what was going on in Stratford and he replied, "His blood pressure is such and such, his pulse is . . . . " I was getting through.

A couple of guards were kind of angry. One said he knew all about it; his brother-in-law was a farmer and I suppose in his eyes was doing quite well. Most of them, however, were working-class people and understood the problems of the interest rates, and the problems of the farmer.

I received numerous telegrams of support, quite a stack of letters from all across Canada. I discovered two cousins: one I hadn't heard from for years and the other I didn't even know I had. Some people sent money. People came to visit me. The federal Minister of Agriculture Eugene Whelan phoned me; I had numerous phone calls from MPs, and tremendous support from the Labour Union Movement.

I sat in jail for eight days with no food. On the eighth day I was brought into court. I felt quite strongly that the bill would pass through the house that day. I was torn between going back to jail, knowing the implications, driving back there, getting a change of clothes — it was about a four-hour process to get in and out of jail. So I signed my release at the court hearing, and continued my fast until about three or four o'clock that afternoon, when the news reached me that the bill had passed second reading.

Coming off the fast I was told to start very slowly with consomme. A problem arose when the press arrived, because they all wanted a picture of me eating my first bowl of soup. So for the press I started three different bowls. Trouble was I couldn't stop until each was finished. Almost made myself sick!

So the hunger strike was very successful; I think we accomplished a few things. Afterwards there were meetings at the banks who said that any branch which gave an opening for a penny auction would see heads roll. We actually lined up a couple after that, but the banks — whether they got wind of it or decided to settle — didn't try too much intimidation. They realized I guess that every time they swung at us, they would give us another soapbox to stand on. They did back off.

During my time in the Stratford Jail, the rest of the organization rallied support in a large Sunday church service, outside the jail. Then they went to Ottawa to lobby. We've had a lot

My first bowl of soup, after the 8-day hunger strike. It wasn't steak but it sure tasted good.

of compliments on the way our lobbies are organized and conducted. Of course this is helpful to the people involved, to see an organization that has things together.

Special mention must be made here of my wife Wendy. She has been very supportive throughout our married life, particularly in the Survival Association. She was doing a lot of the work — answering calls, using our home as an office, that sort of thing.

During the hunger strike lobbying Wendy brought home to the politicians, and to the nation as a whole through the press and especially television, the human element of the suffering that is going on. This was one message that she could get through, while the others couldn't. Wendy usually helps as a quiet, behind-the-scenes person. When I'm speaking to an audience she'll sit at the back, making notes of what I have missed, and noting down comments she hears in the audience, and recommending as to what we should cover at the next speech or meeting. Unfortunately, she sometimes gets too involved with the emotional stress on the people, too deeply involved with the problems of others. She doesn't like publicity, but with the hunger strike she took on a good chunk of it. She was on Canada AM, and the National News, that sort of thing.

Women have had a great influence on farm movements through history, and I see it quite often in my work. Most initially follow the traditional arrangements whereby the man will be carrying the burden of worry to the point where he can't anymore. Women of course realize the problems, and some are involved in farm management. When the man starts to break, the women will take on the battle. Their energy is inspiring. I was told a long time ago that if you want to get any work done, a woman is the best one for the job. I generally find this to be true. Men have the ambition and demand recognition, but women do the work.

Back in the 1880s one of the major farm leaders in the populist movement in the U.S. was Mary E. Lease. She was the one that came up with the "Raise less corn, raise more hell" slogan.

Agnes McPhail in the 1930s was the first Canadian woman MP. She was a fighter, and a very strong leader. Agnes was from Grey County. We have a history of rebels from this area: one of the leaders of the suffragette movement, Nellie McClung, is well known; Walter Miller, former head of the

Concerned Farm Women stage a demonstration in Port Elgin, fall 1981. Farm problems are family issues.

National Farmers Union, lived three miles away from me. Eddie Sargent, our MPP, is the most ejected member of our provincial legislature. People sometimes blame the water in our area for the number of its rebels.

Five of the ten farmers arrested at John Hill's farm gate defense were women. Other outstanding women in our own organization are Jean Lipton, who started organizing on her own in eastern Ontario; Sharon Rounds out of Oxford County, is a tremendously intelligent person, a good negotiator and also a good fighter. Shirley Conlif, who attended the Ottawa hearings for the Farmers' Creditors Arrangement Act, is a good resource person who sent out letters to all the townships and counties, asking for support for the Act. These things take a lot of imagination.

The "Concerned Farm Women" started up in our area out of concern for the pressures on farm families. They acted as an outlet, doing valuable research and providing companionship and counselling. Giselle Ireland, of Teeswater, has had a tremendous influence on the farm movement. Both she and her husband Brian have been very vocal. She is the author of *The Farmer takes a Wife*.

Eugene Whelan making false promises to Concerned Farm Women in Port Elgin, Ontario. "If I do not solve your problems, I will not remain your Minister of Agriculture."

"Women for the Survival of Agriculture," is headed up by Diane Harkens. Diane is a tremendous, energetic person. She is a wonderful speaker, very into the farm problems and solutions, who has a dramatic impact.

Carol Hodne, from the U.S. Farmers Association, has been the backbone of the coordination of the North American Farm Alliance.

The backbone of the farm has always been the farmer's wife. She is the one who fills in for the hired man, looks after the house, does the cooking and gardening, raises the children, constantly runs to town for parts, drives the tractor when it's necessary, and of course receives hell when things don't go right.

The increase in financial pressures on the farm resulted in an increase in the work load for the wives. The danger of having people (men, women and children) driving equipment which they are not used to, or capable of handling in an emergency takes a terrible toll. But saddest is the children who at a tender age are not just doing regular farm tasks, but jobs way beyond their years: a six-year-old was trampled while herding cattle; recently a three-year-old, who was with his father because there was no money for a hired hand or a babysitter, smothered while both parents worked. Of course there are no daycare centres in rural Canada.

Initially the pressures exerted by the very existence of the Farmers' Creditors Arrangement Act subcommittee were tremendous for us. We had settlements all over the place. They would ask for case histories of problems, and every time I turned around these people were getting settlements. So it had a very good impact. A lawyer phoned me and said you'll never know how much good it did in changing the banks' attitudes, with the tension brought on by the realization that the whole world is watching.

I tried to make this government bill known, so that farmers across Canada who hadn't been in touch with us would realize that there is some hope. Despite all the hubbub of the penny auction and the hunger strike, two days after I got out of jail and was in Manitoba, I found that a man with three children had shot himself the night before. I don't know how you reach these people, because when they get that desperate I guess they don't read the newspapers, they don't watch television. All we can do is try.

Raid

24

*The society of money and exploitation has never been charged
so far as I know with assuring the triumph of freedom and
justice* — Albert Camus

At 7:30 on December 17, 1983, while I was in Toronto getting
ready for a meeting with people from the Provincial Treasury
Department, a knock came at our door at home and my fifteen-
year-old daughter Tracy answered it. Three policemen in
trench coats forced their way in and started shouting and ordering my family around. My wife Wendy shouted down that they
should wait in the entrance until she got dressed. They hollered
back that they had a search warrant and could do what they
liked. They sent the search warrant up with my daughter and
proceeded to go through our house. My wife came down and
phoned our two lawyers. The police went through our whole
house until my wife objected that she wanted to be present as
they did their search — to make sure they didn't pick up
valuables, or worse, plant something.

The police did not let my wife examine the search warrant,
which they are supposed to do, but rather gave her a copy. They
had the lawful authority to search and seize financial records
pertaining to cattle, hay and barley, (plus a copy of my
signature). Now my financial records were in a drawer in the
desk but they only glanced through the papers there and took
a few copies of my signature and then proceeded to search
through our kitchen cupboards, refrigerator and under the carpet
— typical places that one would look for financial records. They
even stepped over boxes in the basement clearly marked "income tax files" to look in the deep freeze. These officers were
from the anti-racket squad in Toronto and I suspect were more

used to doing drug searches. But this does not excuse their methods.

To seize the records from a normal business does not include a search of the owner's home. Much to her surprise, Wendy quickly found out through our phone network that five houses in the Grey Bruce area were suffering similar raids. I feel these were done deliberately when the men were not there. I was in Toronto to meet with the government; George Bothwell was in Toronto for a Co-op meeting; Al McKinnon was caught before leaving for the day so his wife was saved from the ordeal by the fact that he would not let them in until his wife and children had left for school. When they did search they dumped all the drawers on the floor and left the place looking as if a cyclone had hit.

At George Bothwell's home, his wife Azelda was upstairs with their four small children when the phone rang, saying the police were at the door. She had not heard the knock. Before she could get the baby's diaper changed it rang again and she said "Just a moment until I get dressed." They broke in the door and searched for five-and-a-half hours. They also searched George's parents' house because the dummies did not realize that George's wife and mother had the same first name. And even though there was nothing on the search warrant permitting them to seize the elder Bothwell's books, these too were taken. Al McKinnon's sister was likewise terrified.

Now the interesting facts started to come to light. We knew that George and Al had been raided by the RCMP about a year and a half before, and investigated for ten months with the constant fear of a knock on the door which might be an arrest. Their books however, revealed no wrongdoings. They were returned and the RCMP said, "This is just a civil action between you and the Bank of Montreal." I feel they were influenced by the Bill Wolfe hearings.

When I questioned the OPP on the matter, they pleaded that they did not know the outcome of the RCMP investigation. Al McKinnon had pointed to the boxes of records the RCMP had returned and said, "The government already has a lot of money invested there — help yourself." But they still ransacked the house.

There had been no business dealings between myself and George and Al. I dealt at the Royal Bank and the others, at the Bank of Montreal. The only common denominator was the

Survival Association. The full intent was to terrorize and intimidate. We remembered the Bill Wolfe case where it was done to create the proper political and local climate and to facilitate a cooperative attitude from the farmer. The banks try to turn the local populace against people who fight back by instigating the criminal investigation. In Canadian law this is called extortion. The banks hoped that we would be embarrassed and not tell anyone so that they could carefully leak it to the press and discredit us — well, they pushed on the wrong people.

Immediately after I got the call from Wendy I located George in Toronto and we went to the Ontario Legislature. Eddie Sargent nearly got ejected for accusing the Attorney-General of extortion. Eddie was angry at the police acting as a collection agency for the banks, and at the continual harassment the Survival Association was receiving.

In 1981 10 OPP officers came to Bruce County from North Bay to investigate the Survival Association. When the provincial Minister of Agriculture spoke to farmers at the annual Grey-Bruce Farm Week 1984, the police had at least 17 undercover police in the audience, and took video films of the farmers. "Big Brother" is watching.

I then started to dig into what had prompted the raids and since the search warrant had been issued by a J.P. — that's right, not a judge — I started there. I found that our J.P. is supposed to protect us from the police and is not only underpaid but is paid piece work for this sort of thing. In other words, they are paid ten dollars, or whatever, to examine the information. Now, they get paid this whether or not they sign the warrant. But the fact is if they don't sign, the police don't go back to that J.P. and he goes hungry. It is common knowledge that the police will drive many miles to a local J.P. who signs everything without reading it, whereas others, who are conscientious, are avoided. A very corrupt system, but as you delve into our legal system it gets worse.

On attempting to get a copy of the information on which the police had obtained the search warrant, I found that it was unavailable until the police had returned the objects and had made a report. There was no time limit on this. Also, they could make a return, not to the J.P. who signed the warrant in Owen Sound, but rather to any J.P. in Ontario. This is in fact what they did — to the J.P. in Toronto, 130 miles from Owen Sound.

It took a week for the returned objects to get to Owen Sound, when I could finally get a look at the information. *Look,* mind you; no copies could be made, unless I wrote it out in longhand. This document contained no less than a dozen papers. So in order to get a copy to my lawyer I had to copy it in longhand — talk about obstructing justice! It was further complicated by the Christmas holidays — banks always do their dirty work days before Christmas. In John Otto's case, the bailiff attempted to seize all his livestock and equipment four days before Christmas. A Walkerton farmer got a letter two days before Christmas, saying that the Royal Bank was coming to pick up his livestock, equipment, and furniture. In New Lissgard the Bank of Nova Scotia seized a family's machinery and livestock, including the children's horses, just days before Christmas. I know that this is deliberate policy. If they can break your spirit, it's easier for them to foreclose.

The reason for the raid on my house started about the same time as the Survival Association. It was a result of the education provided by the Association, and questionable bank practice. I had been deliberately lied to by the bank in order to get more security. Also, the guarantee the bank presented against Wendy's half of the property was signed by a lawyer whom neither of us had ever met.

I, as did many Survivalists, maintained my farms, my equipment, and my livestock, while the banks kept their papers. A fair deal, I felt, for they seemed to get adverse pleasure out of pieces of paper, while I enjoyed my farms. Of course, they wanted my farm as well, and contested the ownership of my assets. While I, in turn, contested their papers. An obvious case for the civil courts, one would think.

But the banks are not comfortable in the civil courts, with just reason. Every time, in other cases, we got to litigation their lawyers wanted to settle out of court. Realizing that a negotiated settlement should be the proper outcome, I proceeded with the settlement I proposed. The bank refused to settle with me, although we managed numerous settlements with the Royal Bank under identical circumstances and they have acknowledged losses of millions of dollars. I was determined that if we couldn't get a reasonable settlement, we would expose the banks through the court system. These proposals were always one-way: me to them; seldom the other way around. Our last proposal for a reasonable settlement was recommended not only by the local bank lawyer, but by the big city lawyers as well. But because of my position, the case went to Roland Frazee, President of the Royal Bank. Not only did he turn it down, but it certainly looks like, in collusion with the Bank of Montreal president, he decided to attack using the criminal process. Again, this is usually called extortion.

This not only saved the bank lawyer's fees in civil court, but is designed to cost the farmer tremendous legal fees for his defense. Again, bank policy is to bankrupt in order to conquer.

It is perhaps worth mentioning here that when they move to enforce their authority their actions are no different than those of a Mafia loan shark — if the enforcer breaks both of your arms you cannot possibly pay. But everyone else in town gets the message. So it is with the banks. At first I couldn't understand why they would not limit their losses with a settlement but it became quite clear by the way the receivers destroy, that their real purpose is to impose terror. As Al McKinnon said, "When I was a kid the Mafia wore pin striped suits, charged 25% interest and carried a violin case. Now they have traded the violin case for a banker's desk."

The theft charge at the penny auction was the same thing: just pure b.s. But still, I have no recourse to damages from the Crown. It amazes one that they can continue to find Crown Attorneys stupid enough to do their dirty work. It is hopeless for a person without funds to fight a protracted criminal case, unless he or she can find a sympathetic lawyer who will work for little money. The information against me laid by the police was based mostly on false bank documents and statements. Also peculiar was the fact that they wanted a copy of my signature. The OPP said they were acting on a complaint from the bank, but the bank denied any involvement. Of course the banks have as much respect for the truth as my dog has for car tires.

The good part came in February 1984, when Judge Robson (the judge that sentenced Marv Black) stated that the Royal Bank's lawsuit against me should have been settled out of court. The bank's lawyer protested that there were extenuating circumstances, whereupon the judge dismissed herself from the case, on the grounds that she had money in the Royal Bank. She then refused to set another court date for an out-of-town judge. The bank's lawyer simply shook his head with disbelief.

(He had told people two-and-a-half years before that they would put me out of business.) I don't know what was in the judge's mind. Perhaps she too was disgusted by the banks carrying on. However, this was the second judge to reaffirm my belief that we should not give up on the judicial system; that justice is available if one stands up and reaches for it.

It was a foul blow against my family — and no one can appreciate this until it's happened, for a house search of a woman's home when she is alone is as frightening as rape. She is completely helpless. All your intimate things are examined. These are men who can do as they wish.

The Way Ahead

25

There are three ways a nation can become wealthy. It can make war and take the wealth of another by force. It can trade freely and make a profit by cheating. Or it can profit through agriculture, whereby planting a seed we create new wealth as if by a miracle. — Benjamin Franklin

The following article in *Macleans Magazine,* January 23, 1984 issue, accurately describes the situation:

. . . as 1984 dawned, ominous signs abounded that many Prairie farmers may have trouble surviving. The Canadian Wheat Board announced this month that final grain payments to Prairie farmers were $409.7 million in 1983, the lowest in five years and $173 million less than a year ago. That discouraging report, combined with poor prospects for 1984, underlined the fragile state of the region's entire agriculture sector.

After suffering a drop in net income of $150 million last year, farmers in Manitoba, Saskatchewan and Alberta face the prospect of continued weak grain prices due to a world surplus and an even more competitive international market. At the same time, farm bankruptcies on the Prairies are climbing at a yearly pace of nearly 100%. And in the wake of the turbulent demise of the Crow rate, freight rate costs are expected to double by 1985, and the financial situation of many farmers is worsening.

> The assessments vary slightly, but the forecasts
> for the farm economy are all strikingly similar —
> no one expects a swift recovery.

The governments continue to substitute a dollar of credit for an earned dollar, trying to prime the pump of a dry well. The public and private debt of the U.S.A. is near $7 trillion. At 10% interest, this would claim 22.8.% of the total income of the U.S.A. for 50 years; spread out over 100 years, it would still take 22.6% of gross income. In Canada, the per capita debt is worse. We are going to see drastic measures by government as they grasp for straws.

Economic collapse will affect us all, especially if it follows the normal course of a depression — war.

The problem certainly goes beyond the immediately affected farmers and the unemployed, expanding as poverty spreads in the face of plenty, as government and private debt destroy financial institutions. These parts of the economy which produce the new wealth must be properly recompensed before economic recovery can take place. It is the first step towards the solution of our social problems.

Research tells us that when feed grain production is controlled and priced properly, an orderly livestock production and price will follow. The answer, therefore, lies in control of the foundation of the food supply, grain, and the price thereof.

How do we obtain this? There are lots of vehicles. The attainment of 100% of parity in the U.S., using their existing legislation, will have a major impact on the world price. However, if this is not done, we have the potential in Canada to protect our internal economy with supply management, but it must cover all major agricultural products. Legislation and precedents are available and can be implemented.

This will not just happen. Governments do not act, they react. Here is the major problem: getting people involved. People need to believe that solutions and progress towards them are not beyond their control. They need to realize that we cannot avoid the problems of food supply any more than we could of oil. What is happening is the result of definite policy and as such can be changed.

As farm populations and incomes decline, funding for schools, medical services and cultural opportunities becomes increasingly difficult. Rural Canada is not only deprived of services most people take for granted but it is becoming increasingly dependent on handouts from the central government.

The tendency to larger and larger farms, with their tenant farmers and absentee landlords, has negative implications far beyond the social decline of rural Canada. Large-scale farming necessitates the wasteful and destructive use of excessive chemicals, undiversified monoculture and other land use techniques which are harmful to the soil and water.

Every hungry nation on earth is characterized by the concentration of land ownership in the hands of a few. The tool used to destroy our farmers, the marketing system, is a throwback to colonialism. It is nothing more than a raw materials procurement and distribution system: a system designed to buy raw materials as cheaply as possible and re-sell products on the basis of all that the traffic will bear — regardless of cost, efficiency, supply, demand, fair price or concern that non-renewable resources will be available to future generations.

If farmers failed to produce enough food to feed our people, then we would have a farm problem. However, when farmers go broke because they are producing "too much" food in a hungry world, when we have starvation in the midst of plenty, then we have a marketing system problem, not a farm problem.

The current farm marketing system has much in common with the "fur trade" with the Indians. The fur trade was not established by the Indians or designed to give them a fair price, and it didn't. It was designed to make some people rich and it did. We farmers as yet have as much leverage against "the merchants of grain" as the Indians did against the Hudson Bay Company.

As we go to press, the various levels of government continue to annuonce new programmes and promise help, and the incidence of respiratory problems in farmers escalates as they hold their breath waiting. Survival members face three obstruction charges and three theft charges, and we will continue to fight these in the courts and in the political arena because they really are political charges.

The Farmers' Creditors Arrangement Act, as well as general revisions to Bankruptcy C12, died with the last session of parliament. New bankruptcy legislation is being introduced but literally the federal government is playing games with the banks, calling the shots. After all, they used the Liberal majority to push the controversial Crow Rate charges through when the railways wanted it. Meanwhile farmers and laid-off workers, such as White and Maislin employees, get shafted by lack of the same.

The farmers that have the survival spirit will continue to hold their land and the means of their livelihood, and will continue to form a column of mutual defense and support.

The opposing forces are very powerful and have a great deal of wealth; they not only control governments but have influenced the minds of the people to the point where truth and reason do not always win out. But our worst enemies are some of our fellow farmers. I think of how the hound has been trained to hunt and kill his cousin, the wolf, simply for a pat on the head and a few table scraps. Our vanities, selfishness and greed have been used against us for years. Occasionally, there are men and women who overcome these weaknesses and conquer the chains of fear. ''For fear is the first enemy, and the first duty of a man is that of subduing fear, for a man's thoughts are false, he thinks as a slave and a coward until he has got fear under his feet.'' It has been my pleasure to work with such individuals and my life is much the richer for it.

> If you will not fight for the right when you can so easily win without bloodshed.
>
> If you will not fight when your victory will be sure and not too costly.
>
> You may come to the time when you will have to fight with all odds against you and when you have only a precarious chance of survival.
>
> There may be an even worse fate.
>
> You may have to fight when there is no hope of victory.
>
> Because it is better to die than to live as slaves.
> — Winston Churchill

> Never fear to negotiate.
> But never negotiate out of fear.
> — Motto of the Canadian Farmers'
> Survival Association

Tips On Survival

If the bank calls your loans or asks for more security, such as third party guarantees or mortgages, RELAX. Welcome to the club. You are now in for a long negotiation process, but you can gain more dollars through negotiation than you can farming. The only thing you have to conquer is your own anxiety, for this will be used against you. Remember, the bank has a problem, you don't.

WALK to a good lawyer, one that is properly recommended and qualified. Check with the Survival Association if in doubt.

BUY a copy of *You Can Negotiate Anything*. It is a good book, explaining how the banks negotiate and how you should also. The banks know these tactics and are experts in this field, so be prepared.

DON'T sign anything. Do not take your wife to the bank where she might be intimidated into signing anything. Do not allow her to sign anything. If asked to sign, think first. Take the documents home for at least one week and read and understand them. If in doubt check with your lawyer. Do not allow yourself to be pressured by threats to bounce issued cheques, a common bank tactic.

BE honest with yourself. Things are not going to turn around overnight. The depression of agricultural prices is going to get worse. Do an accurate assessment of what your assets are worth. Know if you are broke. Know what bank losses will be if they do liquidate (don't forget their costs of lawyers, auction, real estate, receivers etc.), which will be borne by them if you are bankrupt.

APPLY to Farm Credit Corporation for assistance regardless of prospects. Their evaluation is based on cash flow ability and may seem low but there is no sense jumping from the frying pan into the fire. Be realistic. Do not reach too far just to relieve the emotional stress or you will be in the same problem but a worse position next year.

If you are turned down by FCC, CONTACT all your elected representatives and get them personally involved in your case. We need the government to be aware of the problems.

DO NOT accept debt-set-aside provisions. Realize that you shouldn't start below zero. Your settlement should never be above existing values, minus bank recovery costs. Remember they have a vested interest in keeping your assets off the already flooded market.

NEGOTIATE from a position of strength. Refuse to liquidate assets and do not make any further payments until a final settlement has been reached. Do not give the bank any money. The Bank of Nova Scotia asked one man for $100,000 deposit of good faith to start negotiations. Once they had that they decided they didn't want to talk.

NO ONE should guarantee another person's loans. If your friends or relatives want to help let them buy the livestock or equipment so that they can retain the first security position. This will give you the advantage of the use of their money with no risk to them. If a guarantee is in place put a limit on it immediately through a lawyer. Remember there is no need for anyone in Canada to lose their farm if they are determined and well informed. Your creditors want some kind of negotiated settlement as much as you do.

REMEMBER, the price for our product is the real problem — you cannot pay a debt without a profit. Unless we solve the problem of all commodity prices any debt settlement is only temporary.

The purpose of the Canadian Farmers' Survival Association is to give you access to good legal and financial advice as well as necessary moral support. You are not alone in your struggles and the Survival Association is a network of other farmers who have already fought the battles you are beginning to undertake. Feel free to contact us at any time. Box 218, Tara, Ontario, N0H 2N0.

My special thanks to all those who have been involved in this struggle for freedom and justice. The Canadian Farmers' Survival Association membership gets my first thanks and the following are some of those individuals who have assisted us in our fight for the family farm.

AAM, all the members
Adams, Barb and Jim
Alderman, Ken
Almond, Bill
Appenheimer, Ed
Ash, Brian
Ash, Nancy
Atkinson, Jeffrey
Bailey, Betty
Barfoot, Stew
Barfoot, Teddy
Barfoot, Ab
Barlow, Allan
Barnes, Phyllis
Belliveau, James
Belliveau, William
Belliveau, Jack
Belliveau, George
Black, Keith
Black, Clarence
Black, Keith
Black, Pat
Black, Marvin
Black, Clarence
Boak, Jim
Bothwell, George
Brady, Greg
Brady, Ruth
Bridge, Cecil
Bridge, Gayle
CAM, all members
Calhoun, Leonard
Calhoun, Eloise
Campbell, Colin
Camplan, Reg
Cazabon, Robert
Christian, Peter
Clark, Tom
Coil, Nelson

Conliff, Shirley
Conliff, Don
Corbett, Rick
Cossell, Joe
Coueslan, Jim
Cozart, Thayne
Crowell, Aubrey
Crowell, Ronald
Curtis, Gary
Dailey, Doug
Dailey, Jerry
Dailey, Pam
Dalton, Cletus
Davis, Bill
De Vault, George
De Vries, Pieter
Deichman, Don
Deloire, Paul
Di Emmanuel, Ezio
Dixon, Langille
Donnelly, Jim
Durant, Erva
Easter, Wayne
Eleich, John
Emmerson, Allan
Enestoedt, John
Ferris, Don
Fischer, Joe
Fisher, Mrs. Roma
Fisher, Ada
Fisher, Ross
Forbes, Ruby
Forbes, Eugene
Forbes, Ronald
Fowler, Cary
Frazier, Susan
Fritz, Bud
Gallagher, Larry
George, Roger

Gibbons, Vic
Gregory, Wilf
Gurbin, Gary
Hamilton, Hal
Hansen, Merle
Harkins, Diane
Harris, Lem
Harris, Leon
Hemson, Fred
Henry, Bob
Hijink, Henk
Hlady, Gary
Hodne, Carol
Holgerson, Don
Ireland, Brian
Ireland, Gisele
Irvine, Bob
Jago, John
Jannone, Errico
Johnston, Barbara
Kanten, Anne
Kanten, Charles
Keazler, John
Kelly, Ken
King, Walter
King, Carol
King, Robert
Klages, Harold
Kling, Lou Anne
Kotter, Kevin
Kramp, Emaline
Kramp, Leonard
Krebs, A.V.
Krohn, Melvin
La Blanc, Sandra
Lacina, Mary and Jim
Lamont, Roger
Langman, Jim
Lathan, Jake
Lau, Dorothy
Lemaresquier, Thierry
Lemkie, Allan
Levitas, Daniel
Lipton, Jean
Lucier, Don
MacDonald, Leone
MacDonald, Wray
MacDonald, Duncan

Malone, Phillip
McArthur, Dale
McClung, Doug
McCoy, Michael
McCurdy, Dave
McDermott, Dennis
McEwing, Doug
McIlhargey, John
McKinnon, Allen
Miller, Les
Moller, Thomas
Moonie, Father
Mooney, Pat
Morris, Andy
Mosser, Herb
Muff, David
Muffets, Jacqueline
Mulland, Brian
NAFA, all the members
Naylor, George
Nickerson, Kirby,
Nickerson, Darrell E.
O'Kane, Joe
Odell, Ron
Orosz, Andrew
Ostendorf, David
Otto, John
Otto, Debbie
Ovens, Doug
Paul, Doug
Perry, Chuck
Peterson, Wayne
Philips, Ron
Platt, Yvonne
Polzine, Bobbi
Pope, Dan
Price, Fred
Pruder, Doug and Jennifer
Pyke, Bridget
Quinn, Tom
Rabe, Roy
Rattai, Pat
Rattai, Richard
Reimer, Wolfgang
Rennie, Alonzo
Reshe, Alan
    and the slough club
Reske, Henry

Ricketts, Robert
Ringer, Derrell
Riordan, Jim
Ritchie, Mark
Robertson, Wayne
Rogers, Neal
Rossiter, Vince
Round, Sharon
Ryder, Larry
Sargent, Eddie
Satoshi, Akiba
Saunders, Tommy
Schneider, Brook
Scotland, Ken
Seabrook, Norm
Sears, Eddie
Shelton, William
Shelton, Mae
Shibish, John
Shoebottom, Tom
Sigda, Walter
Skelton, Jackie
Slatts, John
Slumskie, Tom

Slumskie, Beth
Smith, Bob
Staloch, Ken
Stover, Fred
Talbot, Marcel
Taylor, Ken
Thomas, Richard
Toby, Al
Torrie, Alex
Underwood, Jack
Van dan Brand, Arie
Verdonk, John
Vogal, Sarah
Voorend, Peter
Wainman, Gordon
Want, Don
Watson, Ben
Weddig, Bill
Welty, Howard
Wiehoff, Dale
Williams, Keith
Wilson, Brian
Wolfe, Bill
Wunder, Haleh

And to all those others whose help was invaluable but who must remain anonymous.

Suggested Readings

Acres USA. Monthly newspaper, P.O. Box 9547, Kansas City, Missouri, 64133.

American Agriculture Movement Reporter. Box 434, Floydada, Texas, 79235.

Cohen, Herb. *You Can Negotiate Anything.* Lyle Stewart, 1980.

Devalt, George. *The New Farm.* Dept. 61081, Emmaus, Pennsylvania, 18049.

Hyams. *Soil and Civilization.* State Mutual Book, 1980.

Ireland, Gisele. *The Farmer Takes a Wife.* Concerned Farm Women, Box 457, Chesley, Ontario, N0G 1L0.

McConnel, Grant. *The Decline of Agrarian Democracy.* Atheneum Publications, 1979.

Moore Lappe, Francis, and Joseph Collins. *Food First.* Ballantine Books, 1979.

Morgan, Dan. *Merchants of Grain.* Penguin Books, 1979.

North American Farm Alliance Publications, Box 8445, Minneapolis, Minnesota, 55409. (612-827-6056):

Ammo: up-to-date clippings of agricultural actions as reported in the press.

Newsletter

With a Grain of Salt: what U.S. farmers are being told about world situations.

The Trilateral Commission Takes on World Hunger: a critical look at the Powers that control.

The Farmer Takes a Holiday: a history of the Farmers' Holiday Movement and strike of 1932.

Farm Borrowers' Handbook: your rights (American).

The Loss of Our Family Farms, Mark Ritchie.

National Organization of Raw Materials Publications, Mr. Ken Staloch, 16039 Prairie Villa Street Southwest, Tenino, Washington, 98589. (406-653-1496):

Borrowing Our Way out of Debt?

Printed in Canada